3

83

4

Sins of the Fathers

BY THE SAME AUTHOR

A Time to Learn:
A Guide for Parents to the New Theories in Early Childhood Education

TO MY MOTHER

Contents

Author's Note

Throughout *Sins of the Fathers* I have followed the customary usage of 'he' and 'him' to refer in general cases to both sexes. As a liberationist I resent the fact of having to do so, but the constant use of both male and female pronouns is cumbersome and awkward. My apologies to militants for opting for the male pronoun.

R.I.

Introduction

When I showed my sister and American researcher, Louise van Agt, the manuscript of this book for her opinion (much valued by me), she exclaimed: 'Why Sins of the Fathers? Why not Sins of the Fathers *and* Mothers?'

I considered this a sound question, which showed her fairness to the male sex (a fairness unmarred by an equally strong loyalty to the cause of Women's Liberation), and hastened to explain that by 'fathers' I meant, of course, both parents. The title of my book refers to the Biblical 'fathers' and the sins they visit upon their children. In fact, where physical child abuse is concerned, I have appeared to cite more cases of abusive mothers than of violent fathers (not a deliberate intention to lay emphasis on one sex more than the other). Suffice it to say that disorders in parenting have no sexual bias.

The comments people make when you are toiling over your book can be irritating, something like having the bricks knocked over as you are halfway through building a wall. You have to pause and think hard before continuing to slap on the liquid cement with the same resolution. My sister's remark was not of this nature, but others were.

I remember one in particular, made by a psychoanalyst at the Hampstead Child-Therapy Clinic. When I told her that my book was about physical and psychical damage to children, she looked askance. Why was I going to bother to make parents even more anxious about child-rearing than they already were, she asked sternly.

This touched me on the raw. In fact, I have long resented some of the more Olympian professionals for their view that parents are either half-moronic creatures, unable to understand anything even when it is explained to them, or hysterics who are best kept in the dark. Parental hunger for knowledge about child-rearing is insatiable and healthy, and I think most parents are quite strong enough to read about the reasons for mental and physical cruelty to children.

I have not written about psychic and physical abuse in order to harrow. One of the most hopeful aspects of child abuse – and one which I think I have substantiated with all the available British and American data I could find – is that parents are very responsive to help. There are far too many eager, functioning, self-help groups for formerly abusive parents in both countries to confirm that disturbed parents are desperate to alter their abusiveness and to find out what caused it in the first place.

Insight is all. Once abusive parents begin to have a glimmer of what in their own past has distorted their parental behaviour, their treatment of their infants and toddlers tends to improve.

The number of helpful psychiatrists and social workers in the United States and Britain today who are anxious to share their knowledge concerning the roots of certain kinds of aberrant parental behaviour, gives parents a great advantage over their Victorian forefathers.

In my first two chapters, I have tried to show that cruelty to children has always been with us. When Thomas Hardy in *Jude the Obscure* wrote with documentary realism of young Jude's earning a few farthings a day for the onerous job of becoming a human scarecrow, he was probably not trying to tear at our heartstrings, but simply recounting life as it was. When Jude stopped waving his tired arms about in order to watch the birds and was soundly thrashed by his farmer employer, this too was an unremarkable occurrence; unthinking violence towards children was a prominent feature of life in those days. It was even furthered by the dictates of certain despotic child experts, such as the German doctor Daniel Gottlieb Moritz Schreber, as I will show in a later chapter.

Although cruelty to children still exists, it is no longer treated with such bland acceptance. In the eighteenth century children went to the gallows at the age of eight; young teenagers are still given the death penalty in some states of America today. But there is a difference in attitude. Today, we may well read outraged editorials about the continuance of the death penalty for young people; a hundred years ago, it would have aroused no emotion whatsoever. We do progress.

In choosing the Biblical title referring to parental 'sins', I should like to emphasize that I am not thinking of sins in the virulent, deliberate way this might suggest. I would prefer to speak of the 'blindnesses' or 'inadequacies' of the 'fathers' or parents.

Their mistakes are 'blind' in a very literal sense: they are often transmitted from generation to generation and are not 'visited' upon the children in any conscious manner.

In the rather heavy language of sociology, such transmission of parental behaviour has been called 'intergenerational continuity'; that is, the continuing of learnt behaviour from one generation to the next. This kind of unintentional transmission of behaviour from generation to generation is damaging to a degree. It could be called the 'cycle of abuse'. It seems that if one has been treated badly as a child, far from breaking this cycle ('I was mishandled, therefore I shall be a better, more kindly parent'), one often *repeats* the pattern of abuse: this is particularly true in the child-rearing sphere.

This is not to say that a child who has had a deprived, wretched background will automatically grow up to be an abusive parent. Many people break this unhappy cycle. Children of criminals, alcoholics, battering parents, do not always grow up to become carbon copies of the sad people who sired them. In fact, one could equally well write a book on 'the good seed': those children who emerge from appalling backgrounds without an apparent scar, free of their parents' self-destructiveness, patterns of violence, or addictions.

But this is not my book. For every delightful child who emerges apparently unscathed from a disturbed family background, unburdened by an unconscious need to repeat his background, there are ten who do not. And it is this kind of neurotic transmission that concerns me and forms the core of my book.

I have been questioned about the validity of such 'intergenerational continuity'. Does it really happen? Do parents impart a certain neurotic set of behavioural characteristics to their children which are then repeated in the next generation? Can neurotic behaviour in the home produce its own form of family-induced madness? There is an overwhelming amount of data which shows that such behavioural legacies are indeed transmitted from generation to generation (one distinguished piece of research referred to in later pages, the monograph by two child experts called 'Five Generations of Ill-Treated Children in One Family Pedigree', sums this up in its title).

Confirmation of the transmission of neuroses and certain forms of aberrant behaviour has recently come from a learned source, two psychiatrists trained in the complicated skills of measuring sociological and psychological data. Michael Rutter, Professor of Child Psychiatry at the University of London Institute of Psychiatry, and Nicola Madge, fellow psychologist at the Institute of Psychology, conducted a survey of all known British and American research on such 'cycles' and published their findings in a book called *Cycles of Disadvantage*. They found that while economic and educational 'continuities' were not always certain to be transmitted, emotional and neurotic behaviour was very much more likely to be so:

> With all conditions the likelihood is that troubles will not persist into the next generation of the same family. Nevertheless, considerable continuity is evident with respect to conduct disorders in childhood and personality disorders in adult life. With the most severe of these it is quite common to find persistence of problems across several generations. Adult depression and chronic neurotic disorders also show a tendency to intergenerational continuity.

Such a view, expressed by this scholarly team, could be depressing. Can we never break out of our patterns? Is our behaviour preordained? Thankfully, the answer is no. As I have tried to show in my section on child abuse and the further chapters on emotional abuse and family therapy, these patterns, if identified, *can* be broken. But it requires many disciplines to do so: community help, social worker contact, individual insight, a caring friend, kindly teachers, psychotherapy, group therapy sessions. One of the more optimistic aspects of learnt childhood patterns bequeathed from generation to generation is that they are reversible.

Equally encouraging is the new respect for children's rights, which we see on both sides of the Atlantic. There is a definite *child-centredness* now governing the legal profession in matters relating to the child and his family. Legally, children are beginning to have a long-overdue voice in the management of their own lives, particularly where family placement is concerned. The 'best interests of the child' are being seriously considered in the courts where, in the past, parental voices were the only ones heard and heeded.

In a number of states in the USA, for example Colorado, a 'guardian *ad litem*' is appointed specifically to oversee legal matters regarding children in the courts, and to speak as their advocate. In Britain, the new Children's Act, implemented in stages and not yet fully operational, will ensure that children cannot be placed in a succession of foster homes in a capricious way, nor adopted without welfare supervision. As long as a child is verbal, his wishes will be heeded when one of his parents remarries after divorce and the step-parent wishes to adopt him (previously he had no say in the matter; his natural, non-custodial parent's consent was all that was needed). This means that a child will no longer be forced to live with, or to take the name of, a step-parent with whom he feels in discord.

While the child is being protected legally with more assiduousness than ever before, there is also an increased feeling in the community that children must be watched for signs of abuse, and that such abuse should be reported to the correct agencies. Thirty years ago, the sight of a three-year-old, bruised and ragged and playing alone in the streets, might have occasioned neighbourly outrage, but no more. Today, with an increased awareness that every child is our responsibility, we can, without undue intrusiveness, make sure that his plight is quickly brought to the notice of the correct officials, who are there to protect him. Thus, in every way, the modern child is getting a fairer deal than he had before. But it has been a long, slow voyage to this new state of compassion.

I should like to show how this increased humanitarianism towards children has developed over the past two centuries, starting with the early, brutish beginnings.

1 | Early Attitudes to Children: Early Cruelties

There are so many cases of child abuse reported in our newspapers almost every day, that there is sometimes a tendency to forget that cruelty to children, like poverty, has always been with us. Today's variety of child abuse is covert, explosive, the product of neurotic isolation in modern society, the ugly spin-off of the nuclear family. The only consolation in contemplating the contemporary type of child cruelty, the child battering which is discussed with so much heart-searching by government committees, social service agencies and psychiatrists in every country of the Western world, is that there is a keen awareness of its existence and a serious attempt to understand and prevent it. Abusive parents themselves are usually sunk in feelings of self-hatred for their own seemingly inexplicable behaviour.

No such public or private awareness of wrong-doing was in existence before this century and, viewing the mortality rates of children and the types of labour they were forced into if they did survive, one wonders how the concept of 'blessed childhood', described in the literature of the eighteenth and nineteenth centuries, ever came into being. One can only conclude that a happy childhood, like leisure, education, culture and luxury, was a privilege enjoyed exclusively by the well-to-do.

Perhaps one of the greatest myths to have come down to us over the ages, is that motherly or fatherly love is something that happens

14

instinctively, a quality there for the tapping, like some blessed underground spring. Unfortunately, facts have never borne this out. 'Home is where the hate is', was a sharp slogan used by the National Society for the Prevention of Cruelty to Children (NSPCC) in Britain in the late 'sixties and, brutal though this sentiment is, there is great truth in it. In former centuries, parental abuse was usually occasioned by the harshness of life itself – the widespread ill-health caused by wretched hygienic conditions, the subsistence existence on farms, in small towns and big city slums, and the corrosive effects of this poverty. The Industrial Revolution in Britain, beginning in the 1760s, heralded the possibility of slight material betterment for working families; parents rushed into the mills and factories to pick up lean wage packets, making sure their progeny scrambled into the mills, too. In fact, they exploited their children shamelessly, using them as financial assets and taking all the money they made. The idea of a children's savings book, of preserving at least a fraction of the wages a child earned for his or her own future, was an alien one to poor parents. The concept of children's rights was as remote to them as moon travel.

This does not mean that there were no reformers ready to complain of the injustices done to children. Their protests, although initially ignored, slowly began to produce protective legislation for the young, effective at least by the beginning of the twentieth century. One of these was R. Fletcher who, in 1886, pleaded for legislation to prevent children from being exploited in the factories. In his book *The Family and Marriage in Britain* he wrote that such protective legislation would help very young children who were 'kept at their protracted and injurious labour . . . by their parents. It is unhappily to a painful degree apparent . . . that amongst no persons do the children of both sexes need so much protection as against their parents.'

Poverty is no humanizer, as we know. In nineteenth-century England, feelings of indifference towards a child's welfare in the midst of general economic misery, were further blunted by a numb familiarity with infant death. The Registrar General's Report of England and Wales for 1831 states that 'of 1,000 children born alive, [only] 737 attain the age of five years.' And the high incidence of infant death spread right through the class spectrum. The wealthier classes comforted themselves with sentimental, cherub-adorned headstones to mark their babies' graves, but they, too, tended to impose a self-protective coolness upon themselves in the face of so much mortality. Sometimes their *sang-froid* was so total that it smacked of icy indifference.

Mary Shelley, wife of the poet and author of *Frankenstein*, made the following laconic entry in her diary in March 1815, when – at the age of seventeen – she lost her first baby, a premature girl: 'Find my baby dead. A miserable day.' She became pregnant again about eight weeks after the event so succinctly recorded. The second baby, a son, also died. Victorian motherhood was like this. As one matter-of-fact working-class recorder of childbirth noted in her diary at the time: 'Eleven was born but we died down to six.'* The large families remembered with such nostalgia in the present days of the tight nuclear family, were very hard to achieve.

The effort of repeated confinements, and the endless deaths that followed, had their attritive effects upon attitudes to children. One might call it the psychology of exhaustion. Poor mothers had no time for cosseting those of their young who survived, for stories at bedtime, for games in the park, for teddy bears and birthday teas. If a child was sufficiently tough to reach the age of five, he was considered sturdy enough to be treated as an adult – and this meant, of course, that he should *work* as an adult. Two assiduous contemporary chroniclers of that period, the British social historians Ivy Pinchbeck and Margaret Hewitt, express their conviction that children in pre-industrial and industrial Britain were regarded as 'little adults . . . little attempt was made to soften life for them.' They write:

> Until modern times, children dressed as their parents, their dress reflected their social status. In industry the children of the poor worked the same long hours as their parents, hours which were matched by the 11 or 12 hour day spent at school by the children of the more prosperous parents. . . . For parental cruelty of any kind the law provided no remedy until the 19th Century. . . . Thus, among the poor, the labour of the children was exploited, among the rich their marriages were contrived; all to the economic and social advantage of the parents.

* From John Burnett (ed.), *Useful Toil: Autobiographies of Working People from the 1820s to the 1920s,* London: Allen Lane, 1974.

Side by side with this uncompromising view of children as miniature grown-ups, there existed the sentimental, over-indulgent 'children as pets' view adopted by the often lonely and eccentric rich – a legacy of earlier times. John Wesley, the founder of the Methodists, had a somewhat unmethodist, indulged upbringing in the early part of the eighteenth century, being fed only on spoon meats. Later in the same century, Robert Southey, the future poet laureate, was spoiled to a repulsive degree as a child and allowed to drink himself into a coma (an inebriated tot was often found to be an amusing spectacle among the upper classes).

The 'child as doll' concept was very much in evidence in the paintings of Thomas Gainsborough and other artists of the time, who showed beautiful, wealthy, impassive children in satins seated with their parents in idyllic meadows and glades. A century later, in Frances Hodgson Burnett's *Little Lord Fauntleroy* of 1886, we have the apotheosis of the 'pretty child' – an almost unreal object of upper-class adulation with his 'lovelocks waving about the handsome, manly little face, whose eyes met his [benefactor's] with a look of innocent good-fellowship.' These idolized children were often a little mischievous, a look of impishness creeping into their invariably blue, forget-me-not-coloured eyes. They could be coltish, too, graceful and fleet of foot. They were never plain, fat, pimply or pigeon-toed, or plagued with adenoids or bow legs.

Little Lord Fauntleroy had his female counterpart, 'The Little Lady of Lavender', created by Theodora C. Elmsie in 1891. She was a 'small maiden with a pretty, pensive face, thoughtful eyes of grey-blue, shaded dark by lashes, and a wealth of golden-brown hair that reached below her waist.' As the British children's author Gillian Avery writes: 'It had suddenly become important [for children] to have curly hair, blue eyes and pearly teeth, and too often this was linked in the author's mind with innocence.'

Meanwhile, Yankee versions of Lord Fauntleroy and Lady Lavender proliferated in America, trussed up like their British cousins in buttons and bows but democratically bereft of titles. In *The Sentimental Years,* E. Douglas Branch reports on a social development and a new attitude to the child in 1855:

The fashion plates in the ladies' magazines are eloquent of the change; for the children are very often in there, in preposterous clothes imitating mama's and papa's but with their hoops, ropes and dolls. The little ones are at play, and the grown-up ladies, stiff though they be in the latest frounces from Paris, are beaming at them.

In a very real sense, adults treated children like dogs,* with behaviour patterns veering between extremes of indulgence and savagery. The rich pampered their offspring, dressed them up in frills and furbelows, fed them teacakes and strawberries and cream, put ribbons in their ringlets, petted them and fawned on them. The poor starved, beat and neglected theirs, or worked them cruelly beyond their capacities, for their own material gain.

Coming as it did after so much economic deprivation, the industrial boom in Victorian England produced an ugly acquisitiveness in the nation's parents. The country exploded into wealth on pyramids of coal and cotton (in 1880, forty-six per cent of Britain's exports were textiles). Magnificent country mansions were erected and filled with delicate china ordered specially from the Orient, exquisite mahogany furniture, and large numbers of domestic servants (there were 1,310,000 servants working for the well-to-do in 1851). Meanwhile, the children of the poor wove their woebegone way through this get-rich-quick society, at all times having to prove themselves useful. They were sent up chimneys from the age of five (the smaller their frames the better suited they were to squeeze up the constricting flues), there to contract lung cancer, damaged eyesight and twisted bone structures. One investigating committee of the time reported that some chimney-cleaning bosses – or 'masters' as they were called, because they were purported to be teaching the boys a trade – hastened the passage of the children up the chimneys by lighting straw beneath them. The tasks the

* In the US, the Society for the Prevention of Cruelty to Children actually *grew out* of the Society for the Prevention of Cruelty to Animals. The children's protective society developed from the dramatic case of Mary Ellen in 1875, a child who was cruelly beaten by her guardians. As there was no appropriate legal way of removing her from her cruel caretakers, she was drawn to the attention of the courts by being called a mistreated 'animal'. The Society for the Prevention of Cruelty to Children was organized in New York City after this. In England, the National Society for the Prevention of Cruelty to Children (NSPCC) and the Royal Society for the Prevention of Cruelty to Animals (RSPCA) are still the largest protective societies.

very young were forced to perform became increasingly bizarre as industries, both agricultural and urban, grew in prosperity. Thomas Hardy, in *Jude the Obscure,* relates how the young Jude was employed as a crow-scarer in a wheat field, earning 4d. for a twelve-hour day (children rarely worked for less than eleven hours daily).

Children's very smallness seemed to ensure their economic worth. It meant that they could bend readily over low coal barrows in the mines, tunnel more effectively in the underground ore faces for rich veins of coal, and be on an eye-to-eye level with the bobbins and spools in the textile factories. In 1840, toddlers of three and four were employed in the cotton mills to creep around picking up cotton waste, their natural prehensile skills and crawling abilities being deemed valuable assets.

Ironically, the very skills a toddler or kindergarten-aged child possesses (one can almost paraphrase the child development manuals on the subject: 'at three, he will enjoy crawling on the floor and picking up bits of fluff with his fingers', 'at four he will like stringing beads,' etc) were just those used by parents for monetary gain. In the factories, sweatshops and home garment industries of North America, from Maine to Manhattan Island, children of nursery school age, particularly those of immigrant parents, were plucked from their playpens and put into workshops to help swell the family coffers. Child slavery boomed in the coastal towns of Maine where small fingers were found to be particularly adept at placing herrings into tins in the so-called 'sardine' factories. In the home slipper factories in New York, little girls of under five spent eleven or twelve hours a day stringing beads to adorn those glittering 'Late Ninety' shoes, purses and fancy hats. Wrapping cigar papers around tobacco to make 'stogies' was also something the under-tens were induced to do. An American author, John Spargo, writing in 1906 about working children, described the varieties of industry to which children were placed with a voice of passionate indignation:

In New Jersey and Pennsylvania, I have seen hundreds of children, boys and girls, between the ages of ten and twelve years at work in the factories belonging to the Cigar Trust. Some of these factories are known as 'kindergartens' on account of the large number of small children employed in them. It is by no means a rare occurrence for children in these factories to faint or to fall asleep over their work, and I have heard a foreman in one of them say that it was 'enough for one man to do just to keep the kids awake'. . . . In the woodworking industries (of Pittsburgh, Pa.), more than 10,000 children were reported to be employed in the census year, almost half of them in sawmills, where accidents are of almost daily occurrence, and where clouds of fine sawdust fill the lungs of the workers. Of the remaining 50 per cent, it is probable that more than half were working at or near dangerous machines, such as steam planers and lathes. Over 7,000 children, mostly girls, were employed in laundries – 2,000 in bakeries; 138,000 as servants and waiters in restaurants and hotels; 42,000 boys as messengers; and 20,000 boys and girls in stores.

In the works of Charles Dickens and Charles Kingsley, the plight of the overworked British child, up the chimneys, down the mines and in the factories, is so eloquently described, that one tends to forget that American children were subjected to similar forms of hardship, differing only in detail because of the contrasting trades and work techniques. Boyhood in America at the turn of the century was not the Mark Twain dream of international imagination. The 'breaker-boys' of coalmining Pennsylvania, for example, were a long way from Tom Sawyer and Huckleberry Finn and their sunny fishing days on the Mississippi River. Crouched over anthracite coal chutes, boys of ten and twelve picked bits of granite and other refuse from the coal as it rushed by to the washers. They worked twelve hours a day and made fifty cents, many ending up with deformed backs, asthma, and miner's consumption. From the breakers, the boys graduated to jobs deeper down in the mines, becoming door tenders, switch-boys and mule drivers.

As in Britain, children in America were constantly being placed in difficult niches which suited their size. As a result, their bodies became deformed, much as did the backs and legs of London and Manchester chimney-sweeps and Lancashire coal-barrow boys. A record of the measurements of some 200 children working in the factories and workshops of Chicago in 1893-94, showed them to be undersized, rachitic and consumptive. The jobs often had respiratory and skin side-effects to add to the body deformation. Girls and boys packing matches suffered from phosphorous necrosis, or 'phossy-jaw', a gangrene of the lower jaw. In type factories, boys contracted lead poisoning; in caramel factories, girls who spent hours in the refrigeration department suffered from bronchial troubles – and so it went depressingly on.

The health of the children suffered and, in turn, affected the quality of family life. The working youth of the Victorian era seemed more like somnambulists than active, high-spirited young people. It is significant that, in the stories of Dickens, young boys are perennially getting their ears boxed by their bosses for being inattentive. The children of these times spent their lives like horses, asleep on their feet. I have often wondered whether Lewis Carroll's drowsy dormouse was not some kind of conglomerate of all the sleepy children; certainly Carroll's reading audiences of the time recognized and revelled in this particular tea-party guest and the shovings he received to wake him from his perpetual torpor. Descriptions of sleepy infants and wan, pubescent girls and boys abound in the reform literature of the day. John Spargo's pity was particularly aroused by the spectacle of drowsy little girls at their labours in the US in the late 'nineties. In *The Bitter Cry of the Children* he speaks of two of them:

> In Maryland there are absolutely no restrictions placed upon the employment of children in canneries. They may be employed at any age, by day or night, for as many hours as the employers choose, or the children can stand and keep awake. In Oxford, Md., I saw a tiny girl, seven years old, who had worked for twelve hours in an oyster-canning factory, and I was told that such cases were common. . . . In the sweatshops and more particularly, the poorly paid home industries [in Maine], the kindergartens are robbed to provide baby slaves. . . . Take the case of little Annetta Fachini, for example. The work she was doing when I saw her was wrapping paper around pieces of wire [for beading]. . . . She was compelled to do this from early morning till late at night and even denied the right to sleep.

Sleep, or lack of it, was the prevailing flashpoint between parents and children and often the only point of prolonged parent-child contact. At dawn, in preparation for the day's work, boys and girls were shaken, screamed at and beaten out of their beds by frenzied mothers and fathers; at night, when they returned, numb with fatigue, they were capable only of swallowing some bread and milk, or porridge, before falling into bed. Evidence given to reforming committees concerned with working children during the 1830s, highlights the impoverishment of family relationships. One vivid description of family life, or the lack of it, was written in a report to the British Government in 1832 by the reformer Richard Oastler, who claimed that it was:

> almost the general system for the little children in these manufacturing villages to know nothing of their parents at all excepting that in the morning early, at five o'clock, very often before four, they were awakened by a human being that they are told is their father, and they are pulled out of bed (I have heard many a score of them give an account of it) when they are almost asleep, and lesser children are absolutely carried on the back of the older children asleep to the mill, and they see no more of their parents, generally speaking, till they go home at night, and are sent to bed.

When family contact was reduced to angry pummellings out of bed in the mornings, it is not difficult to understand why actual cruelties, both parental and from society at large, were correspondingly swift and savage, especially among the poorer classes. And the law had always been remarkably languid in its punishment of child cruelty. At a trial in 1761 in London's Newgate prison, for example, a woman called Anne Martin was given a sentence of only two years for putting out the eyes of a number of children, something she had done to help excite the pity of passers-by as she took them begging.

The law was equally indifferent concerning the punishment of the children themselves. Few things emphasize more sharply that children were regarded as 'little adults' rather than as a special age group with their own rights than the eighteenth-century laws governing capital punishment. Children were hanged as readily as adults and for equally minor infringements of the law. The authors of *Children in English Society* tell of pathetic ragamuffins crying for their mothers on the scaffold, and describe how 'on one day, in February 1814, at the Old Bailey Sessions, 5 children were condemned to death – 2 boys, aged 12, for burglary; 3 boys aged 8, 9 and 11 for stealing a pair of shoes.'

As the authors point out, cruelty to children was not the exclusive province of the poor. They cite the case of a Mrs Montague, 'a lady of position' who was sentenced to a year's imprisonment in 1892 for having tied up her little girl in a locked cupboard, resulting in the child's death, presumably from asphyxiation. In her defence – which must have been eloquent to have netted her such a light sentence – her counsel said that every parent had a right to chastise his child in the manner he saw fit.

The prevailing view that every parent had the sacred right to punish his offspring (and presumably work him into an early grave as well) prevented the passage of many humanitarian bills protecting children's welfare in the factories as well as in the home. Parents, especially fathers, were seen as godheads, patriarchs and all-powerful monarchs in their own homes, and interfering with their right to rule was regarded as unwarranted. In a recent work, the American children's liberationist, Richard Farson, speaks of parents as a child's natural 'political enemy'. While this may have the ring of an emotionally overloaded remark, one must also look at it in the light of the comments of the so-called reformers of the nineteenth century who were supposed to be working for children's protection. Even the most liberal of them campaigned tentatively for protective legislation, tiptoeing hesitantly into the public consciousness, holding firm to ideas about 'the sanctity of the family' and 'the right to chastise'. These two convictions, resolutely held by the charity and church leaders in the face of much parental cruelty, sabotaged many attempts at humanizing a child's world. A spokesman for one powerful British charity of the mid-nineteenth century, dedicated to educating young children, gave the following reasons for opposing the provision of free meals in schools, institutions which were run by voluntary charities such as his own:

> It is better, in the interests of the community, to allow in such cases [undernourished children], the sins of the parents to be visited on the children than to impair the principle of the solidarity of the family and run the risk of permanently demoralising large numbers of the population by the offer of free meals to their children.

Another 'reformer', Whately Cooke Taylor, in 1874 invoked the sanctity of family life when questioned by followers as to why strong legislation had not been passed to help reduce the high infant mortality rate. While he conceded that there was a connection between the high death rate and the phenomenon of mothers leaving their babies inadequately supervised while they went out to work, he proclaimed: 'I would far rather see even a higher rate of infant mortality prevailing . . . than intrude one iota further on the sanctity of the domestic hearth.'

This belief in the 'sanctity of parenthood' made it very difficult for the British NSPCC to get through Parliament their 1889 Bill prosecuting cruel parents. It became law only forty-four years later, in 1933, in the form of the Children and Young Persons Act, which decreed that anyone over the age of sixteen who 'wilfully assaults, ill-treats, neglects, abandons or exposes him [a child] . . . in a manner likely to cause him unnecessary suffering', is deemed guilty of misdemeanour. *

Laudable as this long-overdue legislation was, continuing strong adherence to the concept of the sanctity of the family made the law very difficult to enforce and the sentences correspondingly light. According to one British Home Office Research Group report in the 'sixties, the average prison sentence imposed on persons convicted through NSPCC action was four months, the fine £35. Since it has been discovered recently that psychiatric counselling is more effective as preventive action for abusing parents, the relatively light sentences may, with hindsight, have been fortuitous. The cases unearthed by the NSPCC, although they caused revulsion in the public mind, did little to shake the belief that every parent had the inalienable right to shape, punish or reform his child as he saw fit.

The belief in this right dies hard. Only in August 1973, in Basildon, Essex, Max Piazzani, the four-year-old son of two gifted musicians, died in hospital weighing fifteen pounds. His parents were subsequently sentenced to the prescribed two years' imprisonment for 'wilful neglect', in accordance with the 1933 law. Although neighbours were vociferous about the scandal of this

* Though concerned church workers both in the US and Britain had to battle to spread their conviction that cruel parents should be punished by law, the American reformers fared slightly better; the first SPCC in the US was established in 1871 in New York and protective legislation was passed in that State five years later. The first British NSPCC was established in Liverpool in 1883, fifty years before legislation was passed.

'Belsen' baby in their midst, few reported it. Even fewer rapped on the parents' door and demanded that he be fed. Why? Because, they argued, it was really none of their business. The starving child belonged to his parents.

Obviously, the blood-tie relationship continues to be revered. Cases abound where children are wrenched from loving foster-parents and sent back into homes of deprivation, neglect and out-right cruelty because of the old totem belief that 'blood is thicker than water'. Two sadly famous little girls, now dead, Maria Col-well, from Brighton, Sussex, and 'Roxanne' * of Manhattan, N.Y., would undoubtedly be alive today if the authorities in both countries had not held the conviction that mother's care is best. This is by no means always the case, as I hope to substantiate later.

But we carry with us many unhappy legacies from the past. Let us see what some of them are and how our ideas regarding punishment and nursery care developed from the nineteenth century to the present day.

* In the US, the identity of murdered children is often protected and only first names are given in court case histories; hence only the name of Mary Ellen in 1875, described on p. 18.

2| Early Attitudes to Children:
The Unsparing Rod

As we have seen, children were at a disadvantage in every respect in the past. They were treated as 'little adults' and were expected to work as unflaggingly as their elders, but they shared none of the privileges of adulthood. Children could not be trusted; indeed there had long been a suspicion in the grown-up mind that children were somewhat sensual and unbridled creatures who had passions that had to be suppressed.

With hindsight, it is probable that the spectacle of developing sexuality – whether in the milder forms of infant and childhood sexuality, or as revealed in the more dramatic hormonal explosion of adolescence – repelled and frightened our Victorian forebears. The sight of developing sexuality can make even the most modern parent feel apprehensive and threatened, giving rise to emotions he hardly dare analyse. How much more it must have harrowed the puritanical souls of eighteenth and nineteenth-century parents. This fear of youthful sexuality was probably the largest underlying cause of repressive behaviour in adults. Yet they hid it from themselves, concealing their sternness and restrictiveness behind the sanctimonious façade of 'doing their best for the child's spiritual welfare'. The pronouncements about child-rearing from parsons and vicars in the 1700s, added to by schoolmasters and educators in the following centuries, were based on the assumption that many natural traits in children were undesirable aberrations, which had to be eradicated or 'broken'. The analogy between raising children and breaking horses permeated the literature of those times. One seventeenth-century educator who expounded it with gusto was a New England preacher called John Robinson:

> Surely there is in all children (though not alike), a stubborness and stoutness of mind arising from natural pride which must in the first place be broken and beaten down so the foundation of their education being layd in humilitie and tractableness other virtues in their time be built thereon. It is commendable in a horse that he be stout and stomackfull being never left to his own government, but always to have his rider on his back and his bit in his mouth, but who would have his child like his horse in his brutishness?

Surrounded as we are these days by child care manuals, we sometimes forget that our ancestors were not given much, if any, written advice on how to rear children. Women tended to rely on advice from grandmothers and aunts, on hearsay, on their own instincts – and a great deal on luck (with the high rate of infant deaths, the children who managed to survive were indeed lucky; undoubtedly more fit than their less fortunate sisters and brothers, they were true survivors). Also, such advice as was given, centred on the social behaviour of children rather than on their personal well-being. The manners and morals of their offspring counted for far more with parents than intellectual or emotional growth. Children were to *behave,* and this overruling concern guided parental attitudes to the young.

Just how children were to behave was usually outlined in verses, tracts, homilies and horrific tales with sober moral messages. Somehow the feeling was conveyed that an offence against a parent was tantamount to an offence against the good Lord himself. Religion and filial piety blended together, creating an awsome mixture. As the early Victorian, Isaac Watts, wrote in his *Divine and Moral Songs for Children:*

> Let children that would fear the Lord
> Hear what their teachers say:
> With reverence hear their parent's word,
> And with delight obey

Have you not heard what dreadful plagues
Are threatened by the Lord,
To him that breaks his father's laws,
Or mocks his mother's word?

Children's stories held thinly-veiled moral lessons and were filled with tales of symbolic figures coming to gory ends because of their carelessness, disobedience or arrogance (Humpty Dumpty and his great, shattering fall, for example).* When a character in a nursery rhyme came to his customary catastrophic end – the baby in the treetop (the snapped bough and fallen cradle), Jack and Jill (the broken crowns) – there was a feeling of irreparability about their disasters. Humpty Dumpty couldn't be put together again, cracked heads weren't much helped by vinegar and brown paper, the baby in the cradle was most assuredly dead after that crash, and so on. Child analysts today tell us that the most damaging aspect of a tragedy heard or seen by the very young is the thought that the accident or catastrophe cannot be remedied. If this is the case, those nursery rhymes of the past might have had the desired effect of harrowing their young audience and frightening them into model behaviour. (Today's child is more likely to be amused by them: their old-fashioned ring, and the use of symbols whose meanings are no longer clear in a modern context, place them in the comfortable realm of fantasy.)

The Germans, during the early years of Queen Victoria's reign, were especially adept at wrapping up moral lessons in deceptively engaging packages. *Struwwelpeter,* by the Frankfurt pediatrician Dr Heinrich Hoffman (published in 1845), must have kept thousands of German children spellbound and yet quivering, filled as it was with stories of naughty little boys growing their nails too long, being absentminded, bad-mannered, disobedient, and revealing undesirable habits of almost every kind. And the penalties meted out were unremittingly savage. In the case of Conrad of 'Little Suck-a-Thumb', to cite one fairly typical instance of retribution, we have 'the great, long red-legg'd scissor-man, Oh! children, see!' coming in and wielding his scissors – 'Snip! Snap! Snip!' – and off comes the offending thumb, 'never to grow again'.

* These rhymes had political connotations too, as we know, but they were too sophisticated, obviously, for their child audiences.

There are obvious sexual overtones in the tale of Conrad. Sucking a thumb is warm, pleasant, a surrogate teat easily found, giving a child simple oral gratification (not a long way off from that other sensual pleasure – that of playing with his or her genitals). The German Victorians were having none of this auto-erotic pleasure. Off with his thumb! (This could equally be interpreted as 'Off with his penis!')

The savagery inherent in these pious verses and blood-stained nursery rhymes was reinforced in the schoolrooms, where corporal punishment in many terrifying forms was inflicted on children with adult abandon. Illustrated English lesson books as far back as the seventeenth and eighteenth centuries invariably show stern, bearded schoolmasters wielding a rod with a mixture of severity and obvious pleasure. The written comments below the cartoons usually congratulate the teacher on his actions. One, below a drawing of 1831, picturing a bespectacled, pinch-mouthed master beating a small boy whom he holds up in mid-air with his left hand while he whips with the other, reads: 'He that chastiseth one amendeth many.' While boys and girls could not have appreciated these endless schoolroom blows, it is not unusual to read of the victims in later life saying it did them good. Even the acerbic Dr Johnson, recalling that one master who beat his pupils unmercifully tended to shout as he flogged: 'This I do to save you from the gallows!', allowed that he was grateful for the beatings. He owed his knowledge of Latin to them, he said.

The tools of punishment were made with loving care and, according to one book on 'Oldtime Discipline', 'birch rods were tauntingly sold on London streets with a cry by pedlars of "Buy my fine Jemmies; Buy my London Tartars."' Schoolmasters in colonial Boston were conscious of the need to maintain the great English tradition of 'education through pain' and, if anything, added refinements to the flagellant tools they had inherited from the old country. One Bostonian invented an instrument called a 'flapper', a heavy piece of leather six inches in diameter with a hole in the middle which was fixed to a wooden handle. Every stroke on a bare bit of flesh raised an instant blister. Other Massachusetts masters sent their grade school pupils out to the New England woods to find their own birch rods, made splits in the ends and forced those they thought needed singling out for ridicule to stand pinched in the clefts for hours. 'Whispering sticks' – wooden sticks with pieces of string at each end placed in children's mouths like horse's bits – were also used to keep children from whispering among themselves during lessons.

In *Child Life in Colonial Days,* Alice Morse Earl describes some of the devices used in Pennsylvania schools:

> One whipped daily and hourly with a hickory club with leather thongs attached at one end; that he called the 'taws'. Another had a row of rods of different sizes which, with ugly humour, he termed 'mint sticks'. Another, named Tiptoe Bobby, always carried a racoon's tail slightly weighted at the butt-end; this he would throw with sudden accuracy at any offender, who meekly returned it to his instructor and received a fierce whipping with a butt-end of raw-hide with strips of leather at the smaller end. One Quaker teacher in Philadelphia, John Todd, had such a passion for incessant whipping that, after reading accounts of his ferocious discipline, his manner and his words, the only explanation of his violence and cruelty is that of insanity. . . .

Cruelty is contagious and was often copied from the masters by older students, taking the form of savage bullying. Flashman, in Thomas Hughes's *Tom Brown's Schooldays,* has become one of literature's most famous school bullies.* Hughes's description of him literally scorching the smaller boy, Tom Brown, by pinioning him against an open fireplace, has etched itself on many a young reader's mind. Hughes meant to shock his readers with this episode, but there are blander recollections of his Rugby schooldays which conjure up little degradations, made all the more shocking by the author's mild acceptance of them:

> The Sixth-form boys had not yet appeared, so to fill up the gap, an interesting and time-honoured ceremony was gone through. Each new boy was placed on the table in turn, and made to sing a solo, under the penalty of drinking a large mug of salt and water if he resisted or broke down.

* We can see his bullying descendants in *If* . . ., Lindsay Anderson's brilliant, if dangerous film of revenge, where the whipped hero turns a sten gun on his tormentors at the end. This film of the late 'sixties had a profound effect on adolescent audiences, no longer in mood to passively accept bullying from anyone, older peers *or* teachers.

School punishment wasn't necessarily sexist in nature. Although it seems as if boys received the worst of it, girls could also be cruelly humiliated and physically hurt. My mother's reminiscences of her grade school years at the 'little red schoolhouse' in Kensington, Maryland, always both intrigued and appalled me, as stories of cruelty told in tranquillity, parent to child, tend to do. A pretty little brunette with an upturned nose, she had already begun to draw the ardent admiration of boys at the age of ten. One day her schoolmistress found a love letter from one of them addressed to her, and made her stand on a stool in a corner of the room – on one leg, with a book on her head – for an hour. She never told me what happened to the writer of the letter, but I always assumed that he had been wise enough to leave his billet-doux unsigned.

Reminiscent of my mother's punishment was one which was meted out by a Miss Hetty Higgenson in her school at Salem, Massachusetts, also at the beginning of this century. Girls who had misbehaved were made to hold a heavy book, a dictionary or a Bible, by one leaf. If they moved, the page tore, of course, and further indignities were heaped upon them in front of the whole classroom.

Miss Higgenson both punished and rewarded – a system, in fact, upon which much of the old-style school discipline had been predicated. When pupils were good, she would divide a single strawberry into minute sections among half a dozen or so girls, giving the strawberry portion to the child along with a 'buss' or kiss. It is difficult to know which part of this offering was the more off-putting; the mashed bit of strawberry or the old maid's kiss.

Then as now, punishments and rewards always seem to be charged with ill-disguised sexual voltage. If whipping didn't have a sexual aspect, why the need for the bottom to be bared? Why else would flagellation be a form of sexual deviancy, especially as is believed, in countries where corporal punishment has been the norm in early childhood? ('Spanking Lords', who admit to acquiring a taste for the rod and who are willing to pay prostitutes handsome prices for each lash, have been part of the British vice scene for centuries; their tastes are often explained by the existence of physically punitive nannies in their early years.) Desmond Morris, the British anthropologist, suggests that the redness produced by the beating can excite the beater with its appearance of a sort of displaced flush. It is also possible that the mere sight of a naked bottom in itself is sexually exciting, and that the whipping is the next best thing for the deviant to prolonged and actual erotic contact. Presumably for a sexually frustrated teacher with a lonely life and a load of grievances (insufficient status, money, recognition, social contact), the wielding of a whip on an appealing backside can relieve a multitude of suppressed emotional problems.

Schoolteachers battling to keep the right of corporal punishment alive in Britain's schools today – and there are a great number of these* – maintain that the need for the rod is purely disciplinary. They dismiss out of hand suggestions of sexuality in the act of caning and emphasize that British 'Blackboard Jungles' and truancy are on the increase and that teachers are powerless to maintain order without force, especially with aggressive young male teenagers.

However, there are signs of awareness that caning on the buttocks may contain sexual connotations as many British local authorities advise against beating against the bare flesh. There is widespread confusion about how to retain corporal punishment without actually appearing to be regressive and Victorian. The outcome is a situation full of embarrassing anomalies and inconsistencies. In Cornwall, for instance, the school authorities warn against the whacking of hands, suspecting permanent damage to finger joints. Other local authorities say that the buttocks may be caned but that head zones should be left alone. Whatever the confusions, a large majority remain adamant about keeping their right to the rod. Liberal legislators make little headway even with suggestions to phase out the system in educational areas requiring special compassion. In 1968, Patrick Gordon Walker, the Secretary of State for Education, tried without success to ban corporal punishment for the mentally or physically handicapped; the Bill failed again a few years later when Baroness Wootton attempted to revive it.

Although corporal punishment is banned in many US schools, the more subtle forms of cruelty and punitive measures continue to flourish. Only recently, I heard of a co-educational boarding

---

* Primary schools and Junior schools abolished corporal punishment in London in 1972 as a three-year experiment. By January 1975, press reports revealed that four-fifths of the teachers wanted it restored.

school in Maine for high school children, which had special 'diet tables' for the fatter girls and boys. Undoubtedly this would be explained by its directors on the grounds of facility; the right foods could be more easily served to those in need of them in one central position, and so on, but whatever the reasonable explanations for such 'diet tables' might be, I suspect some residual cruelty here, the 'singling out' process that has pervaded all forms of discipline since the very idea of punishment in schools began, the dunce with his cap in the corner being a kind of apotheosis of this (as if children's learning capacity could be seriously improved by punitive ridicule!).

Whatever the confusions and anomalies inherent in the retention or non-retention of corporal punishment in British schools, the fact remains that there are serious doubts about the validity of using physical force on children to maintain discipline. While British parents are more awed by educational authority than Americans – as well as traditionally more compliant about how the establishment chooses to treat their children – there are nevertheless signs of parental dissent. News stories abound about mothers and fathers withdrawing their children from secondary school rather than allowing them to suffer various indignities (being beaten, having their hair cut publicly, being chastised for wearing slacks). And local school authorities have to report their canings in detail (before a ban was imposed on caning in London schools, for example, one school with a student body of 360 reported twenty-seven canings in a school year). So, in contrast with Victorian times, when no brake was placed upon teacher violence and the instruments of school punishment proliferated and grew with sickening diversity, even when corporal punishment is allowed today, it is being closely monitored.

3/ Some Gurus of the Nursery

It is not really surprising to find that the first guru of the nursery was as savage in his approach to child-rearing as the times in which he lived. Certainly the Victorian atmosphere of cruelty to children was an accommodating one for a martinet. And into this vacuum stepped the brutally repressive German 'health and beauty' expert, Dr Daniel Gottlieb Moritz Schreber (1842-1911). Before the advent of Schreber, there had been no single adviser on child-rearing of any note. From the way he was welcomed, it seems as if Victorian parents had been waiting for him, almost as the ancient Hebrews had awaited Moses and his Commandments.

Reading his dicta now, one's mouth tends to go dry. Can he honestly have meant what he was saying? It appears that he did. And, what is more, he had followers – millions of them in his native land and a great many in France, England, and America.

Not all of his advice was damaging. He wanted people – especially those in their middle years – to limber up with callisthenics, urging sedentary businessmen, especially, to exercise in the fresh air. He also believed that city people needed to garden and was the first to suggest that urban dwellers tend small allotment gardens on the outskirts of the towns, where land for tilling was obviously more readily available than in the town centres.*

* Allotments in Germany came to be known as *Schrebergärten,* and thousands of Germans and Austrians still belong to Schreber Associations today.

But his advice on infant and child care is chilling. He regards babies as bundles of untamed badness – squirming, red-faced sinners aching to shape their own destinies through the sneaky, undercover routes of will-power, passion and plain 'orneriness'. Babies were an adult's natural enemy, to be suppressed and moulded. It was his belief that the main responsibility for the result of a child's upbringing lay with the father.*

To gird oneself for this early struggle against a baby's dangerous, capricious, even evil will, he advised parents to employ the 'law of habituation' and to start using it *right from the beginning,* at five months old. In a passionate treatise written in 1858 on educating one's child towards beauty and balance, he expands on his favourite law, in which parents should learn to:

> *Suppress everything* in the child, keep everything away from him that he should not make his own, and guide him perseveringly towards everything to which he should habituate himself.
>
> If we habituate the child to the Good and Right we prepare him to do the Good and Right later with consciousness and out of free will. . . . The habit is only a necessary precondition to make possible and facilitate the proper aim of *self-determination* of free will. . . . If one lets the wrongly directed habits take root, the child is easily put in danger; even if he later recognises the Better he will not have the power any more to suppress the wrongly directed habit. . . .

In *Soul Murder,* a compelling analysis of how Dr Schreber managed to drive his own son, Daniel Paul, to madness (and another son to suicide), American psychologist Morton Schatzman interprets 'habituate' as meaning that parents should programme their children to obey his, Schreber's rules: 'the aim is for the child to do what the *parent* wants, while thinking he does what *he* wants.' He calls this Schreber's 'peculiar psychologic', and no one would quarrel with him. Brain-washing would be another perfectly good term for it.

Like so many child experts after him, Dr Schreber concentrated

---

* This was a firm Victorian belief, shared even by the more pleasant fathers. One only has to recall Clarence Day's father's benign despotism as depicted in his *Life with Father* to be reminded of a similar advocate of parental domination.

on such nursery matters as a baby's bathing, sleeping, playing, eating and posture. This sounds benign enough until you examine his exact stipulations in these areas. As Schreber avowed, his major goal was complete submission of a child to his parent, especially his father. Some authorities on Schreber have related the growth of Hitlerian sadism to a father-dominated upbringing of this kind, suggesting that the way for a malign, dictatorial government was paved in autocratic homes where blind obedience to a 'higher' fellow being was the rule. But this does not explain why cruelty and autocracy flourished in English and American homes as well (Elizabeth Barrett Browning's father, 'Mr Barrett of Wimpole Street', also practised the 'divine right of fathers'.) My own feeling is that Schreber was popular because he suited the overall Victorian mind and ethos, and to hold him even partially responsible for a psychopathic régime which sprang up seventy-five years after his writings were in vogue, seems less than fair.

Dr Schreber was too involved in crushing what he described as a child's 'innate barbarity' to be greatly interested in matters of actual physical health. A mother of his day would therefore have learned little of how to cope with her baby's measles and mumps from his tracts. The suggestion he did manage to convey was that, if the child's behaviour was model, good health would be bestowed upon him as a godly gift in return. There lurked in Schreber's mind – and in the minds of his contemporaries – the superstitious belief that ugliness, disease and accident tended to befall evil-doers in divine retribution for their social shortcomings. (Hoffman's children in *Struwwelpeter* fell into rivers, lost limbs and became ill because they transgressed manners and morals, not because of any misfortune or ill luck.)

But when Dr Schreber left his murky philosophizings to give instructions on how to force a child to develop 'self-determination' (most of his edicts held built-in paradoxes of this kind: you 'prepared' a child for 'free will'), he could be quite specific.

On eating, he was unequivocal – a child must be made to clean his plate: 'One should *never* give in; one should not give the child a morsel of anything else until he has *completely* eaten the refused food. . . .' (The italics are Schreber's.)

On cleanliness, Dr Schreber reiterates his familiar theme that 'discomfort is good for you': '. . . starting about three months after birth *cleansing of the infant's skin* should be by cold ablutions only . . . in order to physically toughen up the child.'

On posture, Dr Schreber careered dizzily into the realms of his own obsessions and individual madness. In fact, much of his active adult life was spent devising harnesses such as 'sleeping belts', 'head-holders', 'shoulder-bands', and 'straight-holders' to keep a child from slumping or stooping or letting his head fall to one side. These devices consisted largely of ringed belts, straps and harnesses which kept a child fixed in one position; if he slumped, relaxed, or pulled in any other direction than the desired one, he would be pinched or have his hair pulled by the mechanism in which he was encased. The 'straight-holder' was one of Schreber's proudest and most ingenious inventions. It was an iron cross-bar fixed to the table where a child sat to study. The bar squeezed the collar-bones painfully if he sat crookedly.

Dr Schreber was obsessed with the idea of keeping children from making quick or untidy movements, and from wriggling (touching themselves?). A straight back was his idea of godliness; even when a child slept, he insisted that it must be flat on the back, not curled in any pleasurable ball, knees to chest on one side. On this favourite obsession, his writing is fiery, explicit, impassioned: 'One must see to it that children always sit straight and evensided on both buttocks at once . . . leaning neither to the right nor left side. . . . As soon as they start to lean back . . . or bend their backs, the time has come to exchange at least for a few minutes the seated position for the absolutely still, supine one. If this is not done . . . the backbones will be deformed. . . .'

Writing about a child's early sexuality, he becomes unexpectedly coy, as if abashed by the strength of the subject itself. He calls nocturnal emissions 'pollutions' and sperm 'seeds of passion'. In a section from *Medical Indoor Gymnastics* (1899), he suggests a battery of sixteen arm-circling, arm-striking, arm-raising and elbow-bending exercises to help keep straying hands well away from that possibly inviting member or genital area, the stimulation of which he refers to as 'unhealthy, weakening and polluting'. He wanted adolescent boys to keep themselves in a ferment of activity in order to distract their desires from thoughts or deeds of self-contact which he seemed convinced were uppermost in their minds. He advised that the wind-milling arm exercises be performed 'four to one-hundred times daily', the amount presumably depending on the boy's own record of indulgence or self-denial. If all else failed and the wheeling around proved ineffective, he tells the offender to 'take a hip-bath of a temperature between fifty-four and sixty degrees Farenheit for six to eight minutes, or a simple water enema of the same temperature, which should be retained as long as possible . . . in the morning, wash the parts around the sexual organs and the perinaeum with cold water.'

Dr Schreber's obsession with masturbation did not stop with the adolescent child. He had a conviction that little boys and little girls, allowed to lie in bed in the mornings under the covers, would most assuredly find their genitals. This was not to be tolerated: 'One must strictly see to it that children', he wrote, vaguely admonishing their parents as well this time, 'rise immediately after wakening in the morning, that they never stay lying awake or half asleep. . . . That is because with this is mostly connected the temptation of thoughts into an unchaste direction. The secret sexual straying of boys as well as girls, well known to doctors, teaches us that we must keep keenly aware of this [activity even] many years before the development of puberty. For this very reason . . . sleeping in un-heated rooms is absolutely to be preferred from now on if this is not already the case.'

The German doctor's belief in the efficacy of cold water, cold air, exercise, and an ever-present edge of discomfort in the child's life, along with flesh-pinching harnesses to crown the entire puni-tive approach, appealed enormously to his generation. If children were mischievous, disobedient and sensual, there was nothing like a douche of cold water or the touch of a leather harness to bring them up short. British and American boarding schools were – and still are, in many cases – heavily influenced by his dicta, available in numerous pamphlets and handbooks: iron bedsteads with hard mattresses, runs through the frosty dawn before breakfast, cold showers, callisthenics, outdoor sports in all weathers.

One finds evidence of Schreber's influence everywhere – and in some very unexpected quarters. Edith Sitwell wrote of her miser-able childhood in harness because of her 'poor posture', undoubt-edly a legacy from Dr Schreber. An Anglo-Irish friend of mine who was sent to a Sussex boarding school in 1921, at the age of five, tells me of having to walk around the playground for hours with a

pole stuck through his belt at the back (ostensibly to cure his stoop –
it never did). And boarding schools today continue to make a fetish
of the supposed salubriousness of cold showers and draughty dorm-
itories. While it has been tempered with time, there still lurks about
some minds the idea that burgeoning sexuality can literally be
cooled off. The outcome, however, is more likely to be an increase
in the number of colds suffered than reduced sexuality. Dr
Schreber notwithstanding, love does continue to thrive in a cold
climate.

Frederick Truby King, a New Zealander, was born in 1858, the
year in which Schreber delivered his most influential treatise on
child care or, to be more precise, on child suppression. When I first
moved to London from Boston in the late 1950s, accompanied by
my toddler daughter and armed with my Spock manual, I heard
the name Truby King on many mothers' lips. They made him
sound like a true bogey, something their own mothers used to
frighten them with when they made errors of judgement in their
child-rearing efforts. A Truby King mother would have had her
baby toilet-trained by the time he was six months old; she would
not have given in to those hunger cries before the mandatory four-
hour feeding interval had elapsed, and so on.

I hadn't read Truby King then, but I have since, and I have a
feeling that he was badly maligned. Not only does he sound like the
soul of sweet reasonableness after the extreme measures advocated
by Schreber, but, considering his times, I think he had his priorities
right. Unlike his predecessors, Truby King was not primarily interested in a child's behaviour. His overruling aspiration for a mother
was that she should observe certain fundamentals of infant
hygiene. He was far more concerned that a baby should be reared
in a germ-free environment than that it should be sternly ruled.
Unlike Schreber, he did not attempt to be a sort of Napoleon of the
nursery. He was worried to the point of obsessiveness about cleanliness, sterilization of bottles, and powdered milk formulas. And
who can blame him? The infant mortality rates in the countries
where he practised – chiefly New Zealand and Great Britain –
were appalling. Almost single-handedly he helped to lower these

in many areas. In Dunedin, New Zealand, for example, the death rate from infantile diarrhoea dropped from twenty-five per thousand in 1907 to less than one per thousand in 1922 – due to his widespread teaching of the basic rudiments of infant hygiene.

The infant mortality figures in Western countries in the early part of this century, now seem hard to credit. But in 1911, nearly 3,000 babies died in London in one hot summer month alone, undoubtedly as a result of drinking unrefrigerated, unsterilized cow's milk and contracting severe gastric ailments as a consequence. Like some dedicated missionary entering the outer reaches of the Congo, Truby King set about trying to instruct London working-class mothers on how to maintain better hygienic standards. He appears to have been the consummate scientist, caring more for theory than for actual humanity. His interest in feeding babies was sparked off originally by his work with livestock in New Zealand where he instituted what he called 'rational, scientific, artificial' feeding for 3,000 calves, concentrating on the 'protein ratio' in their intake of cow's milk. With his scientific precision, he applied the same principles of 'percentage feeding' to babies, so that a certain chilliness of manner pervades his work – as if his experimental mammals (pigs, calves and rabbits) were as important to him as the human variety.

His cool objectivity didn't prevent him from making some valuable pediatric rounds in the East End of London in 1913, where he helped to lower the high infant mortality rate. As his daughter writes in her affectionate biography, published after her father's death: 'They [Truby King and his wife] began with thirty babies whose parents lived on the very margin of subsistence in houses which had been condemned for their lack of sanitation . . . but despite the adverse circumstances under which they lived, the babies were found to gain weight with unfailing regularity once the mothers understood the necessity for regular weighings, regular feedings, fresh air, cleanliness and the basic necessities of health.'

He kept detailed case histories of each baby visited, which his daughter reprinted. Here are a few:

31/7/13. Saw Mrs C. of Brady Street. Baby six months old. Got first tooth last Friday. 12 noon, fed for five minutes. Sucked 2¼ oz. Feeding was started before we arrived, and was disturbed and only

nursed for a short time. 3 p.m., fed for 10 minutes and got 3½ oz.
6 p.m., 1 oz. in 5 minutes. Did not want more. 9 p.m., had a good
drink. Baby weighed with clothes before and after feeding. Bowels
moved. Baby had a dummy. Advised mother to throw it away.

14/11/13. Mrs F., Barnsley Street, Bethnal Green. Baby boy aged
3 weeks. Naked weight 7 lb. 11 oz. Mother feeds baby from one
breast only. The other gathered. Mother not very well. Baby
received 16½ oz. in 24 hours.

28/11/13. Gain in fortnight, 8 oz. Mother much better. Father out
of work this week. Food scarce. Total sucked in 24 hours, 21⅜ oz.

These case histories reveal Truby King's reluctance to allow
emotion to enter his endeavours ('father out of work') but, in fairness, perhaps he had no time for it. He was, after all, trying to keep
babies from dying.

Truby King believed that motherhood was a 'craft' rather than
a natural gift. 'No woman is a perfect "born-mother" ', he wrote,
'she has to learn how.' The rather fey word 'mothercraft', still used
in certain commercial contexts (mothercraft stores which sell baby
clothes, for instance), was his gift to Great Britain. He only mentioned mother love in order to discourage it – at least, any flesh-to-
flesh form of it. It was no good, he tended to believe, for a mother
to slot a bottle into her baby's mouth, with love flowing along with
the milk from the rubber nipple, if the formula was wrong, the
bottle dirty, and the combined effect likely to lower the infant into
a premature grave. Today, his advice appears rigid to a degree. In
view of what we now know about an infant's need for physical
contact and verbal communication with his parent, the New Zealander's injunctions against too much touching and cuddling can
be seen as seriously damaging.

Truby King made much of what he described as a baby's 'nervous excitability' or 'hypersensitivity'. He felt that this had something to do with the 'delicate structure of his brain' at this early
stage of development. Mothers are cautioned to restrain themselves from playing with their babies before bedtime for fear of
over-exciting them and rendering sleep impossible. And such
'spoiling' could have long-term effects, he warned sourly. 'Half the
irritability and lack of moral control which spoil adult life originate
in the first year of existence,' he wrote in his book, *Feeding and*

Care of Baby, a volume published in 1913 which had gone into seven editions by 1932, when its popularity finally subsided.

His dictates concerning the various facets of child care are similarly dour in tone. Truby King's ideal mother followed a schedule as rigid as any railway timetable. Feeds were to be given five times daily; if she nursed her baby, she was to use a left breast at one four-hourly feeding and a right breast at the next, being careful to stimulate and empty each breast during feeds. The baby care manual shows a clock face which sets out the following routine: 7 a.m. to 10 a.m., food, exercise and bath; 10 a.m. to 2 p.m., sleep, exercise and food; 2 p.m. to 6 p.m., sleep, exercise, wash and food; followed by SLEEP. For Truby King, a baby shut down at a certain time like a TV set. He warns a mother strictly against 'night-feeding', suggesting that a baby can quickly develop a little wiliness and become deliberately fretful when picked up too often, having divined that his mother is a soft touch. The idea that a baby used his cries as a capricious weapon to manipulate and dominate his mother was first implanted into a mother's mind by this expert.

Truby King's dietary suggestions were admirable and would pass muster today: a great many protein-rich ingredients such as eggs, fish, chicken; citrus fruits for Vitamin C, such as oranges and grapefruit (juice); warnings against fatty foods, starches and follies like raw onions and cucumbers. Mothers are cautioned against tea, coffee, cider and beer for their infants, and begged to avoid giving them fruit that is several days old in summer. All very sound.

On toilet training, he loses his good sense, advising mothers to begin holding their babies over potties at two months, after the early morning and evening feeds. If the baby doesn't get the idea, he suggests enemas of the small 'bulb' type. If the Freudian psychiatrists are correct and a rigid adherence to potty training at an early age does produce psychic disturbance in the older child or in later life, Truby King must have laid the groundwork for many a neurotic, anally-obsessive and compulsive adult. Certainly my parents' generation seems to have been over-concerned about the desire for 'regularity', administering enemas to themselves, swallowing endless laxatives, topping up each morning on castor oil, living on prunes and figs. An English uncle of mine would pace in his bedroom for an hour and a half each morning, inhaling deep

puffs of strong French cigarettes as he did so, awaiting the arrival
of the all important movement. One had the uneasy impression of
waiting for the birth of something (and Truby King *had* said it
should be delivered daily; my uncle was well trained).

On the subject of play Truby King was confused, unable to
decide whether or not it was good for a child to be touched and
played with or not (although he was firmly opposed to contact
before bedtime; no confusion there). As we have seen, he emphasized that too much playing could make a child excitable. At the
same time, he had an inkling that a passive existence for a baby
wasn't the best plan for him either, and inadvertently touched on
some of the most up-to-date thinking on early stimulation when he
wrote: 'Babies who are allowed to lie passively in their cots and
who do not get sufficient "mothering" tend to be pale, torpid,
flabby and inert.' It is frustrating for the reader to see him back
away from this revolutionary and prophetic reasoning once again
and revert to his warnings and convictions that 'meddlesome interference' was to be avoided in any contact between mother and
baby.

But while he was unfeeling and misguided when he declared
that 'fond and foolish over-indulgence . . . may be as harmful to an
infant as callous neglect or intentional cruelty', he was the first to
emphasize that motherhood was a vocation – and not one to be
undertaken lightly. We have turned full circle since the advent of
Truby King. While we can discard much of his rigidity, there is a
return today to his belief that motherhood is an exacting, difficult
job that isn't necessarily everyone's forte. With much evidence of
child abuse to discomfort us in the 'seventies, his almost sonorous
comments on the role of parents suddenly make sense again. He
wrote: 'theirs is the most sacred trust and privilege in the world –
to mould and shape the destiny of a new human being.' No one
would quarrel with him on this.

However, on the emotional content of being a parent, he was
ever the remote laboratory experimenter, the scientist more at
home with clocks, schedules, healthy, balanced diets and liquid
intakes, than with interrelationships. He had no time for developing psyches, if he thought of them at all. Also, he was deeply influenced by the edicts of a group of his contemporaries, American
pediatricians who were practising and writing from their training

hospitals at Harvard and Columbia Universities. Chief among these, very much a high priest of the 'don't touch' school of parenting, was L. Emmett Holt of Columbia, also chief physician to the New York Babies' Hospital and the New York Foundling Hospital.

L. Emmett Holt's book on baby care, *The Care and Feeding of Children,* enjoyed the same massive popularity that Schreber's and Truby King's manuals shared, suggesting that parents have always felt uneasy about their roles as child-rearers and have habitually sought advice with touching eagerness. First published in 1894, Holt's book went into six editions before 1914, being enlarged and revised with each new version (in much the same way as is Spock's *Baby and Child Care*). It is much more concise and crisp than Truby King's, with fewer meanderings, footnotes, and untidy cross-references. Holt fires a rhetorical question at a parent ('What are the most essential things in the clothing of infants?', for example) and then answers the queries unequivocally and dogmatically. On the subject of clothing, for instance, he suggests covering the baby with fine flannel, supporting the abdomen with a broad flannel band (those tiresome 'belly bands' that afflicted most babies throughout the first quarter of the century and more), avoiding the use of pins and tight clothing and supporting the babies' petticoats with shoulder straps.

Reading Holt's book is like journeying back into the elegant world of tea dances at the Ritz, summers at Newport, Gatsby-like champagne parties on the lawns at Easthampton. Baby, with his or her petticoats and 'fine flannels', was not brought into the fun, like today's infant on mother's hip at midnight parties, but kept in the higher reaches of the mansion with nurse in charge. So unquestioning was Holt of the affluence of his reading audience, that his baby care book carries the sub-title: 'A Catechism for the use of Mothers and Children's Nurses'.

'When is it advantageous to heat milk to 212 degrees F?' he asks. And answering his own question: 'For use upon long journeys, such as crossing the ocean.' Holt mothers and nurses tended to know their way about luxury liners.

But the opulence of his parents' diet did not find its way into a
Holt baby's dinner dish. He was given a wide variety of gruels
instead, made from wheat, rice or oats. Here is a typical mid-
morning Holt breakfast for a baby of a year and a half: 'Cereal:
one, later two or three, tablespoonsful of oatmeal, hominy or
wheaten grits, cooked for at least three hours and strained; upon
this from one to two ounces of thin cream, or milk and cream, with
plenty of salt, but without sugar.' Holt keeps his babies on this
almost geriatric diet until they are three. His prejudices against
edible food are violent. 'Omelets are objectionable!' he declares
at one point. Relenting a little for the seven- or eight-year-olds, he
concedes on the subject of cakes: 'A stale lady-finger or piece of
sponge cake is about as far in the matter of cakes as it is wise to go
with children of this age. . . .' We have come a long way since then.
One only has to observe today's two-year-old happily gnawing on
a chicken leg to feel great sympathy in retrospect for those babies
of the 'twenties and their form of suppression by gruel.

Holt mirrors Truby King's obsession with sterilization, devoting
thousands of words to the rinsing, cleansing, boiling, filtering and
stoppering of bottles and teats. Teats and bottles are to be boiled,
then rinsed in cold water, kept covered in a glass containing a
solution of borax or boric acid, daubed with refined, non-absorbent
cotton wool balls, and stood on a table covered with a plate of zinc
or tin. No wonder a nurse was needed!

Germs were an ever-present fear in this New Yorker's mind.
Throughout his book there are suggestions that there is no better
germ-carrier or upsetter of digestions than an emotional parent. 'A
Mother's uncontrolled emotions cause colic in a child!' he an-
nounced, touching on something very significant, though not for
the right reasons, I suspect. (I cannot find any previous link in any
of the other baby care manuals between a mother's psychic state
and its effect on her infant: so Holt was stumbling onto something
big. But like Truby King, with his admonitions against a too
passive life for a baby, he backs away from this significant pro-
nouncement, returning to his safer and more familiar fixation with
cleanliness.)

When I was bringing up a baby in the late 'fifties, there was a
distinct swing away from the Holt laws concerning cleanliness and
endless sterilization. Instead, there was much talk about America's

children having to develop 'natural immunity'. The boys in the Korean war of the early 'fifties had gone down like the proverbial ninepins with every unfamiliar epidemic or bug encountered. We were being told that we had hermetically sealed our children by giving them a too clean, all-American upbringing and, so the pundits of the day told us, not doing them any favours by this.

But before this turnabout in thinking, Holt had held sway. And the cleanliness obsession of this guru of the upper-class American nursery led him into some deep sillinesses. In a lugubrious chapter called 'Foreign Bodies', he declared that kissing infants could transmit a variety of desperate illnesses: 'Tuberculosis, diptheria, syphilis, and many other grave diseases'.

Related to the belief that babies could contract a venereal disease from a fond mother's kiss, is the attitude towards masturbation as a loathsome and dangerous pastime – 'the most injurious of all the baby habits . . .' as he called it. Slightly more compassionate than Schreber, however, Holt does say that punishment and mechanical restraints are of little avail in trying to stop the child. He advises the giving of 'rewards' to the child who shows restraint after being warned. What kind of rewards, one wonders. A stale ladyfinger?

For the generations of Holt and Truby King mothers who had been deliberately refraining from kissing their babies or from picking them up, who had been forcing early toilet training upon them, feeding them endless gruels, Dr Benjamin Spock emerged as a kind of saviour. When his *Baby and Child Care* first appeared in 1946, telling a mother to 'trust herself' ('You know more than you think you do!'), it was the most liberating sentiment she had heard on the subject of parent-child relations for a century.

More than that, it was liberating and solacing for the child, too. For the first time, babies were to be treated like human beings with feelings. Spock's advice must have poured over his readers like warm oil: 'When a child is hurt he wants to be comforted. This is *natural* and right'; 'Keep bedtime happy. Don't rush it. . . . Let a child keep a woolly animal in bed'; 'Let him get dirty sometimes (in mud or sand). . . .'; 'In the infant [handling the genitals is] wholesome curiosity'; 'It [masturbation] may be a sign of tenseness and worry at any age. . . .'; 'Why threats [if he doesn't stop] are harmful'; 'Readiness for toileting depends on the age and the individual child'; 'You don't have to boil everything'; 'It's a great mistake to get into an argument with a baby about his first solid food'; 'Be quietly companionable with your baby'.

I was fortunate in 1969 to be working as a journalist in London when British interest in 'Spock-the-baby-doctor-turned-Vietnam-protester' was at fever pitch. It enabled me, first on *The Observer* budget, to have a thirty-minute transatlantic telephone conversation with him and, later in 1970, to interview him personally for two hours in New York for the London *Evening Standard*. His English devotees wanted to know why their revered oracle, the embodiment of common sense, had switched, as one headline put it, 'from potties to protest'. The memorable 1967 photograph of him being led away by a New York policeman after his arrest for taking part in an anti-draft demonstration outside an induction centre in Manhattan, had etched itself on millions of minds, both in America and abroad.* The defiant thrust of the jaw of this huge, kindly Connecticut Yankee pictured at the side of a tough New York cop, alarmed his followers. Had the dear old boy perhaps gone a bit soft in the head?

Not a bit of it. My lengthy telephone conversation with him cleared this up fairly speedily (he might have speaking to me from the other side of the street; his voice echoed over the transatlantic cables with complete clarity). The elegance of Spock, I found, was in his consistency. *'Why,'* he boomed, 'should you bring up children healthy and happy and then make a world in which they can't stay alive? They're *my* kids fighting out there in Vietnam. I don't want to see them get *mashed.'*

We are now left with many unanswered questions about Spock's influence in infant care history. Did he, by returning a degree of

---

* In January 1968, Spock was charged with four other men with conspiring to counsel young men to avoid the draft; in Boston the following July he was convicted. The trial was bizarre – the judge elderly and vaguely scolding – the jury all-white and male. Spock was acquitted soon afterwards after an appeal. It was decided that the men had not 'conspired': they had never been together privately until after the indictment. The trial itself was a damp squib; it did nothing to define the legal limits of dissent.

casualness and spontaneity to parent-child relations, help create the permissive society and the druggy, drop-out, alienated, adolescent brigade of the 'sixties – the 'Spock-marked' generation as one unpleasant punster put it? Or did he, by his concern for infant sensibilities, open the way for the children's rights movement of the 'seventies?

I doubt it. It is significant, I think, that Spock spoke of 'his kids' out there in Vietnam. Nothing that the young were doing in the 'sixties made a serious dent in Spock's pleasure in them (except perhaps their reputed sexual promiscuity which did disappoint him; and even this, he has always interpreted as a mild losing of the way, nothing venal). When I met Spock, he repeated constantly that he didn't mind 'the dirt between the toes' of his young marchers and followers. What he respected most about them was their idealism, their rejection of their parents' material values, their repudiation of 'gunboat diplomacy', of international strength through attrition bombing. And in a sense, the dirty toes, and all, expressed their belief in a return to simple virtues, communal harmony, delight in untrammelled nature. These features did not spring from a Spockian rearing so much as from a reaction to decades of material affluence and parental pragmatism.

Spock himself is disturbed to find that so many have dubbed him the father of permissiveness. It is not what this benign, paternalistic and rather puritanical figure would want in the way of an international image. In fact, as he explained during our conversations, he is convinced that his link with the so-called permissive generation is erroneous. In his pediatric practice at Columbia's College of Physicians in the 'thirties, he had become convinced that Freud's theories about sexual repression in infancy made good sense and that strict toilet training and inflexibility generally did nothing to contribute to a child's mental health.

He transcribed these feelings into his child care book which he began writing in 1943 when he was a medical officer in the navy. At about the same time that his book was published, a report came out attempting to prove that a baby could set his own feeding schedule ('demand feeding', as it has come to be known). His own manual became confused with this report.

'Parents thought that if you could let a baby decide how to eat, then you could let him decide *how* to sleep, *how* to play, and so on,'

Spock explained to me. 'I was *alarmed*. There should be firm leadership from a parent to make a child happier.'

Spock is very conscious of the need for parents to be models for their children; if he puts the emphasis on parent-child companionability, it is because he feels that a child is more likely to mimic a beloved model than a feared one. In his own psychoanalysis, part of his internship training in the 1930s, he discovered through his dreams that the one person he had been afraid of and resented was his father. He speaks of his father, an official of the New Haven Railroad, as an exceedingly 'grave' man. His home was happy and stable but never gay, he says: 'Laughter and gaiety always seemed to be out there, somewhere else.' Dr Spock Senior was not the only Victorian paterfamilias who had something in common with Dr Schreber. He was not to be disobeyed – ever. And, like the German, he had a touching faith in bitterly cold surroundings for growing children. Spock's teeth almost chatter when he speaks of sleeping out on a porch in the winter nights with nothing between himself and the snowy air but blankets. Significantly, his *Baby and Child Care* advises a comfortably warm room even for a sleeping baby (no lower than 60 degrees at night, and between 68 and 72 degrees for an awake infant; requirements which could only be met with central heating, as far as I can see).

In the most human way, Spock's ideas developed largely in relation to his own upbringing. He resented his father's gravity, the sombre atmosphere he created, and he was critical of his mother for a variety of reasons, disliking her arbitrariness, control, rules and severity. His parents appear to have been highly inflexible. By reaction, he stresses the need for parental adaptiveness to a baby's or child's physical and emotional needs, the necessity for being able to bend like a reed to the changing winds of a child's growth and demands.

Spock is acutely aware of the 'sins of the fathers' being visited upon the children, and is very critical of his own attributes as a father. He now feels he was sometimes too domineering and severe with his own two boys. Mike and John, now in their middle years.

'I think I was probably a difficult father, especially with Mike,' he told a colleague on *The Observer*. 'I think I disapproved too strongly, and showed it. I can remember a few episodes, for instance, when Mike was three or four years old and he cried because he was hurt or disappointed. I jumped on him too hard, because being a crybaby was one of my own problems as a child. It is typical of all fathers and mothers to be overly tense in situations which relate to their own childhood.'

In subsequent works, *Decent and Indecent,* and *Bringing Up Children in a Difficult Time,* Dr Spock emphasizes and re-emphasizes his belief that the happiest children come from those families where the parents have the most unequivocal beliefs and are not afraid to pass them on. But while his unchanging beliefs in the perfectibility of man, woman and child continue to be uplifting to hear, his excursions into philosophy on such subjects as divorce have come to feel more and more remote from the realities of contemporary society; this in spite of his attempts to remain in the radical forefront (as exemplified, for instance, in his endorsement of the legalization of marijuana).

Reading parts of *Bringing Up Children in a Difficult Time* made me feel as if I'd been pulled by the hair back into the 'forties and made to sit through an Andy Hardy movie. On the all-important subject of divorce and single parenthood, he has this folksy tip to make to the freshly-divorced mother: 'It is preferable, I think, for a mother not to have any obviously romantic dates for a few months after the divorce. . . . This doesn't mean that a working mother cannot have lunch with a man or see him occasionally in the evening in the home of mutual friends. . . .' Where is the gnawing sexual hunger of the lone parent, the adjustments to loss of status, the housing rearrangements, the financial deprivations? Where are the millions of husbandless black and brown mothers in inner-city ghettoes trying to cope with fractious adolescent sons? Not in Spock's *Saturday Evening Post* world.

It is a pity that he has gone from spare common sense to vague, florid sermonizing. We can only be grateful for his original, incomparable gift to the world, his *Baby and Child Care,* which is still selling briskly (over twenty-five million copies sold so far and in thirty different languages). After all the harrowing advice given to mothers by the Gothic Schreber, the chilly Truby King, the hygiene-fixated Holt, how delicious was – and is – his message to a woman concerning her child: 'Don't be afraid to love him, and enjoy him.' And to have this revolutionary remark backed with all his lucid advice on the medical side as well!

With his emphasis on the value of the one-to-one relationship, mother to child or father to child, Spock has been blamed for making Western parents become too child-centred, for hastening the isolation of the nuclear family. I cannot subscribe to this view. My guess is that the nuclear family was on its way already, especially in the America of the late 'forties, when affluence was at its peak and American families tended to become rich transients, travelling from state to state, making money, cutting extended family ties.

Spock's manual was a comfort to lonely mothers; it certainly did not create them. He was embraced on such a universal scale because he filled a sad vacuum in society. His avuncular, reassuring voice took the place of an absent relative; it did not *displace* a relative. He was the right child authority for the right time.

I would conclude by saying that most of the gurus of the nursery, past and present, have been creatures of their times. Schreber was suppressive and brutal in his attitude to children, but so were the Victorians – they were given the child expert they deserved. Truby King and Holt were trying to advise mothers on how to prevent babies from dying; they didn't have time to dwell on the importance of the emotional side of the parent-child tie. By the time Spock appeared, standards of public health had risen beyond their imaginings (it is said, for example, that wartime British children had a more perfect diet and were in better health at that time than they have even been before *or* since). The spectre of infant mortality had nearly vanished. We were ready for Spock.

But Spock has now been overtaken by his own revolution and appears to be stranded somewhere in a polite WASP backwater, irrelevant to our times. The complexities of single parenthood, child-rearing in poverty situations, family dynamics, the complicated learning processes of the pre-school child and his need for early intellectual stimulation, the pressures on parents in nuclear families, the bewildering growth of the phenomenon of child abuse – all these have passed the good doctor by.

Is the world ready for a new guru of the nursery, waiting to step in at the right historical moment once again? Could it perhaps be a woman this time (now that women feel secure enough to trust another woman's written advice)? I think not. As the problems of modern family life are more diffuse and complicated, so is the need to synthesize all the many findings that arise, rather than to expect a single person to unravel the complexities in one or two concise manuals. The era of the lone nursery oracle is over.

4/ Child Abuse: The Background

While the gurus of the nursery preached their various gospels of good behaviour, cleanliness, sound diet and, with Spock, enjoyment of the baby, one thing they all tended to gloss over was the fact that, for the great majority of women, the very concept of a nursery must always have been a luxury. Mothers confined to a small kitchen as their day nursery – today a situation not necessarily applicable only to those with low incomes – are hardly likely to have either the time or the inclination to read about perfecting their maternal competence (the ability for mothering being a gift, in any case, as Truby King observed), or to reach for their 'how to' manuals when feelings of frustration and anger overwhelm them.

What kind of mother abuses her child? From all the research that has been done to date, it would appear that there is no specific type – that it is a mother's own past nurturing, rather, which contributes to the possibility of an eventual breakdown of the normal parent-child bond. Bad or neglectful nurturing in childhood may then be exacerbated by environmental pressures in later life, when the neglected child herself becomes a mother, further weakening the bond.

The mother most liable to abuse her child, whether she be rich or poor, urban or rural, is the one who is the most isolated. Potentially or actually abusing parents are those who live in states of alienation from society, couples who have carried the concept of the shrinking nuclear family to its most extreme form, cut off as they are from ties of kinship and contact with other people in the neighbourhood.

This isolation may be combined with – and heighten – a number of other negative feelings about mothering: many young mothers, cooped up in small flats, feeling persecuted by their querulous off-spring, may suffer from a deep sense of betrayal. Is this all? Those secretarial jobs that they have left in order to marry may now loom in retrospect as positions of high glamour. In comparison, looking after a baby is drudgery.

One Chicago psychoanalyst, Irene Josselyn, suggests that many women's disillusionment about mothering, when they discover how difficult it can be, springs from a conviction that they are indeed in a secondary role to their more fortunate men, house slaves toiling away at an occupation that carries little prestige and few rewards.

Added to this self-denigratory belief, fed by current social philo-sophy, is a sense of great disappointment. A number of mothers suffer from a 'Madonna Complex'. If they had fantasies about being mothers when they were young adolescents – and this dream is normal among pubertal girls – they tended to picture them-selves in a roseate light, arms encircling a rubicund, cherubic and motionless child, resembling the seraphic duo in Raphael's 'Mad-onna of the Tower', or the coloured portraits of Mary and Jesus found in primary school scripture books.

The truth, as we know, is often dramatically different. A baby can fret all night, appear to be repudiating the comfort a parent is extending, vomit up the food he had swallowed protestingly, soil its own clothes and sheets the minute after he has been cleaned, move ceaselessly, sob and screech on a piercing, unending key (in this context, referring to prolonged crying in particular, it has been explained that abusing parents often hit a baby's head, causing brain damage in many instances, because the noise which inspired such panic in them is issuing from this vicinity).

A rewarding result of intensive study of mother and child rela-tionships over the years is the realization that the ability to mother an infant satisfactorily doesn't necessarily come naturally. For a mother who is already experiencing negative feelings, and who is also unable to produce an affectionate response from her baby, the wriggling, squalling, demanding, perplexing infant shouting at her for attention can be an object of terror and loathing rather than of love – a red-faced, wrinkled, living reproach. And when the infant grows into a toddler, the inadequate mother is not necessarily in a happier position; she has then to deal with the problem of keeping him or her from danger, from burning on the gas rings of the stove, from falling downstairs or out of windows.

There is reason to believe that later patterns of maternal behaviour are already formed during infancy by what is known as an early imprinting process. The term 'imprinting' was originally conceived by a German naturalist O. Heinroth, who wrote in journals of ornithology in Berlin in 1910 explaining his theories about the imitative or 'following response' which is a marked learning characteristic in baby birds. Heinroth believed that, in the human as well as the animal world, a young baby becomes fixated on his keeper, who is usually his mother. Konrad Lorenz, the German ethologist, took these studies further, in particular in his observations of greylag geese,* when he hypothesized that this learned behaviour was confined to a certain period in an animal's life and that, if it was missed, there was no way in which the process could be reclaimed. In his animal studies, Lorenz showed that, if an animal had missed that period of 'object-fixation' with his mother and is isolated from his kind, he will transfer his fixation to his human keeper. (During an interview I had with Konrad Lorenz at his zoological laboratory outside Munich in 1969, he whistled for a Muscovy drake. The sleek, multi-coloured creature waddled excitedly over to Lorenz and proceeded to try to make love to his arm. Lorenz explained that the duck had been 'human imprinted' in infancy and so its strongest urges, such as the reproductive one, were freakishly directed towards human beings. This behaviour, most significantly, was irreversible. He was to be a pervert for life, it seemed.)

Lorenz's work in Germany was echoed in America by the work

* See Konrad Lorenz's descriptive passages on the habits of the greylag goose in his book, *King Solomon's Ring*, for highly readable insights on imprinting.

on rhesus monkeys conducted by Harry and Margaret Harlow. The German scientist's work, like the Harlow studies, examined both the mother-child link in animals and the reasons for breakdown.

Working in 1962, the Harlows observed two groups of baby monkeys who had been raised in strikingly different ways – one group by real monkey mothers, the other by cloth and iron-mesh surrogates. The Harlows wrote of the results:

> Four females that had been raised in the partial isolation of individual wire cages – and successfully impregnated in spite of the inadequacy of sexual behaviour – delivered infants within three weeks of one another. This made it possible to set up a playpen group composed of these 'motherless' mothers and their infants. *The maternal behaviour of all four mothers was completely abnormal, ranging from indifference to outright abuse.* Whereas it usually requires more than one person to separate an infant from its mother, these mothers paid no attention when their infants were removed from the cages for the hand-feeding necessitated by the mother's refusal to nurse. . . . As for the infants, the extremes of sexuality and aggressiveness observed in their behaviour evoke all too vivid parallels in the behaviour of disturbed human children. . . .

I italicized the sentence about the abnormality of the four monkey mothers because the gradations of neglect 'ranging from indifference to outright abuse' are amazingly applicable to inadequate human mothers.

There is by no means a consensus about maternal deprivation and its consequences. Some experts claim that the importance of the early mother-child link has been inflated – especially by the British psychologist John Bowlby, who vividly chronicles 'separation grief' in children parted from their mothers by illness or other unhappy circumstances. However, so much has been written supporting the view about the crucial need for parent-child contact during the first three years of a child's life, that the aware parent may find such telling information difficult to brush aside. If the findings of many sociologists and psychiatrists studying child abuse are to be believed – especially their conviction that the inability to mother is a response to earlier maternal neglect – future generations could be in for massive doses of parental neglect, particularly with the modern mass exodus of mothers from the nursery to offices and factories.

It is significant in this context to read from the Harlows that the neglected baby monkeys who were rejected by their own socially deprived mothers were somewhat compensated by contact with peer groups. Not to extrapolate too wildly, monkey to man, one's thoughts do however take a leap to the kibbutzim children of Israel who have minimal mother-child contact during infancy but who are encouraged during their school years to have fulfilling relationships with their child contemporaries, and who, to all intents and purposes, grow up to be reasonably unneurotic adults. (I say 'reasonably unneurotic' because according to the American observer Bruno Bettelheim, in his book *The Children of the Dream*, the kibbutz graduates are somewhat emotionally flat. They have what Bettelheim calls a 'fear of feeling', a legacy, he postulates, of early maternal deprivation.)

It may be that Western mothers who wish to return to work while their babies are still small will have to concentrate on the creation of more sophisticated alternative care arrangements than presently exist, where peer group association is cultivated as assiduously and carefully as it is in the kibbutzim as a compensating factor for lack of extensive mothering.

While no one knows exactly what process is at work in the satisfactory mother-child union, it does seem possible that a mother who has been lovingly mothered during her own babyhood, becomes a better parent herself because she has osmosed the tactile feelings and emotional warmth in this early period of association and is therefore able to reproduce them with her own offspring later in life. Whether this is the correct answer to why some appear to be endowed with an adequate mothering facility while others are not, is not known. What *is* known is that, in the majority of cases, mothers who have *not* been properly mothered in infancy are incapable of adequate parenting when they themselves have babies.

It is not too far-fetched a proposition to suggest that another aspect of malfunctioning in the mother-child relationship may begin right back in the womb, so that the mother herself is the unconscious cause of bearing a baby who is undernourished and bony, with wizened skin.

We have always been led to suppose that the womb is a sealed, safe envelope, protecting its slumbrous inmate from all outside stresses. The casual phrase 'back to the womb', voiced by anxious adults at times of longing for escape, has meant to signify a return to the cosy, the protected, the enviably calm.

But a relatively new science, foetal medicine, suggests that for a great many babies the womb is not the snug harbour of popular belief. It has built-in hazards of its own, causing some doctors to describe it as the most dangerous environment in which humans have to live. In Great Britain, where one million normal births occur each year and the infant mortality rate is among the lowest in the Western world, there are still over 20,000 annual infant mortalities,* a figure far too high for complacency or comfort. Five thousand of these deaths are caused by toxaemia – foetal oxygen starvation occurring in the last weeks of pregnancy. In toxaemic circumstances, the womb, far from being cosy, becomes a poisonous chamber from which the baby has to be freed immediately, or irreversible brain damage may occur.

Many obstetricians say that toxaemia in the womb is caused by overactive, highly-strung mothers. It is significant that with all the technology that doctors have to hand, the most consistent advice given to potentially toxaemic mothers is to go to bed and stay there. Bed rest is the only known cure for the condition.

Another fear for the doctor concerning the unborn child is that a rapid fall-off in the growth of a foetus may occur in the last three months of pregnancy: these unborn babies are classified as 'small-for-dates' – a phrase heard more than any other in the field of foetal medicine. One of the most common causes for a 'small-for-dates' foetus is placental failure – a condition in which the blood from the mother's placenta seems to be nourishing the baby inadequately. If placental failure is severe in the last months of pregnancy, it can cause irreversible neurological damage to the unborn child, resulting in 'backwardness'. Less severe placental failure causes the newborn baby to resemble a concentration-camp victim; but this is a reversible condition and the baby will respond to intensive post-natal incubator care. Once again, when a doctor

---

* In the US, at the last count in 1974, 23,960 infant deaths were recorded.

suspects placental failure in a mother, he prescribes immediate bed rest. A more drastic measure to ensure the survival of a 'small-for-dates' baby whose linear growth line has fallen off between the thirty-ninth and forty-third week of pregnancy, is to deliver him early, even prematurely.

Many of the 'small-for-dates' babies begin to thrive as soon as they are delivered; some, however, do not catch up after birth and may never grow normally. Follow-up studies on 'small-for-dates' babies have shown that some remain at low weight and have a fairly recognizable 'scrawny' appearance which they may carry into middle childhood, even through life. This physical handicap may also be compounded by the far worse advent of impaired mental ability, though doctors are keen to emphasize that this is by no means a general rule.

A growing number of gynaecologists and obstetricians are convinced that a mother's stress contributes to the condition of toxaemia and to a 'small-for-dates' baby. As one Harley Street childbirth expert told me: 'Stress raises the blood pressure and blood pressure causes toxaemia. How can there be any doubt as to the fact that one causes the other?'

While many doctors would agree with this Harley Street expert's opinion that an unquiet, restless mother may produce adverse foetal conditions for her unborn child, some go even further and hypothesize that when she is under stress specific hormones are released in the mother's bloodstream which pass through the placenta and directly alter the physiological processes of the foetus.

A pregnant woman's emotional health is of prime importance to the medical well-being of her unborn child. This often has the saddest of chicken-and-egg consequences in that many young mothers are prey to feelings of fear and depression and yet, being resentful of their pregnant state, refuse ante-natal care and worsen the condition they may have already produced in the womb.

Fear and depression in pregnancy and in the post-natal phase seem to be part of a potentially abusing mother's make-up. It is true that many pregnant mothers are prone to easy tears, both before and after the birth of their child, but the depression of the abusing mother seems to be a more searing, painful business.

Two New York sociologists, E. Pavenstedt and V. Bernard,

studying the behaviour of two groups of mothers, one abusive, the other non-abusive, found that though over half the mothers in both groups were depressed, there was a contrast in the matter of demonstrating their depression. The abusive mothers complained of insomnia and loss of appetite and long crying spells, while the non-abusive mothers described their more straightforward moods of milder depression, unaccompanied by wakefulness or eating irregularities.

It is useful here to examine the nature of depression. What causes it? Many psychiatrists have said that depression is anger turned inside-out, that the effort of suppressing angry feelings is so great that the sufferer is sunk into gloom as a result. Why, one might ask, if these mothers are so angry at the memory of past neglect and at the present frustrations they encounter in their daily lives, don't they give expression to their feelings, thus helping to ventilate their troubled psyches in the process?

Dr P. D. Scott, Consultant Forensic Psychiatrist for the Maudsley Hospital, London, as well as for the Home Office, suggests that battering mothers over-inhibit their responses of anger and aggression, not because they are particularly controlled or well-behaved but because they have no confidence in their own assertive responses.

Dr Scott's assessment of these depressed women and their capped-down feelings is supported by another psychiatrist, Canadian child-abuse expert, Martin Rodenburg. He believes that battering mothers 'internalize' their anger behind a passive façade, engendering in themselves 'a severe depressive illness', springing in no small part from past guilt over their own childhood behaviour: 'The mothers ... had little capacity for expression of anger or self-assertive feelings and this defect seemed to have originated in the relationship to their own mothers who tended not to tolerate any expression of anger.'

In pregnancy, the potentially abusing mother is likely to be apathetic, depressed, intent upon the suppression of her own angry feelings. For some, the state of pregnancy may bring a fleeting sense of worth, of kudos, but for most it is something to be endured stoically in a dispirited way, as just another of life's betrayals.

We have seen that an unwanted baby's foetal chamber can be made hazardous by his mother's restless behaviour in pregnancy, her way of expressing her protest at her condition. By failing to check her own toxaemic condition or placental failure, she may already have produced handicaps in the unborn child. And when the baby arrives, his very appearance, indirectly caused by his mother, will tend to negate his chances of being loved. Thus the strikes against him reach right back into his foetal existence and are compounded when he enters the world, undersized and possibly brain-damaged. Some babies appear to be programmed for abuse, almost from the moment of conception.

Events in the hospital's maternity ward surrounding the birth of the premature baby can further assist in the erosion of the mother-baby bonding process. Underweight and frail, he will be taken from his mother at birth and separated from her for some time. Thus the opportunities for a healing embrace between mother and child, the start of what someone once called 'the life-long love affair' can be damaged from the moment he is born.

The importance of this flesh-on-flesh contact is recognized by many. The French childbirth expert, Frederick Leboyer, in his poetic and emotional book, *Birth Without Violence,* speaks of the baby's first language, 'a language of skin on skin'. He is so convinced of the profound necessity of this first 'skin touch' that he finds any distraction from it almost a violence. In particular, Leboyer detests the noise, clatter and bright lights of the wards; in his opinion these shocks, added to the brutal turning of the baby upside down and the back-slapping, make the baby's initial entry into the world a hell. Leboyer has ironed out these 'flaws' in his own Paris delivery wards and brings his babies into the world amidst dimmed lights and a peaceful atmosphere. After a soft, warm bath for the newborn, the baby is returned, face-down, to lie on his mother's abdomen in a kind of happy, exhausted embrace.

Leboyer's views concerning the all-important aspect of the first few hours of a mother-child embrace are undoubtedly convincing, and the superb neonatal care he has given his mothers has enabled him to carry through into the post-natal period his ideas of im-mediate mother-baby contact (it seems incredible but it appears that out of 1,000 deliveries he has conducted to date, none of them has entailed serious complications).

In ordinary deliveries, complications *do* occur, however. Premature babies are at risk and have to be removed from their mothers and placed into incubator care. Babies with congenital or other deformities may be whisked away without the mother being allowed to see them. Mothers whose births have been induced are too drowsy from the anaesthesia to be entrusted with the handling of the newborn at the outset; women who have had Caesarians are similarly anaesthetized and incapable. Even a mother who has had a forceps delivery, a relatively minor birth complication, will be too drugged to see or hold her baby until a few hours after coming round from the anaesthesia.

While all mothers whose babies are immediately separated from them after birth may have trouble adjusting to them when they are reunited, either in the hospital or when they are discharged, mothers of premature babies seem to have a particularly difficult time in healing the effects of early separation. The very length of time that a premature baby has to stay in hospital – usually at least forty-one days – increases the rift between mother and newborn. Consequently, a baby who has been incubated will be unused to physical contact, his mechanical rearing unfitting him for an easy transference to human arms. His mother may also be convinced that he is more fragile than other babies and be afraid of handling him – and fear and love are often inimical.

There are ways to ensure that bonding occurs even when hospital events seem to be militating against it, and I shall discuss these methods later, when I touch on the matter of preventive measures in relation to child abuse.

In fact, I shall be looking at the phenomenon of child abuse in all its complexity. Having outlined how a mother may be *predisposed* to battering even from her antenatal days, I would like to go into the matter of how the phenomenon was originally identified, what kind of parents are most likely to be involved, what the community can do to help these parents, and what society's attitudes are towards them.

I came into contact with the subject on a personal level when my own second child was a baby of eighteen months. His infant play-mate at that time was a wiry boy who lived in the same West London street as we did. I had become friends with his mother, a lonely, twenty-three-year-old American college graduate living in a bedsitter with her student husband. She was ten years younger than I and seemed very lost in a new country.

I had noticed that her baby was bruised and had felt uneasy about it. But, thinking that the bruises were probably the result of his falls (he was athletically ambitious for his age and literally appeared to climb up walls sometimes, especially when he found a chair's edge to teeter from), I had said nothing. I noticed, however, that he had fingerprint bruises on his cheek one day and I commented on them.

It was then that my young friend burst into tears and told me that she knew she was hitting her baby too hard and that she feared her own violence. She said that she thought living in one room was causing it and that, if she could work off her energies riding in Rotten Row once a week, the vicious smacking would stop. Having help and a roomy house, it was no problem for me to have her baby for one day each week. My friend rode around Hyde Park every Thursday and came back flushed and happy-looking. The hitting tapered off and soon she had her son in a pre-school playgroup which gave her more freedom than before.

At about the same time, in 1967, my magazine editor, Dennis Hackett, was making the woman's journal, *Nova*, one of the most arresting in Britain, exploring social areas that few women's magazines had tackled before. By a curious coincidence, he asked me to write a story about 'The Battered Baby Syndrome'. ('Don't leave out the gory details,' he advised with a touch of journalistic cynicism.)

My first interviewee was the late Professor Francis E. Camps, distinguished director of the London Hospital's Department of Forensic Medicine, who was setting up a study of what he described as 'the psychopathology' of the parents of battered children. In the letters column of the *Lancet* of 11 February, 1967, he solicited information for the study from other professionals, writing that

'In order to establish a true definition of "battered baby", it is necessary for us to have records of as many cases as possible in which the baby died, apart from those in which court proceedings took place.'

My meeting with him in his hospital office on a freezing wet early spring day was a gloomy one. In order to reach his office, one had to walk down a long corridor which held framed mementoes of the grisly findings of 10 Rillington Place, Notting Hill, the floorboards and gardens of which once hid the murdered victims of that modern bluebeard, John Christie (Camps had been the pathologist for the case).

A portly man in his sixties, with a manner that combined uneasily both cordiality and a barely repressed impatience, he seemed more keen to quote from an article he had written for a 1966 volume of *Medicine, Science and the Law* on 'The Battered Baby Syndrome' than to talk extemporaneously on the subject. He had little time for the psychiatric dynamics involved. ('Psychiatric knowledge pertaining to the problem is meagre . . . we have little evidence to suggest that such attacking parents had themselves been subject to some degree of ill-treatment by their parents in their own childhood,' his article, written in collaboration with two other forensic experts, declared dogmatically and inaccurately.)

I left feeling vaguely disquieted by his attitude which seemed too coolly medical and detached. However, I had to remind myself that by the time he examined the children involved in the batterings of which he wrote and spoke, they had already been murdered, hardly a circumstance which would inspire feelings of forgiveness for their parents. In his favour, he did not prescribe prison sentences for attacking parents, believing that incarceration was ineffective, either as a future deterrent or as a cure.

But he and his colleagues did preach the philosophy of detection, imploring hospital staff to have a 'low threshold of suspicion' and to look carefully for any marked discrepancy 'between the clinical findings and the story supplied by the parents'. In one of their pathologist's tables printed in the article, Camps and his associates list twenty-nine parental stories of how a child became injured. Against the 'original story' of 'Fell from pram and caught ear on a handle', they set the probable truth of 'Three blows on face, and then bounced on floor'; for 'Fell and caught stomach against door', they substituted the probable reality of 'Mother kicked him in the stomach', and so miserably on with another twenty-seven examples.

I had a fistful of gory details for my editor, as requested, but I sheered away from writing the story at that time, feeling too queasy. Coupled with the vague conviction that criminal pathologists were not the best people to consult concerning abusing parents, there was also the realization that I, too, could come perilously close to violent anger with my own children (that I never succumbed to it was no ground for complacency).

Having fled from the story like a bolting mare, I was none too happy when the London *Observer* asked me to write about 'Cruel Parents' (their term) two years later, in 1969. But I was more fortunate this time in meeting Joan Court, then psychiatric social worker for the British National Society for the Prevention of Cruelty to Children – an inspired and inspiring disciple of Professor Henry Kempe and his Denver associates. She flinched slightly when I used the term 'Cruel Parents' and politely corrected me: 'We call them abusing'.

She was good enough to give me all the available literature by what I later came to think of as the 'Denver Movement', named after Professor Kempe and his Colorado associates.

One of the articles included Kempe's seminal one on the clinical, radiological and psychiatric symptoms of child abuse, which had appeared in 1963 in the *Journal of the American Medical Association*. It was in this article that the pediatrician had coined the now famous term, 'The Battered Child Syndrome', writing:

> The Battered Child Syndrome is a term used . . . to characterize a clinical condition in young children who have received serious physical abuse, generally from a parent. . . .

However, though serious professional concern became more prevalent in Britain and America after Kempe gave the type of injury its name, it should be emphasized that the phenomenon was being observed and analysed as long ago as 1957, notably by John Caffey. Writing about 'Traumatic Lesions in Growing Bones' in the *British Journal of Radiology* of that year, he offered the possible explanation of parental abuse for the epiphysial separations and long bone fractures. In 1963, two British orthopaedic surgeons, David Griffiths and Francis Moynihan, published further information on the subject, discussing 'Multiple Epiphysial Injuries in Babies' in the *British Medical Journal.*

This growing wealth of material on the subject on both sides of the Atlantic caused hospital staff and general practitioners to be more aware of the problem. They began to be on the look-out for injuries to a baby's epiphysis, a portion of bone attached to another bone by cartilage, which can be discovered by X-rays. These injuries occur and reoccur in the same areas – hence the term 'syndrome' – and are usually a result of severe traction on the baby's limbs.

Parents who bring in a child with this kind of bone damage frequently speak of a bump or a fall but, in the opinion of most orthopaedic surgeons today, a professional can easily detect when a child has been injured by a human hand rather than by an accident. No fall can produce the same sort of epiphysial injury as that exposed by the X-ray film.

Though the term 'Battered Baby Syndrome', and the healthy suspicion engendered by the publicizing of the phenomenon, were novel developments among the professionals (the GPs, the psychiatric and social workers, the hospital surgeons in the accident wards, and so on), it is probably sadly true that this type of battering has always occurred. What was undoubtedly new after the Kempe revelation in 1962-3 (he spoke of the type of injury in an address to the American Medical Association a year before his classic paper was published) was the ability to detect the injury and its real cause.

Professor Kempe, in London on sabbatical leave from the University of Colorado, threw further light on the problem for me in his office at the NSPCC's Battered Child Research Centre, then situated at Denver House in Notting Hill. A mild-mannered man in horn-rimmed spectacles, sporting a natty bow tie, he could have been a commuting Madison Avenue ad man from Westchester County, not the prime mover in the discovery of a major social disorder.

Mother love wasn't instinctive, he said, and it was no good telling a woman that she was 'vile, bad and unnatural' because this love didn't come spontaneously. He told me that in his research into 1,000 Colorado families, he found that about twenty per cent of women had difficulty in 'turning on mothering'. He went on to say that there seemed to be no difference in the way British and American parents interacted with their children – some relationships were marvellous, others were symptomatic of a tragic breakdown. On the 'tragic' side he explained, was the bashing, which occurred in only a very small proportion of abusing parents (only five per cent of neglectful parents are really brutal, coming into the Camps psychopathic category as exemplified in his violence catalogues and 'true' and 'false' stories table).

What Kempe did stress was that abusing parents seemed to share a certain set of characteristics. He touched upon a few during our meeting and I went on to study them myself in depth for several years, referring frequently to the work of his Denver colleagues. Kempe, modest and self-effacing, had left the psychiatric theorizing to his team, he explained.

I hastened to read their works as well as others of a more probing psychiatric nature. I had a hunch that these would shed more light on the baffling phenomenon than Camps had done. In fact, this turned out to be the case.

5 | Child Abuse:
Some Parental Characteristics

The parent does not exist who has not wanted to strike his child, however beloved, at some time or another. Most of us manage to batten down such urges. Some, tragically, do not. What is the psychiatric ingredient that makes one parent stoically tolerate even a baby's worst periods of protracted crying, and another to have a kind of black brainstorm, a fusing of the mind that impels him or her to hit out and use violent aggression against a helpless infant?

More often than not, the abusing parent has had a wretched childhood. The axiom about not being able to love when you have not known love yourself is painfully borne out in their case histories. These mothers, and in some cases, fathers, are often unable to sublimate or redirect their anger and yet everything in their daily lives – brushes with employers and tradespeople, fights with their family, difficulties in budgeting – increases their tension. They spend their days going around the house ticking away like unexploded bombs. A fussy baby can be the lighted match.

Reading through the newspaper reports of abusive parents, one fact emerges clearly. These parents make no distinction between adult and child, nor do they perceive that an infant may be reacting differently from themselves because of his age and differing stage of development. They see these children on an eyeball-to-eyeball confrontation level – a little adversary waiting to be challenged.

A recent example of this kind of blindness to age and behavioural differences can be found in the case of Mrs Pamela
Elizabeth de Gier, a London housewife who confessed to the
infanticide of her nine-month-old son, Jonathan, five years after
the event which had occurred in Boston, Massachusetts, while she
and her husband were residing there. In a report printed in the
London *Daily Express* (28 July, 1975), Mrs de Gier described the
way the baby died: 'We had this big battle about his eating,' she
told the British police, 'I threw him from one end of the dining
room to the other, the whole length of the house. He hit the floor
and his neck broke.'

A significant phrase in this chilling recital is 'we had this big
battle about eating'. It is difficult to conceive that she is referring
to a 'battle' with a nine-month-old baby. In her almost breezy description, this sad woman could be describing a recalcitrant teenager.

Battering parents have the lowest possible tolerance threshold
for a number of natural and inevitable activities: crying, soiling
and periodic rejection of food. In a study of parents who strike out
at their young children, two Denver psychiatrists, Brandt Steele
and Carl Pollock – colleagues of Henry Kempe – found that these
parents yearned for a mature response from their babies, for a show
of love that would bolster their sagging egos and lack of self-esteem.
An infant's apparently rejecting behaviour – crying and vomiting
– sparked off their own feelings of inferiority and made them re-
live emotionally their own unsuccessful childhoods. Describing this
emotional turnabout, Steele and Pollock write:

> From direct observation of parents [who abuse small children] . . .
> it is obvious that they expect and demand a great deal from their
> infants and children. Not only is the demand for performance
> great, but it is premature, clearly beyond the ability of the infant
> to comprehend what is wanted and to respond appropriately.
> Parents deal with the child as if he were older than he really is.
> Observation of this interaction leads to a clear impression that the
> parent feels insecure and unsure of being loved, and looks to the
> child as a source of reassurance, comfort and loving response. It is
> hardly an exaggeration to say that the parent . . . looks to his own
> child as if he were an adult capable of providing comfort and
> love. . . . Axiomatic to the child beater are that infants and children

exist primarily to satisfy parent needs. . . .

An unreal expectation of the infant, as Steele and Pollock stress, is one of several features these abusing parents have in common. A weak and childishly unreal grasp of reality generally, is another trait they share. Having a baby seems a good idea at first, for example, but the consequences of bringing a live human being into the world rarely penetrate their minds.

Two child experts who deal with neglectful families in the rural areas of Wiltshire, England, J. E. Oliver, a consultant psychiatrist, and Mrs A. Taylor, a senior medical social worker, state in their article, 'Five Generations of Ill-Treated Children in One Family Pedigree': 'In our experience . . . the level of maturity and reasoning of some of our parents is comparable with that of a six-year-old girl who states that she would like to have "eight babies, all girls".'

Another parental feature which seemed baffling when first encountered, but now, though still abhorred, seems easier to fathom, is the propensity of a couple to single out one child as the 'scapegoat'. As long ago as 1962, a Massachusetts SPCC official, Edgar Merrill, commented: '. . . normally one child in a family was selected to be abused.'

It is often the case that the child singled out for maltreatment has been unplanned, is one more in a succession of haphazard pregnancies, and is therefore unwanted. The marriage, though fecund, can be on the point of disintegration and the scapegoat child may be used as a temporary form of sealing-wax between the discordant parents. Instead of venting their anger on one another, these parents will redirect it towards the child. In a vivid phrase, US sociologist Sidney Wasserman refers to such a child as a 'hostility sponge', there to soak up the parental rage around him.

The scapegoated child is always a pure victim. The parent may be a perfectly adequate mother or father to the other children in the household but direct all its animosity towards the unfortunate 'hostility sponge'. Newspaper stories are rich in examples of this kind of ruthless discrimination.

In 1975, a NSPCC inspector in the Midlands, Matthew Kelly, stated that he had found one three-year-old girl near to starvation at her mother's home. In the report quoted in the London *Times* (24 January, 1975), he said he had found the young mother of

seven in her home in Flint, Cheshire, happily eating fish and chips
in a warm room with six of her brood, while the three-year-old girl
sat apart in the cold, without nourishment, shivering on a pile of
dirty laundry. The mother told the officer that she had never loved
the child and seemed content to have her removed from her home
into care.

This kind of singling out is always characterized by irrationality
on the part of the parent. Sometimes it happens because the un-
lucky son or daughter resembles a hated spouse (this is particularly
true in one-parent families where one of the spouses has been
physically cruel, or has deserted the home). On 17 January, 1976,
the London *Daily Express* reported the case of a Mrs Carol Elliot,
who had let her eleven-month-old son, Paul, starve to death
because, it was stated in court: 'She did not love him . . . because he
looked like his father whom she hated.' She took perfectly good
care of her two other older children.

When two parents are in the home and child cruelty takes place,
it is usually a case of collusion between the couple. When I met
Henry Kempe, he told me that such parents find one child
'eminently bashable'. In a bizarre way, Kempe suggested, the
'scapegoated child' tends to be the one with whom the parents
identify most closely. In his experience the colluding parents ('one
bashes, the other condones or looks on passively') often describe
the child as 'slow, bad, retarded, even evil'.

As these parents frequently have a low self-image, the 'offending' child may be reminding them obscurely of themselves as
children (where, more often than not, they, too, were cruelly
abused). Stranger still, sometimes the infant will remind the immature parent of his own cruel mother or father. One abusing young
London mother told her social worker: 'When she looked up at me
with those queer grey eyes, she reminded me of the way mother
used to stare at me when she was being really nasty. . . .'

'At the moment of bashing', Professor Kempe told me, 'they
abreact to their own childhood. They themselves have experienced
severe corporal punishment and have had an imprinting of
violence at a very early age.'

Occasionally, a child is victimized, not because it reminds the
battering parent of a hated spouse or parent, but because of its own
bony shape and shrunken physiognomy (those premature babies

described in Chapter 4). Babies singled out for abuse in these cases have sometimes been described as 'provocative', meaning, in this context, that the very physical characteristics of the baby inspire anger and exaggerated feelings of irritation in his emotionally immature parent. The baby does not have to *do* anything; just to *be* is enough to put him in the parental firing line.

The scapegoated child may also be sickly and difficult to care for – scrawny, sleepless and hyperactive.* Joan Court, the former NSPCC psychiatric social worker, has mooted that, in battering such children, mothers are responding to atavistic, instinctual calls to murder the child who is 'not right'. Throughout history, infanticide has occurred when mothers, animal-like, have felt impelled to destroy the odd or imperfect infant. While these babies may have no deformity, their difficult behaviour and wizened appearance can subconsciously convince a neurotic mother that they should be removed in order not to throw a critical light upon herself as his progenitor.

That parents often batter the underweight child is no mere supposition. One of the most intensive studies made of the relationship between child abuse and low birth weight was conducted by two Canadian pediatricians, Michael Klein and Lee Stern. They studied fifty-one cases of children with the diagnosis of 'Battered Child Syndrome' at the Montreal Children's Hospital over a period of nine years, from 1960 to 1969. Of these fifty-one, twelve (or 23·5 per cent) were low birth weight infants (defined as being under 5 lbs. 8 oz. at birth).

This is an alarmingly high proportion of battering of low birth weight babies when one considers that only 7 to 8 per cent of babies born annually in the entire province of Quebec are of low birth weight. In other words, while babies of low birth weight are in a distinct perinatal minority in the Quebec hospitals, the proportion of them selected for parental abuse in the Montreal sampling was nearly a quarter.

Klein and Stern came to the conclusion that an underweight baby predisposes its mother to abuse him (especially, they are at

* Jean Renvoize, in her book *Children in Danger,* says that skinny babies, premature or underweight, are at particular risk from violent parents because they are not cuddly.

pains to point out, when the baby's sickliness is combined with other stressful situational factors such as 'poverty, parental alcoholism, unemployment and social disorganisation').

The abused baby is often the 'last straw' arrival in a crowded family scene already overhung with environmental and emotional pressures. The 'maternal overload', as a succession of unplanned pregnancies has come to be called, has already strained the mother's capacity to nurture to breaking point (and it may well be that it was not a very strong instinct in the first place). The baby's arrival can be like another blow in a regular tom-tom of disasters. Elizabeth Elmer, a Pittsburgh pediatrician, has listed some of the factors which may adversely affect a mother's capacity to nurture: 'disrupted marital relations, out-of-wedlock pregnancies, successive pregnancies at short intervals, strained economic status, lack of immediate support from extended families and isolation from community affairs'.

These young mothers, as I have said in an earlier chapter, have a tendency to be depressed. Their depression is exacerbated by their loneliness and isolation, their inability to reach out to anyone in the community who might help. Dr Phillip Resnick, a Cleveland psychiatrist who studied 131 cases of murder by parents in 1969 (88 mothers and 43 fathers), found that 71 per cent of the mothers had been suffering from depression at the time of the fatal battering of their child. Nearly half of the mothers had gone to a psychiatrist or a doctor before the tragedy and described their depressive symptoms. (It is not a happy thought to reflect that they were clearly giving out warning signals which no one, least of all the professionals, adequately heeded. Would a grandmother, a sister, a minister or priest, not have been better? I suspect that they would. There is something impersonal about a psychiatrist's olympian, objective response to what is clearly a cry for help. I shall describe later how much more effective community help can be than isolated trips to a psychiatrist.)

These symptoms tended to approximate those defined in the case of Mrs A., the thirty-one-year-old wife of a military pilot in Phoenixville, Pennsylvania, who killed her five-year-old daughter, Betty, by beating her repeatedly on the head with a rock. During the weeks proceeding the killing, 'She was hospitalized after taking an entire bottle of tranquillisers but felt she could not establish rapport with her psychiatrist. Covering up her illness with superficial smiles, she was discharged in one week. At home she became agitated, slept poorly, and was unable to complete her housework.'

Depression is usually characterized by early wakings at dawn, violent mood swings, difficulty in concentrating on everyday tasks – large or small – and indecisiveness. Feelings of inadequacy and indecision are often accompanied by irrational fears for the safety of members of the family. Depressed mothers often express most anxiety for the child whom they eventually hurt, a fixation which doubtless occurs because of their own subconscious knowledge that the danger for the offspring lies in themselves. Their husbands, doctors and psychiatrists should take heed of their voiced warning signals: 'I'm sure Martha is going to be run over', 'Teddy is going to be electrocuted', etc. What a pity that these projected fears merely seem to bemuse their male listeners.

It is not too fanciful a supposition to say that the ugliest genie in these women's bottles is the existence of a nameless rage which they are afraid to express. The consequent pressure which builds up in them is like the gas in an active volcano waiting for a moment of explosive escape. The incident causing the final eruption does not have to be very consequential: a child wetting a clean carpet, dirtying her clothes, balking at putting on a sock.

If small children's actions affect these parents so abrasively, why do they have babies in the first place? The answer that springs immediately to mind is simple sexuality, and it is certainly true that some girls, who have been little loved in their own childhood, may seek reassurance and love in the act of intercourse. However, at a time when contraceptives are widely and freely available, and basic sexual needs can be satisfied without resulting in repeated and (certainly to the husband) unwelcome pregnancies, this answer fails to satisfy. Barring those whose ignorance or religious beliefs prevent them from using contraceptives, these inadequate young mothers must be driven by another, less obvious compulsion.

It has been suggested that the overwhelming procreative urge of some inadequate mothers springs from a powerful desire for significance, a need for self-expression so potent that it obliterates all practical concerns for the complexities of life after the child is born.

A tragic example of the procreative urge at work, unrelated to reality and practical concerns, can be seen in the case of Mrs Pauline Kepple. Mrs Kepple, the mother of seven-year-old Maria Colwell, Britain's most notorious victim of child abuse and eventual murder,* has given birth to eleven children in the course of her wretched career as a mother (Maria was the fifth of her children by her first marriage to Mr Colwell; before Maria's ill-fated return to her in 1973, the year of the child's death, all five children had spent periods of time in care or with foster-parents). While her husband, William Kepple, was serving his eight-year sentence of imprisonment for manslaughter (of Maria), Pauline Kepple became pregnant again by a lover and was speaking cheerfully of the 'coming event' to the press. Obviously, this inadequate woman, passive and non-violent herself, takes a certain mindless pleasure in her incessant pregnancies. That the majority of her children end up as charges of the state does not dent her enthusiasm for the new baby on the way. A grasp of reality is not in this woman's make-up.

Many women, made to feel valueless and inferior by their own mothers and fathers during their childhood, appear to be engaged in a kind of 'striking back' action when they become pregnant. Apart from an infantile 'look-at-me-I'm-doing-something-important' view of their own pregnancy, being large (and respected and noticeable) with child, they have an unconscious desire to create a human being who will love and care for them the way their own parents never did ('You didn't love me so I'm going to give birth to someone who will . . . so there!'). They are, quite literally, trying to build a loving parent for themselves to compensate for earlier deprivation.

Writing about ten neglectful mothers of (between them) forty-eight children, Cincinnati social worker Matilda T. Belluci, of the Children's Services Division of the Hamilton County Welfare Department, describes their 'dynamics' as she perceived them during numerous group therapy sessions:

---

* Maria Colwell was beaten to death by her stepfather in Brighton, Sussex, fourteen months after being returned to her natural mother from loving foster-parents (January 1973); this while under the supervision of the East Sussex County Council.

Feelings of worthlessness and the accompanying self-destructive-ness have been consummate problems. . . . Their relationships with parents and parental surrogates have left them with deeply nega-tive attitudes toward authority. . . . They are intensely afraid of their frequently overwhelming anger. . . . Additionally, there are depressive overtones and the need for symbiotic relationships with their numerous children to avoid these feelings.

They have used early marriages and equally early, as well as frequent, pregnancies to find fulfilment. Sexuality is generally equated with pregenital gratification. Activity to ward off depress-ion is another need . . . that their numerous children fulfill.

One of the elements which help to confuse the picture about child abuse, is that there are so many different shadings and gradations of neglect, from leaving a child at home unattended for several hours, to the extreme of bashing. Because of the violent and sensa-tional nature of the 'Battered Baby Syndrome', this single extreme could be said to be the aspect of child abuse that lingers most vividly in the public imagination, providing vaguely titillatory fodder for radio and television plays (as I write this, a British com-mercial TV series called *General Hospital* touts its latest episode, 'Cry for Help', in the daily press. In it, we are told, a small child comes into hospital injured. Is it, wonders Sister Washington, the beautiful West Indian head nurse, a case of baby battering?).

Ill-treatment of children is not just one horrifying, isolated phenomenon, but a complex, diffuse problem, symptomatic of a breakdown in society as well as the breakdown of a family. It is, as three Philadelphia experts on child neglect poetically put it, 'one tree in the forest'.

Leontine Young, a New York child welfare worker, was the first to extend the definitions of neglect from the extremes of the attack-ing parent, who may murder or permanently damage his infant, to a parent whose sheer *indifference* to the child's welfare may consti-tute a kind of abuse. That forms of child neglect are of a multi-farious nature is clearly illustrated in the following excerpt outlin-ing the reasons for the referral of thirty-four mothers to the North Carolina State Welfare Bureau 'to assess their ability to care for their children' (an ability that was obviously in doubt):

The referrals for all 34 of these mothers mentioned one or more of the following conditions presumed to be indicative of physical or moral neglect of children; children reported begging or complaining of being unfed: children frequently reported inadequately clothed, untidy or unbathed: home unsanitary: children's obvious medical needs not met: children reported roaming streets late at night or left unattended at night: children left in care of pre-adolescent sibling during the day: children left alone for several days: children not sent to school consistently: mother often appearing intoxicated in the community: uncontrolled violence by adults in the home (shootings, stabbings): sexually deviant or promiscuous activities in the home: children severely abused physically.

The reference to 'sexually deviant or promiscuous activities in the home' in this rostrum of neglect is significant. Many inadequate mothers are unmarried or divorced, young, lonely and sexually needy, and in perpetual search of male companionship to fulfil their often still adolescent yearnings. There is such a high incidence of children attacked by stepfathers or their mothers' lovers that one assumes that the child or children in question must be viewed as a rival in these men's minds (being as immature in their responses as the women with whom they live).

It is not unusual to read that these random 'uncles' or stepfathers brutalize their adoptive children in the name of discipline, asserting that they are trying to make the offending child more 'respectful' to his mother, or more obedient (William Kepple's fatal violence to the winsome, sweet-faced Maria Colwell, kindled initially by a boozy evening, blazed to its final and tragic conclusion because she was still up watching television when he returned from the pub).

That such inappropriate responses are fired by strong sexual feelings of either desire or jealousy is an unavoidable conclusion. In some cases, these adult male beatings and spankings of young girls are results of stifled and soured sexual yearnings; in other instances, particularly when a close unit of mother and son is concerned, the violence perpetrated on the male child by the lover or stepfather may be ignited by sexual jealousy of the mother, by thoughts of a former union that produced the son, or an inchoate jealousy of the oedipal attachment itself. One abusive stepfather, quoted in the book by Peter and Judith de Courcy, *A Silent Tragedy,* defines his feelings graphically: 'I see my wife grunting and groaning, being balled by another man and loving it. When I feel this way I could kill him [the stepson].'

It has been suggested that overt sexuality, incestuous though it may be, between a mother's male consort and her female child, is often less harmful to the girl than the violent feelings of desire that result in battering. From the research that has been carried out concerning the victims of incest, it would appear that the greatest harm done to the child results from the probing disapproval of one parent or the other, or the opprobrium of the community when it suspects or uncovers incest, rather than by the act itself.

In his study of child sex victims, West Virginian social scientist Leroy G. Schultz states: 'Generally, sexual assaults on children do not have an unsettling effect on the child's personality. . . . By far the greatest potential damage to the child's personality is caused by society and the victim's parents, as a result of (1) the need to use the victim to prosecute the offender and (2) the need of parents to prove to themselves, family, neighbourhood and society that the victim was free of voluntary participation and that they were not failures as parents.'

While I am more than willing to consider Schultz's hypothesis that incest is not as harmful as society's response to it, I was somewhat alarmed recently to hear this kind of thinking propounded by an extremist group in Britain, the 'Paedophile Information Exchange', an organization of some 250 self-confessed paedophiles (adults who are sexually attracted to children). When, in the summer of 1977, I interviewed the PIE's chairman, thirty-two-year-old Tom O'Carroll – a former schoolteacher who was dismissed from his post for admitting his feelings towards an eleven-year-old boy and refusing to undergo psychiatric 'treatment' – one of his arguments for legalizing adult-child sexual union was that, unaggressively carried out, it did no harm to the child. He echoed Schultz in saying that the worst harm in an adult-child sexual union came from the guilt surrounding such contact – caused by the reactions of society when the relationship was discovered.

'Those adults who advocate seducing children on the grounds that it doesn't damage them haven't been on the receiving end!' This was the response of a Hampstead child therapist who heard of the PIE's campaign to reduce the age of consent for children in order to facilitate freer sexual relations between adults and minors. Some of her child patients were in advanced states of disturbance and withdrawal because of sexual molestation by adults, even though it had not been of an aggressive nature. It is possible that the sexual excitation of a large adult, bound to be overwhelming in its nature, would in itself prove fearful to a child unable to comprehend why an adult is behaving so strangely while being touched or touching.

Paedophilia must, by its very nature, be a form of child abuse because it presupposes an egalitarianism of will that cannot exist. How can a child 'consent' to what he does not understand? Children have sexual feelings, of course, but they are not expected to share them with an adult who will be, *ipso facto,* the dominant party in the duo. The 'sickness' of a paedophile must be obvious. A mature, normal adult wishes for reciprocity in a relationship. Let us hope that society will continue to preserve its laws to protect the sexual inviolability of children, and that other countries will follow Britain's House of Commons in legislating against the sexual exploitation of children. The Protection of Children Bill, which received its second reading on 10 February, 1978, will make the production of pornographic material involving children a criminal offence with fines of up to £10,000 or three years' imprisonment or both. In the course of this debate, the Minister of State at the Home Office, Mr Brynmor John, reiterated the British Government's current position on the question of the age of consent: that for the present it remains the same.*

It was originally assumed that the incidence of child abuse was not related to social strata or incomes, presumably because Kempe *et al* worked with neglectful families in the relatively middle-class

* Ages of consent vary in Britain according to gender and sexual activity. Homosexual activity is permissible only between 'consenting adults' over the age of twenty-one. For heterosexual relations the age of consent is sixteen, but 'gross indecency with a child', which presumably refers to caressing, exposure and other sexual contact or incitement to contact, is an offence when committed with a child under fourteen.

milieu of the state of Colorado. Recently, however, the Colorado team has come to believe that child abuse *is* more often associated with low-income families. In a letter to me of 9 August, 1975, Kempe summed up his own view, a reappraisal, on the subject:

> Child battering is more common among the poor because in addition to the internal crises which can lead to abuse they also face external crises which the rich can manage by hiring sitters or going on holiday, returning to work early, etc. It is the poor who often have little confidence in dealing with external forces such as the electric company, the welfare department or doctors.

A significant study into the causes of inadequate mothering has recently been made by two Californian sociologists in a poor section of San Francisco. They decided to find out what made one poor mother a good parent, another an inadequate one. In their sampling of mothers, they tried to select two similar groups, at least in the crucial matter of incomes and living quarters. Up to this point, most studies had been investigations based on comparisons between neglectful families and the general population, with differing backgrounds and incomes involved.

Employing a team of social work students, the two psychiatrists, Jeanne Giovannoni and Andrew Billingsley, interviewed 186 low-income mothers from three different ethnic backgrounds: black, Spanish-speaking and Caucasian. The mothers, already in the casebooks of the San Francisco Department of Health and the Protective Services Units at the Department of Social Services, had not been physically abusive to their children but were rated as neglectful or as potentially neglectful. The interviewed mothers shared certain socio-economic features: all were families with incomes of less than 5,000 dollars a year, came from the three ethnic groups already mentioned, lived independently of their own families and had at least one pre-school aged child in the family.

Certain patterns emerged. The neglectful mothers all stated that they preferred older children to babies, that they rarely sang, spoke or played with their young children (watching TV was the predominant family leisure activity), that their homes were low on 'conveniences' such as a telephone or wrist-watch, or comfortable sleeping arrangements for the children, and that they were largely estranged from their own kin. In contrast, the researchers found that the adequate poor mothers from all three ethnic groups seemed to enjoy rewarding contacts with their relatives. A particularly sad finding was that though the neglectful mothers had impoverished or non-existent relationships with their kin, they did little to try to replace this lack with extended contact in the community. In most cases, the neglectful parents had no idea that systems existed in the community which would relieve their isolation.

The authors of the study emphasize that, while the majority of neglectful mothers were to be found in the lowest income brackets, this did not mean that neglect was the inevitable companion of poverty. An equal number of poor mothers were perfectly adequate in their child-rearing capacities. The chief feature distinguishing the poor inadequate mother from the poor adequate mother was a total lack of family support (and, in most cases, this included the lack of a husband). Happily, many innovative projects have been initiated in Britain and America to try to remedy this lack of family support, projects which I will be discussing later.

A British investigation into the environmental background of abusing or neglectful parents, undertaken three years after the San Francisco study, pointed to some striking similarities in the socio-economic conditions in which both the American and British families lived. Interviewing 214 parents of physically abused children, two University of Birmingham psychologists, Selwyn Smith and Sheila Noble, found that three-quarters of the parents were from Social Class IV and V (categories designating unskilled or semi-skilled working-class groups and financially approximating the 5,000 dollar 'poverty line' annual level of the San Francisco group).

'We often found,' wrote the Birmingham team, 'social stresses such as social isolation and loneliness. Cramped sleeping accommodation, and the lack of one or more amenities, were particularly striking.' Reading such sentences after the San Francisco study, one has a powerful feeling of *déjà-vu*: only the countries are different.

I have tried to look at some aspects of the abusive or potentially abusive parent. But what about the children? Are they mere passive receptacles of all this adult violence directed their way? The signs are that this is far from the truth.

6/ Child Abuse:
What About the Children?

Children react strongly to the violence meted out to them by their parents. Their behaviour is complex, highly responsive (to the psychic or physical injury sustained), frequently retributive.

When one observes how an abused child 'hits back', speaking behaviourally, it is easy to perceive why child abuse can become a perpetuating life-style, a sort of 'emotional plague' in the Reichian sense.* An abused child is an angry child, not letting anyone off the hook for the injustice he has suffered; not his parents, not society, not himself. The sins of the fathers (and mothers) are certainly visited upon the children in these cases. The damage also has a boomerang effect for the parents as the child's behaviour towards them, if he or she remains in the natural home, is apt to be punishing. Obviously some abused children, sunnier in disposition, can be forgiving, but from what the documentation concerning them tells us, the majority of them are not.

---

* Wilhelm Reich, the German psychoanalyst who later settled in the US, postulated that society is the victim of cancerous psychic processes which he calls 'the emotional plague'. Gary G. Forest, US Army psychiatrist in charge of Alcoholic Rehabilitation, Fort Carson, Colorado, has written in his book, *The Diagnosis and Treatment of Alcoholics,* of this Reichian process 'where models both teach and reinforce maladaptive behaviour'. As Forest discovered, alcoholic parents frequently produced alcoholic children: this cyclical process can also be seen to work in abusing families, violent parents producing violent children.

A prolonged and sympathetic study of abused infants' behaviour in hospital was conducted by Dr Richard Galdston, a Boston child psychiatrist. The children were aged from three months to three and a half years, with the largest group ranging from six to eighteen months. Most arrived in hospital with the telltale radiological picture of fresh and old bruises and newly-healed fractures, and were admitted to a medical, surgical or orthopaedic ward, depending on the site of the injuries. Parents spoke either of easy bruisability on the child's part, of falls and accidents, or of blows by older siblings, and left hurriedly, as Dr Galdston says, 'seldom to visit the child again' during his hospital stay.

The behaviour of these babies in the early days in the hospital is pathetic, to judge from Dr Galdston's observations. They have little or no appetite and they cower from adults, hiding under the sheets, showing no expressiveness in their faces. As Dr Galdston writes:

> These children resemble cases of 'shell-shock' in adults. They display a profound blunting of all the external manifestations of inner life . . . they differ markedly from the autistic or schizophrenic child, whose behaviour is bizarre. It appears not so much that their inner life is distorted or idiosyncratic, but rather that it has been completely suspended.

Initially, the children are not encouraged to make contact with the nursing staff but are left alone. When they themselves begin to show signs of activity and to make more facial expressions towards adults, the nurses offer them tactile comfort, frequently carrying them with them on their rounds of the wards. As Dr Galdston says, staff shortages make it impossible for a nurse to establish a one-to-one relationship with an abused child but an attempt is made in the wards at an evenness of the kind of contact preferred; comfortable, bodily, with verbal murmurings from nurse to child. At this point, the children often begin to show a desire to eat, increased appetite nearly always paralleling the wish for increased contact with adults. This return to relative normality is often accompanied by heightened activity. Their attempts to respond to tactile affection are awkward and clumsy, even hurtful, in some cases eerily mirroring the aggressive behaviour which it has been their misfortune to experience at home: poking fingers up the nurses' noses and biting.

While recovering, many of them cling fiercely to any adults who come near them. A sad finding is that, though they may make a complete recovery in hospital, they seldom fully recover emotionally, displaying an apathy towards toys and playing in general, and rarely initiating speech. Underlying their overall behaviour is a pervasive lack of joy, an apparent absence of any pleasure in life.

Few studies have been made on how battered children fare after they are discharged from hospital. Because of this paucity of information, the meticulous cataloguing by Pittsburgh pediatrician Dr Elizabeth Elmer of the way fifty children reacted to their lives with adults – parents, foster-parents and teachers – after they left hospital, is a most valuable piece of research. Selecting the children* on the basis of three criteria for entering hospital – that their X-rays should reveal multiple bone injuries in various stages of healing, that there should be no clinical basis for the injuries, and that there be a background of parental neglect preceding hospital admittance – Dr Elmer and her team studied these children over a period of thirteen years, from 1949 to 1963. It is significant, in view of what has been written about the likelihood of abuse being meted out to underweight babies, that more than half the children were puny and malnourished, with weight below normal for age and sex, a physical state often defined in clinical terminology as 'failure to thrive'. Over fifty per cent of the children were under one year of age – the age, as we have seen, when battering most often occurs.

On average, each child was studied for a period of five years, beginning upon entry to hospital and evaluated afterwards through structured interviews in out-patient conditions. Dr Elmer stresses that the examination of an abused child in this extenuated way is valuable because the social worker involved is able to judge the home with more objectivity and coolness than when she first sees the child – traumatized and injured – in the hospital wards. (Dr Elmer's statement concerning the emotional involvement of social workers, their fight to control their own feelings of animosity and anger towards the parents, is just one of many on this theme in

* Seven of the fifty children later died, three in hospital, four following discharge.

the literature on the subject: that the field of child abuse is one of the thorniest for sympathetic social workers is irrefutable, something to which any young person wishing to enter this area might give some serious thought.)

A pediatric examination of these babies in hospital revealed that fifty per cent of them had some form of neurological damage or retardation upon entry – whether such retardation was sustained through the injury, or existed before battering, could not be established. This backwardness never left the children; years later, at the time of re-evaluation, the same degree of retardation prevailed. While a great many of the abused children showed heartening proof of normal physical development as they reached grade school age, with few remaining signs that they had been 'failure to thrive' babies during their infant hospital stays, intellectual development was consistently poor, with language difficulties being at the top of the list of their social inadequacies in later life.

One Denver expert, Dr Harold Martin, speculates that these children have speech difficulties because they have come to believe that speaking out to their parents is dangerous and that a consequent 'reluctance to expose themselves' is at the basis of this language lag. While I would tend to agree that self-protectiveness might contribute in part to their inarticulateness, I am sure that impoverished verbal contact with their parents is also partly to blame. These children's parents are adults who 'act out' their feelings rather than verbalize them. As speech is a learned skill and the parent a child's first and most important teacher in this sphere, I would think it highly likely that the abused child has missed out completely, being at the other end of brutal expletives and harsh imperatives rather than moments of quiet, affectionate, verbal interaction between parent and child. The ability to handle complicated language patterns helps a child to hone up his own intelligence, language being a kind of necessary muscle with which to flex and strengthen the mind. Battered children often reveal truncated modes of speech and an ability to comprehend concrete rather than abstract concepts. It would seem that, deprived of parental love *and* language, their intelligence levels decline along with their sense of self-esteem.

Weakened in intelligence and ego strength, they appear to grow strong in one emotional area – in their capacity to sustain powerful feelings of anger. This characteristic showed up consistently in Dr Elmer's team of children. They had all built up what she describes as a 'reservoir of resentment', an abnormally high frequency of anger: 'Thirty-two children could be rated on frequency of anger. Of the abused children, eight obtained deviant scores – half because of the complete inhibition of anger and half because of unusually frequent outbursts.'

To illustrate the kind of anger she encountered, Dr Elmer cites the case of a formerly abused five-year-old of average intelligence, whose favourite remark during her psychiatric interview was 'I hit you in the head.' The child also expressed the fear that she might 'accidentally' strike the interviewer with her pencil, something she was obviously desperately eager to do (that she didn't, became proof of her high impulse control, something not many previously battered children possess, impulsiveness being part of their emotional make-up).

Another feature of the formerly battered child's personality is an inability to form deep relationships with an adult, an attitude one child psychiatrist in the field calls 'Hail Fellow Well Met'.* After the first weeks of the post-battering ordeal, many of the children – in hospital and later in adoptive homes (if they are removed from their natural homes) – are as friendly as puppies, talking to everyone they meet, holding hands, smiling indiscriminately. The contact is superficial, but of course charming, often causing the children to become 'ward mascots' with the hospital staff. This outgoing behaviour seems to arise from a lack of trust in more profound relationships, which they have found hurtful.

In psychoanalytic language, such shallow contacts spring from what is described as the child's 'ego-weakness' or 'ego-defect'. A well-defined ego is a strong force for normal, healthy development in a child, the word 'ego' in the psychiatric sense having none of the pejorative connotations which it is frequently given in popular conversation ('he's on an ego-trip', etc.). A damaged child will have a seriously impaired ego, a sense of his own self and value so decimated by his home experience that he doesn't trust his own judgement or feelings and so will pleasantly and easily accommodate

---

* A phrase used by Dr Lenore C. Terr, Professor of Child Psychiatry, Western Reserve School of Medicine, University Hospital, Cleveland, Ohio.

himself to anyone and everyone. An emotionally healthy child possesses powerful likes and dislikes which he doesn't mind expressing – far from it! – and will not be afraid to voice a preference for one friend or teacher, a dislike for another. It is sometimes difficult to remember that an opinionated, definite child ('I *hate* orange juice', 'I *love* that white-haired lady with the blue eyes', and so on) is the one who knows where he stands, who has a blessed sense of his own identity, a knowledge which will facilitate his ability to adapt comfortably to his school and society later on. The best way for a child to develop this healthy sense of self, this strong ego, is to know where he stands with either one parent or another – or if he's really lucky, with both (though one will do). If they have made him feel good about himself, easy in his skin, then he is not afraid to be positive with his peers and other adults.

Child experts describing the behaviour of many formerly abused children starting afresh in new surroundings (after several months or years of intervention and removal from the abusive home situation), make them sound a little like pint-sized prostitutes: solicitous, smiling, endlessly agreeable. Withdrawn and apathetic to begin with, they may then explode into hypocritical, equally distressing 'seductive' modes of contact with adults. As Dr Harold Martin writes:

> Consider for a moment a child who seems to like you immediately, alters its behaviour to be consistent with what you want, is interested in pleasing you and in addition is concerned about your feelings. Superficially, this child seems quite nice and healthy. However, on closer scrutiny the child seems shallow. His external being seems quite adaptive, but his inner self is rarely seen and seems tenuous at best. . . . While no longer apathetic, his investigative behaviour is limited. . . . The rehabilitated battered child often appears quite bright and/or precocious. However, very few of our children have demonstrated superior intelligence scores.

When Dr Martin describes these children as appearing precocious, he is referring to their ease in coping with practical situations. Many battered children, when they are old enough to scurry out of harm's way (few children are battered, as we have seen, after the age of three), become quite adept at reversing the roles, being useful to their immature parents by shopping, dealing with small household chores, waiting on their mothers.*

But in the literature concerning battered children there is little to suggest that any of them 'shine' academically, even after they have left their dangerous environments and have nothing more to fear. While it may be just to say that Intelligence Quotient tests are only diagnostic tools to test a child's potential, not finite scores in any sense, they do give the testers some idea of children's intelligence levels and conceptual grasp. What we find about the IQs of battered children is fairly dispiriting. In one recent survey, for example, a study conducted by the British NSPCC's National Advisory Centre on the Battered Child, IQ scores of a sample of twenty-five battered children ranged from 50 to 80 (80 is just above normal; a university student today must have an IQ of at least 130 to even contemplate coping with his studies and exams, which shows how meagre a score of 80 is in the scale).

Why are the IQ scores of these children so low? Apart from the more extreme cases of brain damage as a result of parental assault, there would appear to be a host of causes why an early damaging environment often seriously impairs a child's capacity for future mental development (see Dr Elizabeth Elmer's list on page 96 and the theory of impoverished verbal contact advanced on page 85). In the present context of seemingly bright and precocious behaviour displayed in practical situations, I should like to include the theory, sometimes advanced, that abused children are unable to develop their mental abilities because of having had to channel them in another direction, that is, developing a kind of agility and shrewdness in order to survive in a dangerous environment.

In contrast with those willing and adaptable children who develop a capacity to 'parent the parent' in acts of role reversal, are the ones who, once they have been returned home under welfare supervision, reject the parent who has abused them. Sometimes the rejection takes an aggressive form, at other times it may be nothing

---

* Avis Brenner, Co-ordinator for Lesley College's Child and Community Program, Boston, Massachusetts area, told me of a visit to one abusive mother where the four-year-old daughter was ordered to make the coffee and serve it to the two older women. The child duly brought two cups of coffee to them on a tray. After she had set it down, her mother hollered at her: 'Damn you, you've forgotten the sugar. . . .' Even the most efficient 'role-reversing' doesn't always please these exigent parents, it seems.

more than a refusal to become involved with the offending mother or father. British investigators Ruth Mitchell and Clare A. Hyman, in their sample of twenty-five battered children who had been returned to their homes, found that the abused children, (most of whom had been hurt by their mothers) had taken up an evasive stance.

Although not openly admitting to negative feelings towards their mothers, they revealed an indifference to them that almost approached a total denial of their existence. In answers to questions about whom they felt closest to in the family, they would often evade the issue by saying 'nobody'. When they didn't opt out of painful queries about their feelings for their mothers by selecting the card for 'nobody', the battered children tended to choose their fathers or their siblings as stated objects of their affection. Hyman and Mitchell defined this attitude as 'indicative of displacement' with a concentration, perhaps unconscious, on the peripheral members of the family rather than the more central mother whom they nevertheless chose to ignore.

It is both fascinating and distressing to discover that even very young children can bear grudges and be retributive in their actions towards erring parents. During the time I was involved in research on children's reactions to neglect and battering, a friend of mine, emotionally disturbed and unable to resolve her own confused love ties in a satisfactory way, especially with the father of her three-year-old illegitimate son, drifted into a state of detachment towards her child – that alienated, dead condition which constitutes a passive form of neglect.*

The little boy had a rough passage while his mother vacillated in her actions (should she leave his father or not?). First, he was farmed out for two months to a nearby London family, then he accompanied his mother on a strange odyssey to Wales where he would be left with lady inn-keepers or whoever offered to care for him while his mother tried to clarify her thoughts in small country pubs with over-generous helpings of Scotch. This hotchpotch of an existence dragged on. Back in London in tiny, unheated digs, still undecided, my friend rang me, sounding worried. Her son was

---

* As Leontine Young puts it in her book, *Wednesday's Children*: 'Toward their children the emotional detachment [of neglecting parents] is predominant. They neglect not out of hatred but of indifference.'

behaving peculiarly, she told me. It appeared that he had acquired a fantasy mother, an 'other mother', as he called her, who lived far away but who could be reached on the telephone at any time. Day and night, the child could be found babbling to this patient, kind, attentive 'other mother' on his imaginary telephone. When his own mother, distracted, tried to interrupt him, he was curt: 'Be quiet . . . I'm talking to my other mother.'

My friend's neglect had been passive and low-keyed and her son had responded in kind with a delicate and somewhat inspired slap. The behaviour of severely battered children can be much more acutely and vividly retaliatory, displaying a retributory violence that is in direct ratio in severity to the aggression received from their parents. Lenore C. Terr, a Cleveland child psychiatrist, studied ten cases of child abuse with the object of following the development of family life after the initial trauma which had landed the child in hospital. She writes:

> Two toddler-age children, Wendy and Douglas, were studied. Because of his severe brain damage, Douglas lay motionless much of the time and did not retaliate. On the other hand, Wendy, age three, repeatedly smeared her feces on the screen door outside the house.
>
> The two five-year-olds, Jonathan and Janice, used more elaborate methods of retaliation. Jonathan spilled ink on his stepmother's wash, cut up his stepmother's dresses with scissors, and defecated into the laundry basket. Janice refused to eat and stole recess food from other kindergarteners and told elaborate lies to others about family atrocities.
>
> The latency-age youngsters, Denise, nine and Gabriel, seven, retaliated elaborately. Gabriel chronically lied, stole food from others, misbehaved, and refused to obey his frantic mother. Denise also lied, stole pencils, failed to complete homework assignments, and frequently reminded her mother about sexual thoughts she was having.

As Dr Terr says, with remarkable understatement, such angry behaviour tends to worsen the already strained relationship between parent and child. Children can and *do* fight back. However, the behaviour, while understandable, is often more destructive to the child than to his parent, which is why it is so tragic. As these children's social attitudes are characterized by hostility, suggestibility, aggressiveness and poor impulse control, it is obvious that the wounds inflicted will in the end be of a self-destructive nature. Such youthful energies as they have are dissipated in acts of savage naughtiness in their early years and in mindless delinquency in adolescence. The victory over their parents, if victory it is, is a sadly Pyrrhic one.

The case histories of maltreated children who are resolutely returned to their natural parents by short-sighted judges convinced that the blood tie will overcome all parent-child difficulties, stud the literature of child abuse. Often children are returned to their homes suffering from the effects of their injuries, effects that make them more difficult to control and even more exacerbating to their parents' explosive temperaments than they were before.

Such a child was Sara Nauck, the fictional name given to a real child in the de Courcys' book *A Silent Tragedy*. Sara, aged six, living in a small American town disguised by the authors for reasons of discretion, was hit over the head by her mother with an electric frying pan. Severely injured as a result – showing skull fracture, impairment of the right leg and right hand and impaired memory – Sara was made a temporary ward of the Juvenile Court pending trial. The injury occurred in early January 1971, and the trial took place on 11 March; thus only two months elapsed between the time of the original assault, the police investigation, Sara's removal to a Children's Shelter, and the trial. During the trial, the judge admonished the mother for using physical punishment but ordered the child to be returned to her home under Welfare Department supervision.

When Sara returned home, her parents observed a great change in her behaviour: 'She was restless and hyperactive,' the de Courcys write, 'and it was difficult for her to fall asleep at nights. Once she did fall asleep, she was difficult to awaken, and she frequently wet the bed.' Her behaviour increased her mother's detestation of her. Further injury, the authors predicted gloomily and probably accurately, seemed inevitable.

It is difficult to comprehend the myopia of court judges who make such dangerous, even fatal, decisions. Once again, there would seem to be a serious gap in the thinking of the professions – in this case, between psychiatry and the law. Over ten years ago,

Dr Leontine Young, one of the most experienced professionals in the field of child abuse, warned that a return of a severely abused child* to his natural home was a risky procedure: 'In none of these cases,' she writes, referring to home replacements, 'was there any change of parental behaviour. The children were, if anything, worse off, and their behaviour in a number of cases, deteriorated rapidly.' She goes on to suggest that the eagerness of court officials to place a child back in his natural home springs from a misguided sense that the parents, having lost their child to welfare departments for several months, will be so relieved to have him back that they will 'come to their senses'. This widespread conviction, she states trenchantly, 'can spring only from an ignorance of their pathology'.

In the fifty cases of battered children studied by Dr Elizabeth Elmer, it was found that a 'changed environment' (meaning removal to a home other than the natural one) inevitably meant a change for the better. The children who were fortunate enough to find foster placements showed substantially better physical and intellectual functioning than their counterparts who had remained with the abusing parents. If they were not abused again in their natural homes, this was probably due to increased age – and, with it, as I have already emphasized, the ability to get out of harm's way – rather than a change of heart on the part of the violent parent.

This is not to say that the child who is placed in a foster-home won't have his share of personality adjustment problems. Many of them, particularly those who become curious about their backgrounds as adolescence approaches, are haunted by a sense of rejection. Were they so bad that their own parents couldn't love them? This is the question that can hang over them.

Kevin, a black high school boy of fourteen living in Vancouver, was beset by such doubts and feelings of insecurity. His story is movingly described by two Canadian child experts, Susan Stephenson and Nerissa Lo, in their detailed case history, 'When Shall We Tell Kevin?' Kevin had been removed from his teenaged

* The milder cases, when properly supervised after intervention, can usually be returned to the original home providing the mother is receiving the support she needs from the social security visitors and the community as a whole.

delinquent mother when he was two, after she had tried to murder him by putting lye in his milk when he was nineteen months old. Swallowing the poison had left him with a permanently damaged oesophagus. This digestive organ had to be dilated at regular intervals to keep it open and he had repeated hospital admissions throughout his childhood. At fourteen, when his behaviour began to reveal his psychic tumult, he was still having to chop up his food in small morsels in order to swallow it, a necessity which, along with heaviness and bigness for his age, made him feel the odd man out. He began to behave belligerently and anti-socially at school, attracting attention to himself with clownish actions and by being a bully in the playground. His caseworker found his behaviour 'counterphobic', particularly his belligerence, as he was really a frightened child with a low self-image, feeling angry and insecure.

At home, his foster-parents, who had been loving during his childhood but who were now older and ailing and less able to cope with his adolescent problems, gave dispirited reports of the boy's increased bed-wetting and hostility towards them to the psychiatric consultant on the case.

It was at this time that the caseworker and welfare agency nurse decided to tell Kevin about his mother. It was obvious that he had entered puberty feeling rejected by his natural parents, about whom he knew nothing. Also, he had been nursing the erroneous notion that his foster-parents were responsible for the lye accident and his embarrassing and painful digestive problems. Kevin had begun to idealize his own parents. Perhaps they wanted him back but were prevented from reconciliation because of his foster-parents? It was decided to check his imaginings against the cruel truth. His caseworker took him to a quiet place and told him of the poisoning attempt, explaining that his mother had been very young and distressed at the time of her action against him. Kevin burst into sobs and said over and over again: 'If my mother didn't want me she didn't have to *kill* me.'

Afterwards, Kevin's attitude to his foster-parents altered dramatically, and though he was still angry and depressed, he ventilated these feelings to his caseworker and was more co-operative at home (politely bringing his wet sheets to his foster-mother when he was troubled by enuresis – a condition associated more with emotional disturbance than with bladder dysfunction – as he still was from time to time). Kevin's next school report was filled with laudatory comments about his improvement, both in his behaviour and academically.

Kevin's story is a happy one, not least because it reveals how one brave caseworker took a calculated risk, which worked. It is also an example of how perilous social work can be in the field of child abuse, and of the strains to which those responsible often find themselves subjected. Kevin was ready for the revelation about his mother and proved strong enough to take it. What if he hadn't been? The consequences hardly bear thinking about. When the writers of Kevin's case history say that the caseworker went through a 'long, harrowing and emotion-laden experience' before deciding to tell him, one believes them.

The placement of a severely abused child in a foster-home may be the happiest solution for him by preventing further assault, but it is not the end of all anxiety. As we see with Kevin, even in a loving home backlash emotions can arise in a young person's mind, especially when events in his childhood are left shrouded in mystery. There are worries for the foster-parents as well. First of all, they may be presented with a retarded and damaged child who comes to them with problems that are not of their own making. As Denver psychiatrist Dr Harold Martin points out, it is frequently a point of personal pride on the part of the foster-parents that the child be shown to flourish under their care, and if the bloom is slow in coming, they can feel hurt and inadequate. The child may need to regress for a while to catch up on stages in development which he missed during his traumatic time with his natural parents; such a period of dependency and clinging to the surrogate parent should be understood and even encouraged. For this reason, foster-parents often need as much guidance and therapy as the biological parents, to help them cope with their complex charges.

Some couples seem to have almost an overspill of the nurturing capacity, possessing not only enough love for their own children but plenty to spare for their foster-child. It is just as well that foster-parents be well-endowed, as they need these strengths. Speaking at a Chicago Conference of Foster Parents in 1971, Dr Ner Littner, a child therapy training programme director, defined the difficult 'juggling' job which faces most foster-parents who have to perform three tasks at the same time: to be the best possible parent, to co-operate fully with the placement agency and its social workers and to maintain a working relationship with the child's natural parents.

The third task, that of keeping in touch with the natural parents, is usually the most thorny, Dr Littner explained, as these disturbed adults often sabotage the foster-parents' best efforts by being un-reliable (not showing up for visits, promising the child gifts and outings which aren't then organized, etc.). However, he believes that foster-parents should try to swallow their understandable animosity, because a child who never sees his natural parents may build up idealized and unrealistic fantasies about either one or both of them (as Kevin did). Such a child may bury separation feelings, and this repression can pose serious dangers to his mental health. As Littner says, 'the effort at keeping them buried [the separation feelings], ties up a lot of the child's energy and thus interferes with his ability to function properly.' So, as he stresses, the occasional sight of the natural parents is a requisite though they may well be viewed by the foster-parents as 'necessary evils' and 'natural enemies'. (It should be emphasized here that not all experts agree with this view. One of these, in particular, is Anna Freud, as I shall explain later.)

While many abused children make very reasonable adjustments to the world outside their home, they share certain emotional characteristics, particularly in relation to the abusing parent, which appear to be lasting. Boston child abuse expert Edgar Merrill has enumerated certain qualities which these children seemed unable to shake off with time: 'a tendency to overreact towards hostility, depression, hyper-activity, destructiveness and fear'. Merrill stresses that these distinguishing features diminish outside the abusive home; he states that in his findings the children show a good ability to relate to teachers, neighbours, relatives, peers at school and social workers. If they are surly and anti-social, it is their parents who feel it most (deservedly, one might think).

Perhaps the most depressing of all the lasting effects of early abuse upon a child's development is the lowering of the intelli-gence, for which so much evidence exists. Of the children Dr Eliza-beth Elmer studied over the years in their improved environments, the majority rarely achieved normal intellectual levels. As she writes:

Fifty percent of the abused study group were mentally retarded upon re-evaluation despite improved environments and recovery from growth failure. Many had suffered at a vulnerable age from trauma, irreversible nervous system damage, starvation, maternal deprivation, or distorted parent-child interaction. Any one of these experiences could have precluded normal intelligence.

Such a gloomy prognosis for their future ('only a few of the children give promise of becoming self-sufficient adults,' she goes on to say) leads her to plead for early intervention. In her own words, 'the serious outcome for so large a proportion of the original study children makes it imperative to recognize abuse as early as possible.'

Nearly a decade has passed since Dr Elmer pleaded for swift help for abused children – the earlier the better. Has this help been forthcoming? It would seem that it has, but patchily and erratically, and sometimes with disastrous results.

I should like to show exactly what *is* being done on both sides of the Atlantic to protect children from being abused, and why, if it is still not enough, this should be so.

7/ Child Abuse:
Social Attitudes and Prevention

If the child most in danger is the one with the loneliest parent, then it would seem to be a community responsibility to ensure that this parent will not continue to be lonely.

A heartening modern trend is the new willingness of the various community services to try to be on hand to assume the responsibility of cutting into family isolation with offers of company, help, counsel and general moral support.

In the past few years we have witnessed a remarkable changeover in attitudes towards the battering parent. While many people still view them with deep revulsion and hope that they will be harshly punished with prison sentences for their violence, there is a newer attitude towards them which is becoming more widespread. This is the view, originally formulated by Henry Kempe and his associates, a psychoanalytically orientated one, encouraging society to prevent abuses occurring in the first place by coming to the aid of these psychologically disturbed parents before illtreatment occurs.

Coupled with this more compassionate stance, with its emphasis on understanding the psychology of abusing parents, is a trend towards increased study of their environmental background. Research in the 'seventies has tended to study the psychiatric dynamics of these parents in conjunction with their socio-economic characteristics.

97

This is not to say that abusing parents are not being punished for their physical cruelty; the newspapers report cases of two- to four-year prison sentences for battering parents almost weekly, sad to relate. But, as far as I can see, efforts towards *preventing* battering seem to be achieving an edge over the punitive approach. A dramatic new discovery is that parents respond to outside help. As one child expert has expressed it, inadequate parents are 'sick but curable'. This pithy phrase could be said to be the rallying call of the new thinkers concerned with abusing parents.

Philosophically speaking, this optimistic outlook carries with it shades of eighteenth-century France, of Voltaire, of a belief in the perfectibility of man, of a disillusion with prison sentencing and a fundamental sense of hope concerning the possibilities of rehabilitation. As far as I can discern from reading the literature on the subject, nothing in the behaviour of the once abusing parents gives rise to a cynical discarding of optimism. They do improve. Recidivist rates amongst abusing parents are low. (Of course, all this is only relevant as long as the abused child has not actually died at his parents' hands. Prosecution rather than psychiatric counselling is the inevitable outcome of child murder.)

As experts in the field now invite the public to regard child abuse as a social problem, a symptom of social breakdown which it is the community's responsibility to help mend, protecting the child has come to be acknowledged as a public obligation.

But community responsibility, in the form of 'community surveillance' – necessary and good though it may be in relation to the safety of the child at risk – is a delicate and complex business to put into operation. The abusing parents, aggressive towards those who wish to help as well as to their children, resent being watched, intruded upon. In Elizabeth Elmer's evocative phrase, the best way the community can help is by administering what she calls 'cool mothering', a process by which members of the community make themselves gently available for help without being too pushy.

This is all very well – but how exactly can it be done? The trouble with the concept of community surveillance is that it must, of necessity, embrace a complex network of social agencies. In the US, since Kempe's coining of the 'Battered Child Syndrome' in 1962, all fifty states have passed legislation for reporting laws. The laws are far from immutable and are being constantly amended; the exasperated-sounding American Humane Association's Revised 1974 Report* refers to the laws as being endlessly 'tinkered with'. So, in the United States at least, the machinery of law has been geared towards quick reporting of abuse in the community. The trouble is that just finding out *where* the abuse is occurring is not enough. You have your law, you find the abusing parent – then what? As Vincent De Francis, Director of the Children's Division of the AHA, says, 'reporting law becomes a meaningless and futile piece of legislation . . . unless the community is prepared to marshal all its resources to help treat the problem situation identified.' But these resources are often so diverse, with so little co-ordination between them, that swift action is made impossible. To use a crude simile, it is like detecting a small forest fire and then trying to co-ordinate over a dozen different fire departments to deal with it. By the time the various departments have sorted out whose duty it is to put out the fire, there might well be an all-out conflagration (or, to come back to the desperate matter at hand, a dead child).

To cite one instance: in 1969, in Buffalo, after New York State had passed a revised reporting law drastically altering its community plan for helping the abused child, Norman Paget, Executive Director of the Buffalo Children's Aid and SPCC, decided to round up all the people in the various services concerned for a conference. The agencies he had to contact were: the Judges of the Family Court, Legal Aid, State and County officials, the Medical Society, the hospitals, the District Attorney, the schools and the police. It is no wonder that Paget expressed his deep concern at the time that the abused child might get 'lost' between the services.

For some reason, society seems to need classic cases of ineptitude and ensuing tragedies before it is awakened to the enormity of

---

* From 1967 to 1970, the majority of US states passed legislation regarding the mandatory reporting of child abuse. The American Humane Association's Children's Division has kept the sprawling, confusing differences in legislation between individual states in some order by publishing an admirable handbook, *Child Abuse Legislation in the 1970's,* the most recent edition being published in 1974. Their job has not been an easy one.

certain social disorders – in this instance, child abuse. In the US, the case of Roxanne in 1969 caused a public outcry which still echoes today, especially in New York City where the tragedy occurred. Ironically, the Manhattan authorities were becoming increasingly aware of the phenomenon of child abuse in the city, so much so that Mayor John Lindsay had ordered the creation of a special Task Force on Child Abuse to evaluate the effectiveness of the 1964 New York State Child Abuse law and the machinery set up to carry it out.*

As if to mock it, Roxanne was found at the bottom of the East River on 25 March, only two months after the Task Force began to operate. The *New York Times,* of 26 March, gave the following brief report under the headline 'Man Held in Slaying of Stepdaughter; Body Found in River':

> A Lower East Side man was charged yesterday with having beaten his three-year-old stepdaughter to death and thrown her body into the East River.
>
> The body of the child, Roxanne Felumero, was recovered yesterday afternoon by police divers. Rocks and pieces of concrete had been stuffed into the pockets of her trousers, presumably to weight the body down.
>
> The police said that she had died Friday, after having been beaten by her stepfather, George Poplis, a waiter. He was charged with homicide and his wife, Marie, the girl's mother, was held as a material witness.
>
> Detectives had been searching for the child since Friday night, when her mother reported having left her 'for just a minute' outside the tenement where they lived at 199 Avenue B, near 12th Street.
>
> After questioning Mrs Poplis again yesterday afternoon, the police turned their search to the East River, just off 12th Street, and the body was quickly found.
>
> Mr & Mrs Poplis have two other children living with them, a year-old daughter of their own and a 5-year-old boy who is Mrs Poplis's son by Roxanne's father.

I have given the news report of Roxanne's murder discovery in full because it seems to me to embody so many of the factors in-

---

* The special Task Force was formed on 23 January, 1969, by Dr Howard J. Brown, commissioner of the city health services.

volved in child abuse cases: the target child, the colluding parents, a weak and lying mother telling a story to the police that is possibly a cry for help (she needn't, after all, have reported Roxanne's disappearance to the police so soon after the murder), the existence of other siblings who are not similarly abused.

Roxanne's tragic story is a classic in other ways. She was, in the rather arch phrase that has become so popular with the Fleet Street press, a 'tug-of-love' child, pulled between her natural mother and doting foster-parents. For the first few years of her young life, Roxanne had spent a happy time with her foster-parents. However, when Mrs Poplis asked the courts for Roxanne's return, she had little trouble in getting her back. With the law courts' customary respect for the blood tie, the judges were quickly convinced that Roxanne's mother had contracted a stable second marriage (one of the reasons Roxanne had been removed from Mrs Poplis in the first place was because she had a history of neglect, drug-taking and violence during her first marriage) and did not cavil at the request. Mr Poplis showed up in court and cut a convincing figure as a prospective stepfather, speaking of his devotion to the little girl and of being gainfully employed (he had no job at the time).

Each time Roxanne's former foster-parents took her out for the day and for the treats she was occasionally allowed, they discovered her body covered in bruises. They reported the injuries to the New York Foundling Hospital, where Roxanne had been born, and in several cases took the child to court to ask for her return. Despite the evidence of maltreatment, the family courts returned the child to the Poplis's (Roxanne herself had told her foster-parents that it was her stepfather who hit her: the child's crime seemed to have been bed-wetting – again, a classic rage-igniter in battering parents).

In her short life Roxanne was 'lost' between the services. Four judges of the family courts had dealt with her case in the two years before her death, and not all of the relevant material concerning her had been given them at the time they had made their decisions. On 2 January, 1969, a doctor on the staff of the New York Foundling Hospital wrote a 'suspicion of abuse' report, but this was not received by the social services protection unit for a week. No one knows why.

In his book, *Somewhere a Child is Crying,* Vincent Fontana, Director of the New York Foundling Hospital and chairman of the New York Task Force on Child Abuse, gives a despairing run-down on the breakdown of communications between the services that existed in Roxanne's case (called Annemarie Lombardo in the book):

> The haphazard division of responsibilities, the faulty coordination, the gaps and flaws in the chain of information, the human weaknesses and errors, these were the things that destroyed Annemarie. At first it seemed obvious that a family court judge was to blame. But gradually it emerged that one social worker had not done *this* and the other social worker had not done *that,* that information in the possession of one agency had not been shared with other agencies; that reports that were to have been sent posthaste were around for days; that investigations that should have been pursued never were begun; that statements that should have been verified by a personal check were accepted at face value; that testimony that should have been produced in court was not produced. . . . This has been the problem not only in the Annemarie case but in every case that has similarly been lost. There has been no communication between the various disciplines.

Four years later in Brighton, in Southern England, seven-year-old Maria Colwell was murdered by her stepfather in a case that is eerily reminiscent of the Roxanne tragedy in its history of inter-disciplinary bungling, lost reports, communication failures and sleepy bureaucratic fumblings.

Like Roxanne, Maria Colwell had loving foster-parents (in this case the child's aunt, the sister of her dead father). She was a 'happy-go-lucky child, always healthy', in her foster-father's words. Mrs Pauline Kepple, Maria's mother, had remarried a Mr William Kepple and assured the East Sussex County Council officials that she was a reformed character (two of Mrs Kepple's older children had been placed in care in 1965, eight years before Maria's murder, because of Mrs Kepple's neglect; she regularly left her children unattended while she went out drinking, it was reported at that time). With the surprising ease with which natural mothers are able to convince the courts that they are changed people, Mrs Kepple was granted permission to have Maria back within a short time of asking; this under the supervision of a young, overworked child care officer with seventy cases on her books, six of them involving abusing parents.

The child's own feelings when taken from her foster-parents were eloquently expressed in bouts of tears, followed by fits of depression, as noted by her family doctor. However, these were ignored by the authorities and she was returned to her mother and stepfather in November 1971. In the next fourteen months, until her death, Maria changed from a 'bonny', normal little girl to a frightened scarecrow of a child, fifteen pounds below weight for her age, nervously explaining away her bruises to neighbours with stories of falls. Tradespeople in the neighbourhood noted that she was sent to fetch a bag of coal weighing twenty-eight pounds – fuel for the Kepple home – each morning (she herself weighed only thirty-six pounds), which she wheeled up and down a steep hill in an old baby's pram. Between 17 April and mid-December, 1972, thirty representations were made concerning Maria to Maria's care officer, to the Brighton Welfare Department and to the NSPCC, mainly from groups of neighbours on the Whitehawk Estate where the Kepples lived.

Sociologists have recently likened such a community reaction to a chorus in a Greek tragedy: there are warning calls and pointed fingers, but too often, just as in a drama by Aeschylus or Euripides, the moaning chorus does nothing to stop an ugly and seemingly inexorable act of fate. Certainly the simile is apt in the case of Maria Colwell. Apart from the deputations from neighbours, there were also the voices of alarmed shopkeepers and shocked school-teachers.

Maria's teacher, Mrs Ann Turner, a state-registered nurse in her late thirties and herself a mother, sent out a constant stream of anxious reports to the headmaster, but these were somehow chan-nelled to the wrong department and never reached him. What had particularly disturbed Mrs Turner was the feel of Maria's under-nourished body. When Maria burst into tears during a class dis-turbance, Mrs Turner took her on her knee to comfort her. She reported later: 'I shuddered when I felt how thin she was. She was like a bird and I was frightened of crushing her.'

Maria also visited the school doctor during her last fourteen months with the Kepples, but his records were amazingly uninformative. On her medical card there was no record of the various care and supervision orders placed on her, and the doctor assumed that her home conditions were normal. A month before she was beaten to death, an appointment was made for Maria to see a doctor at the Brighton schools clinic – at the urging of the NSPCC. When she failed to turn up for the appointment, instead of a new appointment being pressed upon her mother, the card was mistakenly put into a dormant file and forgotten.

The police were also drawn into the chorus of alarm. One neighbour had called a policewoman to check on the house after he had seen three of the smaller Kepple children at their upstairs window saying: 'Mummy and Daddy are down at the pub and we are frightened.' The policewoman 'severely warned' Mrs Kepple that she would be prosecuted if she left the children alone again, but when the same policewoman called on Mrs Kepple the next day, the front door was slammed in her face.

In this context, one sees that the role of the police in the child cruelty prevention scheme is a nebulous one. Raymond L. Castle, Executive Head of Britain's NSPCC, calls it 'one of the most difficult and sensitive areas of all when it comes to co-ordination and co-operation'. The major difficulty is that the majority of police officers have not been educated concerning child abuse and tend to regard it as a straightforward criminal act, requiring an investigation and possible criminal sanctions. Although this is certainly not the case with all police officers – some of whom are very enlightened and happy to refer cases of suspected abuse to the social services – it is a grey area and one Britain's Ministry of Health and Social Security should try to clarify. In other words, do the police have the right to adjudicate in cases of child abuse or not? The question is still unresolved, at least in the United Kingdom. In the United States, the police have been almost totally phased out of the child abuse sphere: while they may be the receivers of information about a suspected case, they now rarely handle subsequent proceedings concerning parents.

In the Maria Colwell case, the policewoman did nothing at all after Mrs Kepple's rude rebuff, and the case continued on its nightmare course to the very end (a month before Maria was killed, her child care officer reported her to her anxious foster-parents as 'improved, and beginning to call Mr Kepple "Dad" '). In character with the entire bureaucratic tangle, it was not until after Maria's murder that the child care officer discovered that William Kepple had a disturbing police record – four convictions for violence before Maria came under his roof.

'A fatal failure to pool the total knowledge of the child's background . . . plus communication failures' caused Maria Colwell to fall through the welfare net, a 1974 Government Report on the case concluded.

If it is possible for children of abusing parents to fall between the services with such fatal consequences, one might ask why children are not automatically placed or retained in foster homes.

Like so many other issues in the field of child abuse, this one is debated passionately between two opposing factions: the supporters of the idea of 'home placement under supervision' and those who favour 'permanent foster placement'. Perhaps the most eloquent supporter of the 'home is best' school of thought is Paul D'Agostino, former supervisor of the Boston Battered Child Unit, Department of Public Welfare, now supervising a mental health programme in Tampa, Florida. Writing in the magazine *Public Welfare* in 1972, while still director of the Boston Child Protective services, he states his view unequivocally:

> With weekly intervention and community support, the child can be permitted to remain in his own home. This is preferable to foster home placement, where both the child and his family must undergo separation from each other. Even though placement is necessary in some cases, it must be remembered that there are many unanswered questions with regard to the long range effects of this type of parent/child separation.

In a recent conversation at his Florida office with my sister, researcher Louise van Agt, Paul D'Agostino reiterated his belief that separating a child from his parents only reinforced the former's feelings of worthlessness and sense of guilt – the conviction that if his own parents couldn't love him, no one else would. D'Agostino believes that this personality damage can be farreaching and difficult to treat in later years, and that community and social service help with the child at his home is preferable to the aiding and abetting of the child's sense of being unloved, which accompanied the removal process. In his opinion the Roxanne type of community breakdown disaster is too rare (perhaps one in twenty) to force society to abandon the concept of home rehabilitation with social service supervision.

But the arguments *against* keeping the child at home can be just as unequivocal. John Reinhart of the Children's Hospital, Pittsburgh, states that many parents are incapable of being rehabilitated,* that their love of their children is not automatic — being a mixture of love and hate, in fact — and that placement programmes are necessary to combat these dangerous feelings of parental ambivalence.

While Paul D'Agostino and his followers worry about the psychic damage done to the child in the process of separation in placement cases, other experts say 'what use is an undamaged psyche if the child may not even live to enjoy his own future mental health?' A recent NSPCC summary of the 'Battered Child Syndrome' puts the Society's case for the primacy of physical safety over mental damage, suggesting that, in any case, physical damage itself can be brutally hurtful to mental health:

> It is a mistake to believe that a foster home or even a good institution is always inferior to home. Where the child's life is at stake the possible damage to his personality development must take second place. In any case our studies of the children show that it is just this personality development which is most damaged by physical assault. ... If necessary, juvenile court proceedings leading to a compulsory care order must be instituted if other alternatives cannot certainly secure the safety of the child.

What does emerge fairly clearly in all the debates about foster placement as opposed to home rehabilitation, is that the major concern is for the children. Few, if any, professionals are after the parents' blood. Punitive action towards abusing parents is becom-

---

* Reinhart cites the research done on a group of 100 British mothers who were placed on probation and admitted to residential training homes after a two-year period after having appeared in the courts for child neglect. Twenty-five per cent of the mothers continued to be incapable of proper child care after discharge from the rehabilitation centres.

ing a rarity (William Kepple's eight-year sentence for Maria's murder was uncharacteristically harsh, no doubt because it followed upon four other convictions for violence).

What society has been working towards is the 'decriminalization' of child abuse (a rather clumsy word meaning that this particular form of aberrant behaviour should no longer be punished criminally; in fact, that social welfare supervision and/or psychiatric treatment should be substituted for prison sentences). One of the reasons for the curious limbo in which the police have found themselves recently, is this very process of 'decriminalization'. While the police are still called upon to investigate suspected abuse, their role after this is no longer clearly defined. It has been – and still is – a hazy position for them to be in and one that should elicit our sympathy.

The process of 'decriminalization' does not mean that abusing parents are necessarily regarded with benign tolerance. Ordinary citizens are repelled by signs of abuse and can feel quite understandably vengeful. For example, when Vincent Fontana later questioned Roxanne's neighbours in the tenement building where she had lived out her last days, he met with anger and horror (her face had 'looked like a balloon' from bruises, they reported). Among prison inmates, where a code of 'honour among thieves' prevails, feelings of fury and retributiveness are so prevalent that child offenders of all varieties often have to be protected by being sequestered in separate quarters from the other prisoners.

Nor do the professionals involved necessarily feel benign about the parents. But their argument in favour of decriminalization is pragmatic, centred on the belief that punishment does not prove an effective method of curtailing abuse. US psychiatrist Dr Irving Kaufman was among the first to suggest that imprisonment was an ineffective deterrent for the abusing parent. He preferred the use of social worker surveillance, though he conceded that inadequate or cruel parents tried the 'mettle, patience and skill' of the protective caseworker. But sentencing them to prison was a waste of time, he wrote in 1962, because:

None of these parents have achieved a level of development which would enable them to feel guilty. They are at a much more primitive stage where aggression is based on unreality and they feel that they had to strike out or that a destructive force would sweep them over, or that they would lose control. Guilt in the normal or neurotic sense does not exist as a mechanism for them. This has major implications for management because any type of punishment or treatment which hopes to mobilise guilt is generally doomed to failure in this type of case.

Dr Kaufman's words have not been ignored. The American Humane Association's 1974 Child Abuse Legislation Report notes that there has been a gradual but impressive nationwide switch for reporting child abuse – from the police to the social services. At the time of their Report, a total of forty-three states required that reports of child abuse be directed to the department of social services, intensifying the trend away from criminal sentencing of the parents.

'The most logical conclusion to be drawn from this trend', says the Report, 'is that it represents an increasing acceptance of the philosophy which favours the use of the helping social work process on behalf of the abused child and a rejection of criminal prosecution of abusing parents as a routine approach.'

Hardly any one state has the same definition of abuse, the same method of reporting, the same penalties for not reporting. Studying the legislation carefully is a fascinating exercise, because it shows clearly the differing attitudes and prejudices held in each state towards the phenomenon. It is also somewhat confusing, because the question of *to whom* to report is a significant indicator of how the local legislators regard abusing parents – as suitable cases for treatment, or as criminals in need of punishment. In Ohio and Nebraska, for instance, the reporting of abuse is regarded as a straightforward criminal matter, and professionals and laymen are asked to report to the police or to the sheriff. In other states (New York, North Carolina, Oklahoma, Vermont, Florida and Massachusetts, to name some), the decriminalization process has become almost complete; the report has to be made to either the county or the state Department of Social Services – not the police.

What about the reporting laws themselves? How mandatory are they? The answer is: moderately. This creates an evident paradox. While the parents involved are being classified as more neurotic than evil, people failing to report them are punished by the law (fines of anywhere from 100 to 500 dollars are imposed, with an alternative of several months' imprisonment). There is irony here in the diminution of the 'crime-and-punishment' syndrome for the abusing parents and the imposition of quite heavy penalties for the innocent citizen who is only the witness and eventual reporter of the abuse. However, the rationale for imposing a penalty upon a professional or a lay member of the community for failing to report is that he may justify his report on the grounds of self-protection ('Neighbour, I hate to do this to you but *I* would have been prosecuted if I hadn't . . .').

Another way in which the neighbour is protected in the US is by the 'immunity clause'. This means that, even if a suspected case of abuse has been found to be baseless, the neighbour cannot be prosecuted (doctors, too, are covered in all fifty states by the immunity law).

However, the situation regarding reports from laymen, or 'any other person' as the neighbour is called in the abstruse language of the law, is far from clear-cut even now. Only thirty states invite reports from that shadowy entity.

One can guess the reasons for this. Presumably, professionals realize that neighbours cannot always be altruistic or totally objective, that they might be motivated by a desire for petty revenge, or simply act as a result of traditional neighbourly intrusiveness (neighbour and 'busybody' often being interchangeably linked in people's minds).

While I write this, a situation regarding a neighbour's report has just come to a head in England, showing how confused the neighbour's role as reporter is in the community. Whereas, until now, the NSPCC has always protected the identity of reporting neighbours, this promise of confidentiality is now being threatened by law (the House of Lords debated the issue in 1976). Pleading for the retention of the promise of confidentiality, Nicholas Stacey, Social Services Director for Kent, wrote in the *Daily Express* at the time: 'Nobody wants a society of tittle-tattlers . . . but the more we discourage people coming forward, the less protection there'll be for innocent lives.'

Many experts believe that neighbours are an essential pipeline to the child at risk and are convinced of the necessity of such reports. When I interviewed Mr Lincoln Bosco, Supervisor of

Intake, Children's Protective Services, of Boston's SPCC, he said with great conviction: 'Referrers from neighbours are frequently valid and understated.' (The 'referrer', in current social welfare parlance, is the person who makes the charge.)

In short, whether one is for or against the reports from neighbours, they are a force to be reckoned with and are gaining increasing recognition in the battle against child abuse. In some states, they are positively encouraged. One can see this in cases where red tape is at an absolute minimum and a telephone report of a suspected case of abuse is all that is needed (in four states – Tennessee, Utah, New Jersey and South Carolina – no written report is required).

However, not all states are as blessedly simple as the four just mentioned in the matter of *how* to report. Again, one falls into the morass of conflicting methods, state by state. Thirty-seven states object to oral reports altogether, inviting 'written reports only'. Others require that the written report be submitted 'immediately' after the oral report; others again are more specific as to time (within forty-eight hours, in Maryland). Michigan law is particularly demanding, requiring a written report immediately and 'in quadruplicate'. The latter requirement would appear to discourage all but the most zealous professional. (It is significant that in this state, reports from laymen are not sought at all.)

The mandatory laws also vary from state to state concerning the age of the child for whom a report of suspected abuse should be made. In Colorado, the statute requires that abuse of any child up to the age of eighteen be reported. In Arkansas, this drops to sixteen years; in California, it plummets dramatically to twelve.

Methods of dealing with a child when abuse is reported also vary. In Kentucky, for instance, the state has an 'emergency removal' clause, which means that after the home has been searched (the mere receipt of a report is sufficient grounds for issuing a warrant) and the abuse confirmed, the child may be removed. If the child is injured and ends up in hospital, and if the physician suspects non-accidental injury, he may hold him in hospital for twenty-four hours without a court order. This period should enable him to obtain the requisite court order and obviates the necessity of returning the child to his parents or custodians for even a brief time.

Other states appear to carry with them the age-old respect for the parental blood tie, and removal proceedings are far more difficult. In Nevada, for example, no child about whom a report has been made may be removed from his custodians before an initial consultation between the disciplinary agencies has taken place (social and medical services, the police, etc.). Only if a child is judged to be in immediate danger by a reporting doctor or law enforcement agency, can he be removed without this requisite consultation.

Three states (Connecticut, New Mexico and Colorado) have decided that the child should be specially protected when in court, and have ordered that he be represented by a 'guardian *ad litem*' – a direct consequence of the growth of the idea of children's rights. The 'guardian' is in court to represent 'the best interests of the child'. His duties, especially as outlined in the Colorado statutes, may be extensive. He may make further investigation as he deems necessary, cross-examine witnesses and make his own recommendations to the court as to what changes should be made to improve the child's welfare after the court hearing.

While Henry Kempe's team appear pleased with this new obligatory appointment, others are wary of it. Vincent De Francis, AHA Chief, considers it to be of dubious worth, preferring, so he writes, a proper attorney to protect the child's rights. (He feels that a guardian may not have adequate knowledge of the judicial process, a process which, he adds, is to decide the child's future, when all is said and done.)

All but six states have Central Registries, offices where lists of children who are known to be at risk are retained in a computer bank, sometimes filed by the police, sometimes by the Social Services. It is to be hoped that the six states lacking Central Registries will soon establish them. They are among the most effective tools for containing and reducing the incidence of child abuse. With a central clearing house in possession of thorough and accurate case histories of each child, the dates of previous abuse, and all other relevant information concerning his family, the chance of a child falling through the net of varying agencies is greatly reduced.

New York State's Central Registry is an exemplary one. It is capable of receiving electronic reports of child abuse or maltreatment, and of providing a statewide child protective service twenty-four hours a day, seven days a week. To cut through the possibility of too many different people receiving reports of abuse and no one acting upon an alarm call because of that age-old deterrent to action, 'Whose Responsibility?', New York State has a single telephone number that all persons may use to report cases. The existence of one Central Registry with a single number has streamlined the system considerably. The minute an electronic record of the reporter's call is made, a check can be carried out to see if the name of the child has been reported before. All the pertinent information concerning the child is thus immediately to hand, and the child protective services can be notified.

The United States is too vast to have anything other than this state by state system. Smaller countries in the forefront of child protection and prevention of abuse – France and Finland, for example – have centralized their systems considerably, using computer banks in the capital cities to store information on each new child born, so that a close watch can be kept on the development of each one. Commenting on the creaking British procedures to prevent child abuse, Dr Mia Kellmer Pringle, Director of Britain's National Children's Bureau, said that she believed Britain could well emulate France and Finland. These countries give cash incentives to new mothers to bring their infants for full pediatric examinations at eight days, nine months and two years. These cash gifts cost France £250 million a year, but the French Government feels that the outlay is well worth it, especially in terms of the future reduction of social security payments for children in care. The scheme may feel like 'Big Brother' to some, but it is, at least, a big 'benign' brother, and fewer children get hurt.

New York State, like France, has an exemplary overall view of its children's welfare. The tragedy of Roxanne galvanized it into praiseworthy legislation. Its legal definition of a 'neglected' child is among the most advanced in the land, distinguishing, as it does, between 'emotional' and 'physical' damage to the child. For example, in the case of an 'abused child', an impairment of his or her 'emotional health' is regarded as neglect.

Just as the death of Roxanne and other unfortunates like her has not gone unheeded, and has helped to perfect New York's child abuse legislation, Maria Colwell's death forced England to tighten up her lax child protective services. The Public Inquiry following

her death, whose Report was published in September 1974, analysed the series of communication breakdowns which led to the
child's murder.

After nine weeks of public hearings in Brighton tracing the
bunglings which caused the death, the three professionals appointed to delve into the case – a barrister, a county alderman and an
Oxford University sociologist – ended up by disagreeing violently
on all points. Miss Olive Stevenson, the sociologist, felt that a
'hierarchy of censure', scolding social workers for their omissions,
was counter-productive. She pleaded for more public compassion
for social workers who were employed 'to perform tasks of the ut-
most difficulty and complexity, under conditions of great strain'.
Miss Stevenson's admonitory message may have made her un-
popular with her colleagues on the commission, at the time, but it
struck a nerve. Was inter-disciplinary wrangling and inter-agency
blame-affixing going to help suffering children? Miss Stevenson's
view that it wasn't, was echoed by others in the field.

As Joan Court had written previously in an article in the
Nursing Times: 'Blaming colleagues is one of the most unattractive
manifestations of the battered child syndrome. Some co-ordinating
committees defeat their purpose by spreading anxiety rather than
sharing information. There may be obsessive preoccupation with
regard to roles and procedures. There is, too, a tendency for these
cases to arouse jealousy and possessiveness among the helping personnel.'

As if in response to these various calls for a more positive
approach, the British Association of Social Workers drew up a
code of practice in September 1975, emphasizing the need for
'swift action' in implementing safety orders for children who
appeared to be at risk. The Code of Practice acknowledged the
difficulties that faced social workers visiting families who were
hostile to them; their proposal for circumventing this was to make
the child a ward of court, with the help of the police and/or the
medical profession. The Code stressed the need for reporting all
visits and telephone calls made concerning children at risk, as well
as the need for inter-agency consultation before returning the
children to their parents.

As there are no mandatory reporting laws in Britain, child protection is often a matter of codes and departmental guidelines.

Largely in response to the public outcry about Maria Colwell, the Department of Health and Social Security wrote a Memorandum in April 1974 to all area health authorities, directors of social services, borough councillors and teaching authorities, calling for increased vigilance in the matter of 'Non-Accidental Injury to Children'. In the area of 'Training and Prevention', the Memorandum states: 'There is a need to ensure that those whose daily work is with young children and their families are familiar with all facets of the problem, particularly the early warning signs.' It calls for increased awareness among doctors in the child health services, hospitals, hospital nursing staff in children's departments and orthopaedic and accident wards, health visitors, home and school nurses, social workers, staff in schools and staff in voluntary day care establishments.

It is apparent that in calling upon principals and teachers, both in Britain and in the US, to increase their vigilance the schools have a larger responsibility in the realm of child protection than they have ever had before in their history.

In the US, one effect of the mandatory reporting laws is to bring schools sharply into the protective role where child abuse might be occurring. In twenty-five states, teachers are called upon to report cases of suspected abuse; in twenty states, 'other school personnel' are deemed responsible (in thirteen states, the two categories are joined, calling for the vigilance of both teachers *and* school administrative staff). Fear of court action has been eradicated by the 'immunity laws', built into the statutes in 1967 – a fact which must make reporting much less onerous for school teachers and personnel than in the early 'sixties.

The kind of abuse that comes to a teacher's notice, however, is not likely to be of the 'battered baby' variety, so long associated in the public mind with the term child abuse. In these older children (usually between six and fourteen), a teacher is likely to uncover 'sins of the fathers' of a different kind: incest, belt beatings, emotional as well as physical persecution from lovers where single mothers are involved, together with frequent injustices wrought by step-parents brought into disciplinary conflict with pre-adolescent and adolescent children. The homes that produce the most abuse visible in the school setting are in the lower socio-economic bracket and in environments where chronic alcoholism is a feature of one or both parents. Teachers are deeply and directly affected by family abuse because a child's learning capacity is depressed, if not altogether eradicated, by neglect and cruelty at home.

In the 'sixties, when schools first became alerted to the fact that they could be prime detectors of abuse at home, the way educators attempted to find out how teachers and principals were coping with schoolchildren from problem families, was to send out questionnaires to the heads of schools. The responses were often laconic, many principals neglecting to send back the question-naires from sheer lack of interest. Two educationists from the West Riding of Yorkshire, Sir Alec Clegg and Barbara Megson, sent out questionnaires to a proportion of the State schools in the vicinity and received 200 replies. Some wrote that they had nothing to report; others were more honest, or more aware. In one instance, the principal described the plight of thirty-one children, a number which constituted about a quarter of his student body:

> We notice children who are withdrawn, a boy who is soon in tears, emotional children, children who cannot express themselves ade-quately. On the other hand, we have children who, on the surface, appear little affected when mother has a change of 'father'. . . . I am sure that loss of potential, lack of success and confidence in school work and relationships, behaviour difficulties, etc., have their root causes in poor home life – and the irresponsible, selfish, restless way in which parents behave towards each other is one of the saddening features of our materialistic age.

This honest and thoughtful response was unusual. Some princi-pals merely stand by and feel helpless and frustrated at the enor-mity of the problem facing them. However, there are systems in existence which support the teacher and make him feel less lost in the face of so much unhappiness.

The Syracuse school system in the US is one of these. A model of its kind, with a decade's record of reporting suspected cases of abuse behind it, it is the greatest single source in the city for un-covering such problems.

Beginning in the school year of 1964-65, the directors of the Syracuse school system devised a simple reporting form asking for the child's name and address, a description of his injuries, and statements from the child and any witnesses. After a referral had been made, the form was given to the school nurse, and she in turn contacted the state children's protective services. According to Dr C. George Murdock, a leading pediatrician and Director of the Health Services of Syracuse City School District, the types of injury sustained included welts incurred in whippings, and lacerations caused by knives and other sharp instruments (weekly showers in schools after games often bring these injuries to light). Dr Murdock discusses the backgrounds to these abuses:

> Upon investigation, the perpetrators of the abuse were frequently found to be emotionally disturbed, mentally handicapped or chronic alcoholics. When step-parents were involved, their relationship was often by common law only and impermanent. Almost all our cases came from the lower socio-economic group, which is contrary to the findings of other investigators.

Although Dr Murdock claims that his findings are contrary to those of some others, particularly in the suggestion that much school-age child abuse comes from economically depressed families, there is a wealth of data to prove that he is correct in this assumption. The majority of neglected and abused schoolchildren come from low income families.

In a nationwide study of 5,993 cases of abuse, Brandeis University sociologist Dr Davil Gil found that 37.67 per cent of the families earned less than $3,500 per year ($5,000 is designated as the 'poverty line'), 51.85 per cent earned less than $4,500, and only 3.61 per cent earned $10,000 or more.

These statistics clearly reveal that only a very small proportion come from comparatively well-off homes. In his findings, Dr Gil also discovered that most of the abuse of the school-aged child occurred in poor welfare families, single-parent families (especially a mother coping alone), large families (four or more children) and where there was a prevalence of 'male caretakers' and stepfathers (nearly twenty per cent had a stepfather at home).

We see here a pattern of domestic violence that is becoming apparent both in England and America, one where poverty, unemployment, unstable emotional relationships and overcrowding (exacerbated by large numbers of children) all contrive to produce unbearable tensions at home.

As so much abuse in the case of older children is perpetrated by father substitutes, one is tempted to conclude that sexual tensions play a decisive part in bringing a situation to boiling point: competitiveness between adolescent male and middle-aged father surrogate in the case of male children, and overtones of incest between adolescent girl and male caretaker in the case of young females. This is not to say that mothers do not also perpetrate abuse (forty-eight per cent in this study), but the figure is misleadingly high as so many homes are run by single women. 'The involvement rate in abuse incidents was higher for fathers or father substitutes,' writes Gil. 'Over 17 per cent of the abuse cases were committed by a male caretaker while the mother was temporarily absent.' It can be assumed that, in many cases, the man of the house is plainly irritated by the plethora of children brought to him by his mistress's former marriage, children of whom he is jealous and for whom he has no natural affection.

There are other flashpoint areas which occur particularly in families where a single mother has taken a lover. If there is a quarrel and the teenagers take the mother's part, which they are likely to do, a fracas can result. An extra dynamic is also created by a young adolescent girl's fantasies about the resident male, the 'cuckoo in the family nest', as is often the case in impermanent mother-lover relationships. Peter Blos, a US psychoanalyst, writing of young female sexual delinquents, says that their promiscuity is often based on a need to cull male admiration coupled with a fantasy that they, the young nubile girl, could succeed where their mother is failing (if the man only slept with *me,* I could cope with him, is the thinking). The pubescent girl in this position may become wayward, promiscuous, disturbed; as a result the mother and the male caretaker become frantic and treat her violently for her behaviour. Both truancy and sexual promiscuity are among the symptoms of teenage disturbance caused by home background disorders, symptoms clearly revealed in school.

Teachers are not only trained to look for adolescent disturbance caused by home chaos; they are also trained to look for signs of neglect and abuse in the very young pupil. Avis Brenner, Co-ordinator of the Child and Community Programme at Lesley College, Cambridge, Massachusetts, tells her young trainee teachers to look especially for the withdrawn child, the one who finds it hard to

join in with a group of playing children (in later life this characteristic is betrayed by an inability to join a group and by habitual
truancy). Teachers can then focus attention on this child, holding
him as much as possible if he is small, trying to draw him out, never
being punitive, attempting to instil feelings of trust at all times. If
the child is young enough to have to be collected from school by
his mother, this is the time to attempt to make contact with her.
You can use almost any ruse to do this, according to Avis Brenner,
even down to the 'What a pretty dress your daughter is wearing'
level. However, if they concentrate too hard on the rehabilitative
side, teachers are in danger of becoming social workers, she
believes. 'One such child in a school year is really all a teacher can
handle,' she told me. 'What she *can* do is to alert other helpful
agencies in the community to the child's plight.'

With older children of secondary school age, one of the tell-tale
signs of a breakdown of the parent-child relationship is when the
parent consistently fails to attend parent-teacher meetings.

'Abusing parents just won't come to school for conferences,' Ms
Brenner says. 'They are very afraid of teachers whom they see as
punitive parents. This is the time to take the initiative and go to
visit them. Either this, or alert a social worker to do so.'

The Children's Division of the American Humane Association
has issued a concise and lucid pamphlet called 'Guidelines for
Schools', which tells teachers, nurses, counsellors and administra-
tors what to look for in the form of a list of key questions and
answers. Is the child aggressive, disruptive, destructive? Then he
may be acting out a need to secure attention. Is he shy and withdrawn? Then he may be crying for help with a whisper rather than
a shout. Does the child play truant? Or does he come too early and
have to be pushed out of school?

On the physical level, teachers are asked to see if the child is
adequately dressed for the weather, if his clothes are tattered, if he
himself is possibly unwashed and odorous. Is it apparent that the
child has had no breakfast? Is he always tired? Is he neglected
medically, needing glasses or dental care? Does he bear bruises,
welts and contusions? The AHA pamphlet implores teachers not
to put these conditions down to poverty entirely, but asks them to
scrutinize the parents of such children. Are they aggressive or
abusive when approached about their child? Alternatively, are

they apathetic and unresponsive? Is their behaviour bizarre?

In the late 'sixties a friend of mine taught ten-year-olds in Manhattan's P.S.87 in the West 80s and had a classroom of poor children whose mothers lived in nearby 'welfare hotels'. She worried about many of the children but particularly about a withdrawn black boy, too large for his age, badly dressed in too short jeans, a little backward, and suffering from culture shock, along with his other handicaps, as he was new to New York from rural West Virginia. He flowered under her patient handling and was beginning to read more quickly when he was transferred to another group. His mother, a wiry, distracted woman, came to the school and pleaded with my friend not to let the school authorities transfer her son from her class. Pathetically, she tried to give her cause more force by bringing my friend the small bribe of an ice-cream cake. Her erratic behaviour alarmed my friend, who then visited her at her welfare hotel – a filthy, two-roomed suite filled with dirty, noisy younger children (she had five altogether). It soon became apparent that the mother was a heroin addict, that her curious ice-cream cake inducement, fuzzy behaviour and tears were symptoms of her deteriorating mental health under addiction. My friend was later able to arrange for her to go to a drug-dependency clinic for help. This is the kind of odyssey an involved and caring teacher can find herself taking when she delves into a child's background.

An innovative approach to the prevention of child abuse, beginning at the nursery school level, has been initiated in the last few years in three different US cities: Denver, Washington and Boston. The three nursery schools (one in each city), each staffed by at least six professionals (social workers and psychiatrists), invite parents to come to school with their children, and to discuss with the staff any problems they might have. Community help, particularly in the realm of child care in the nursery, is sought, with university students and other volunteers helping out. The mothers, many of them single parents, are shy and defensive at first but soon begin to talk to other mothers over coffee, and to give each other support. At present the project is small and experimental, with only a dozen or so families involved in each school, but these therapeutic nurseries may well become a nationwide feature if they continue to prove successful, particularly in re-educating mothers about child-rearing.

What the staff attempt to do at these nursery schools, is to make the parents have more realistic expectations for their toddlers (the children are aged from two and a half to four years). They can re-assure the mothers that their children are developing along normal lines; that the two-year-old can be 'terrible', exploratory and messy, crying noisily at the prospect of bed; that the four-year-old can be disobedient and talk back; that these children are not min-iature adults, defiant and competitive, but children with minds that are different from adults' in their cognitive processes. The emphasis is always instructive, never punitive. Parents are encour-aged to ring the schools if they feel like 'hitting out' (at the Wash-ington therapeutic nursery, eighty volunteers man a round-the-clock telephone hotline for crisis counselling to prevent this hap-pening).

Shirley Bean, project co-ordinator for the Boston therapeutic nursery, believes that these schools form a valuable function in keeping the family together, in preventing the drastic measure of removing an abused child into care: 'Families definitely can change if you bring them the resources,' she told an Associated Press reporter in January 1976.

Another helpful step taken by a number of cities in the US is the creation of a twenty-four-hour emergency service for parents who feel close to violence and who wish to stop themselves from com-mitting abusive acts.* The telephones are frequently manned by volunteers, often para-professionals, though there can be trained social workers at the end of the line as well. An exemplary service of this kind was set up in Nashville, Tennessee, several years ago, funded by the Federal Government ($450,000 over three years). The rationale behind this is the same as that expressed by Boston's Shirley Bean; the aim of the community helpers ready to come to the aid of the potentially abusing parent is to try to protect the child and keep the family intact. Explaining this view succinctly in a Public Affairs Pamphlet, the Nashville project's co-ordinator, Patricia Lockett, said: 'We avoid involving the police, courts and institutions unless absolutely necessary to protect the child. Our aim, if at all possible, is to keep children at home to preserve the family intact. When necessary, certain children are placed in pro-

* Such a service has also been initiated in Nottingham, England, the first of its kind outside London in the UK.

tective custody for a time, while minimizing the traumatic effects of separation. Though we don't condone mistreatment, we always try to make parents understand why they're doing it and to rehabilitate rather than punish them.'

Not surprisingly, Denver, Colorado, where national and international attention was first focused on the problem of child abuse by the work of Kempe and his associates, is one of the most trailblazing of US cities in its services aimed at preventing abuse. Parent Aides, begun in 1970 at Colorado General Hospital, is one of the most imaginative of these. The group was formed when it was decided that the elderly were not being made to feel as useful in the community as they might. As the 'senior citizens' of Denver often found it difficult to cope with spiralling living costs on their old age pensions, it was agreed that they might offer their services to the hospital as 'foster grandparents' for a small fee. When a family was in trouble, with the possibility of violence erupting, the Parent Aides were sent to the home to act as temporary lowerers of explosive tempers. This they helped to do by removing the parents' feelings of being trapped; allowing them an afternoon or an evening off and taking over the baby-sitting duties. Parent Aides are carefully screened by the Pediatric Service for certain necessary qualities – largely patience and a capacity for loving. However, to ensure that the Aide, always a layman, is not given too large a responsibility, many of them work in conjunction with trained social workers.

As in all projects involving lay workers and volunteers, the 'constant availability' theme is emphasized once again. Parent Aides must be available in the evenings and at weekends, and substitutes must be found if they are not, according to the scheme laid down in Denver.

In Buffalo, New York, another enlightened city in its therapeutic approaches to child abuse, an experimental 'Emergency Parents' programme was established in the early 'seventies. This federal-grant project uses caseworkers, homemakers (kindly women who remove some of the household maintenance cares from a stressed, overworked mother), and foster homes for an around-the-clock crisis service when temporary removal of the child is needed. According to the 1974 pamphlet describing their work, the Buffalo Child Protective Services found that 'traditional agency hours and location are inadequate and crisis intervention must be part of any comprehensive programme'.

The term 'crisis intervention', which is used here, is a phrase that appears almost as frequently as the word 'abuse' in the new vocabulary of the 'seventies. It is a loose description for any form of 'rushing in' that is made on the part of the protective services to help disturbed parents. However, the word 'intervention' can be misleading. It does not necessarily mean going into a home and removing the child who is threatened by parental violence. It means that, for that critical moment in the parent-child relationship, there will be a sympathetic person to act as a buffer. In fact, a word like 'buffer' might be more apposite than 'intervention' – a rather muscular-sounding term smacking of imposition. One must remember that, in many cases, the parent has rung an agency to see that no violence does occur: in other words, his wish for a buffer person to stand between himself and an action he fears he might commit towards his child, is as powerful as is the wish of the agency to prevent such an abuse occurring. Crisis intervention, at its best and most dynamic, is a bilateral affair.

It will not have escaped anyone's notice that the American cities with the most effective child protective services are those who are given the most generous grants to run them – either by the Federal Government or by their state. It may be cynical to equate the safety of children with the amount of money expended on them, but this is the reality of the situation. When my sister interviewed Ms Jo Anne Harvey, Casework Supervisor, Protective Services, in 1974 and asked her what she thought would improve the child protective services in the country, she was given the simple answer: 'Government funding.' Ms Harvey added with feeling: 'It would be the answer to so many of our problems. My caseworkers have a very heavy load, forty-three families a week. To do it right, they shouldn't have to help more than twenty-five. Why are they so overloaded? The answer is easy – lack of adequate funds.'

California is one of the states which appears to be generous with its funds. Psychiatric 'out-patient' care and counselling for parents of abused children is being put into practice in some of the large hospitals. The University College, Los Angeles Neuropsychiatric Institute has such a unit for parents who have been charged in court with either abuse or 'maintaining an unfit home'. The parents are counselled by a child psychiatrist and a public health nurse, and the focus is heavily on child care. There are courses instructing parents in normal physical and emotional development patterns, and these are nearly always designed to give parents a realistic expectation of what a child should be doing, as for instance in the matter of toilet training and discipline (flashpoints, as we have seen, in producing violence in abusing parents).

Many other American cities are also trying to make more use of public health nurses to aid in the prevention of abuse in 'risk' cases. In this, they are following the British pattern. The health visitor has always been an important deterrent in cases of potential child abuse in Britain. While historically she was not meant to be sent into homes for purposes of detecting abuse, this is what has happened in practice. In the late 'forties, when the National Health Service came into operation, it was part of the social welfare scheme that health visitors checked regularly into homes to chart the progress of a new-born baby, for about eighteen months from the time of the hospital discharge. Initially health visitors advised mothers on care and feeding problems. Recently, however, health visitors have been trained to observe homes where emotional or physical neglect is taking place and have achieved an important place in the child protective chain of command. (Paranoid, guilty mothers, who might slam a door in a social worker's face, trust a health visitor whose visit is a normal occurrence. It is something of which she needn't feel ashamed, as the new mother down the street can also be receiving regular visits from the same welfare nurse.)

The importance of the health visitor in prevention and detection in Britain can be seen in the recent decision of the Department of Health and Social Security to attempt to reduce the ratio of one health visitor to 3,600 of the population, to one to 3,000, especially in areas where disadvantaged families predominate.

'As a regular visitor to the homes of young children, regardless of social class, the health visitor is in a unique position to observe signs of stress, alleviate them whenever possible, and to detect signs of injury,' writes J. M. Davies, Senior Nursing Officer, (Community Division), Berkshire.

Another area of prevention of future child abuse is in the hospital ward when the baby is born. As parent-child behaviour patterns are fixed right at the beginning of the relationship, the care and attention given to mothers and babies by the nurses and other hospital staff at this early stage are profoundly important. If a baby is not taking to the breast easily and a mother appears panicky, all too ready to give up and start him on a bottle, cool, calm and patient lessons in breast-feeding techniques should be shown the mother by the staff. Many feeding problems, whether the baby is being breast- or bottle-fed, can be clarified in the first week or ten days in hospital.

That improved hospital practices in the lying-in wards could help the mother-child bond is undeniable. Significantly, a recent Sussex report on 'Non-Accidental Injury to Children' (called the Tunbridge Wells Study after the town where it was carried out), puts hospital care high on the list of preventive action in the area of child abuse. The members of the Tunbridge Wells study group concluded that: 'There are some traditional staff attitudes in lying-in wards and some practices, pre-, peri- and post-natal, which interfere, sometimes avoidably, with the development of bonding between newborn baby and mother. This applies especially to low birthweight babies and those other newborn babies whose hospital stay is prolonged.'

The fact that clumsy neo-natal hospital practices can damage the mother-child bond and predispose a parent to battering, is coming to be realized on both sides of the Atlantic. The Canadian pediatricians, Klein and Stern, make a plea for the early entry of the mother into the premature nurseries. They encourage hospital staff to allow the mothers 'to touch their very sick infants', to lessen the customary isolation of the mothers of premature infants and to ease the relationship they will be attempting to forge with their babies after they leave hospital.

Hospital staff might well exclaim in horror at the thought of mothers streaming into their special care units to pick up their premature babies to cuddle. They are, as they might say emphatically, more concerned with the safety of the baby than with the psyche of the mother. In some cases one must sympathize, especially if a baby's life hangs in the balance. However, there is no doubt that many hospital personnel, overworked, their facilities extended, give the baby's safety top priority and tend to neglect too much the mother-child bonding process. A bustling, slightly mechanistic aura pervades most hospital obstetric wards. This lends conviction to those who crusade for home deliveries, where bonding is undoubtedly more quickly and warmly effected, provided there has been no birth complication (the possibility which sadly always places a question mark over the wisdom of childbirth at home).

Those first days or weeks in the obstetric ward are sensitive ones in the prevention and detection of potential mother-child breakdown. Careful observation of mother-baby contact in hospital can often tell a trained professional a great deal about the future prospects of the parent-child relationship. Kempe and his Denver team have recently conducted a study of mother-child relationships in the lying-in wards, asking nurses to observe the interaction. A mother's negative or positive response to her baby can be quite marked and reveal itself in small but telling ways. The nurses involved in the Denver scheme reported that some mothers seemed to be repelled by the very idea of holding their babies, that they screwed up their faces in distaste when asked to bottle-feed them and seemed apathetic when requested to help with the bathing and changing of their infants. The most unresponsive mothers also found it difficult to bring their thoughts round to the idea of naming their babies, as if they could only regard the wriggling bundle of flesh they had produced as a nonentity.

While it could make many young women feel uneasy to think that such close scrutiny in the obstetric wards might become widespread in the Western world (a sort of 'Big Brother-Is-Watching-You-In-The-Wards-1984' movement in the making), the preventive value of such scrutiny far outweighs any intrusiveness it may entail. The Kempe team feel that once a markedly negative attitude is detected in a mother's manner towards her baby, it becomes easier to ensure that a health nurse can be assigned to visit her regularly when she returns home.

Another hospital preventive measure which would direct professional attention to a potentially abusing mother is the 'predictive questionnaire' which Kempe and his associates are currently working on both in Denver and with colleagues in Aberdeen, Scotland. The questions focus on the mother's expectations of her child's future behaviour, the nature of her own upbringing ('How were you punished as a child?') and her own personal feelings of isolation and loneliness. The most significant and consistent information so far gleaned from these predictive questionnaires is that the abusing or potentially abusing mother has little or no social contact outside her own, frequently tottering, family circle.

Nurses, interns and other hospital staff are also asked to observe parent-child interaction when a parent brings an injured child to the accident ward. It may be possible to distinguish between an accidental and a non-accidental injury to a child by the way a parent behaves towards the injured child at the time. When the parent is detached, indifferent, displaying little tactile warmth to the hurt child, only becoming animated when trying to account for the injury (confessions of actual battering at the time of injury are almost non-existent in the annals of child abuse), then a careful report should be made by the doctor in the accident ward, and the follow-up care by the social services should be intensified. Again, it should be emphasized that the hospitals are urging close scrutiny of parent-child interaction in the accident wards not with the aim of 'trapping' or 'catching' the parents in order to punish them, but for the purposes of keeping an eye on the child afterwards for protective reasons.

More and more pediatricians closely involved with the problem of child battering are exhorting their medical colleagues to stop being timid and pussyfooting where an injured child is concerned. (General practitioners, in particular, have been guilty of this, their reporting of suspicious accidents haphazard and half-hearted, their approach tentative; this attitude is undoubtedly a historical legacy from the past, one still coloured by the oath of confidentiality between practitioner and patient.) Dr Grace S. Gregg of the Pittsburgh Children's Hospital felt moved to write what she called a 'comprehensive plan of action for physicians faced with an injured child', adding that all doctors in such cases should have what she describes as 'a high index of suspicion . . . [regarding] every injured child as possibly abused'.

The hospital ward or the doctor's waiting room are vital observation points for professionals concerned with the safety of the child. It may be the only time that the parents, shaken and disturbed by the results of their own eruption, the pain they have caused their child, will not be guarded and coolly evasive (as opposed, for instance, to their behaviour when visited in their homes; the incidents of social workers describing a baby as looking 'bonny' and 'sleeping peacefully' when they visited him at home, and discovering him dead within days afterwards, are too chillingly numerous to make us feel altogether secure about the fully protective capacities of the home visit).

While members of the community, along with helpful school-teachers, improved hospital practices and alert social agencies can combine to help eradicate the problem of child abuse, one of the most important elements in the reduction of the ugly phenomenon is in the realm of 'self-help'.

Parents Anonymous is the most successful of the self-help groups which exist today. A California mother of two formerly abused children, Jolly K., founded the first chapter in Redondo Beach, California, in 1970. Jolly K.'s background is not untypical of that of many abusing parents. Her own mother had called her a 'slut' when she was a child, an epithet which she believed and which did nothing to help her in her own adult emotional life (two disastrous marriages, a 'target' daughter of her own whom she in turn called a 'slut', following in the now familiar generation-to-generation mould of handed-down cruelty). What struck Jolly K. most when she was struggling to keep her hands off her own two children, was the difficulty, if not impossibility, of getting swift professional help.

Modelling itself on Alcoholics Anonymous, the organization offers potentially abusive parents the instant help the professions fail to give them. Veteran members proffer twenty-four-hour telephone 'hotline' help to newcomers and suggest that, whenever a mother or father feels potentially violent, they use the telephone as an instrument for ventilating their feelings of rage and frustration at the child.

One of the most effective methods to prevent violence that P.A. has initiated has been an 'exchange-of-children' scheme: one P.A. member hands over her brood to another and thus the 'target' child is under another parent's care for a twenty-four or forty-eight-hour period. An abusing parent will not feel the same sensations of rage towards another person's child or children, thus with this scheme the all-important matter of removing the 'target' child from harm is effected.

Although the organization grew up because the parents involved felt neglected by the professionals, they do have psychiatrists and social workers at their helm, in many cases. (Denver's Dr Ray E. Helfer is overall consultant for the parent organization in California.) And the idea has gained ground. In the US there are now fifty community chapters in more than twenty states. Chapters have also been set up in Britain and Canada.

An impressive aspect of P.A. is that their 'recidivist' rate is so low. P.A. claims that while some parents might revert to violence after joining, on average only two out of ten do so, according to their calculations. Apart from providing an outlet for feelings of wrath, the success of P.A., like that of Alcoholics Anonymous, is based largely on the inevitable sense of camaraderie that grows out of group therapy, and the minimization of sensations of shame brought about by the knowledge that one is not alone in hitting out in such a seemingly inexplicable fashion. As society still feels repulsed by child abusers, the acceptance of these parents' experience in a group situation is crucial to the building up of their feelings of self-respect and to their eventual cure.

Matilda Belluci, a Cincinnati social worker, describes the elation and extreme pleasure she felt emanating from a group of formerly abusive mothers when she guided them in group therapy sessions:

> The group jelled quickly. The first two sessions were not only spontaneous but almost hilarious. Focus was largely impossible, with each mother mentioning problems others shared. We never knew silence. . . . One member said after missing a group session, 'I felt like I was losing a million dollars.' Indeed, these mothers have been finding through each other something they never had – supportive families and havens of safety. For most of them, urban living is lonely living. . . . The group provides some of the social controls and warm relationships they are unable to maintain with their relatives.

The feeling of fellowship which springs from these gatherings of sad, lonely parents is a real, positive force for prevention of child abuse. Their mutual understanding is all-embracing. Ms Belluci tells us that her group, poor to a woman, still managed to collect cigarette money and a cheering card for a fellow member who was serving a prison sentence for child battering. There was no spiteful, 'We're out and she's in' attitude, but an emotional and material extending towards an unfortunate mate. There is little doubt that such compassion was augmented because they shared a feeling of understanding of what had caused their own inadequate mothering, which only such a group therapy session could bring.

Thus, speaking figuratively, with so many community fire engines clanging out of their firehouses to put out the brushfires of parental abuse, the possibility of gross physical abuse occurring to children is gradually diminishing – slowly, to be sure, but the future prognosis is good.

But what about the other, more subtle form of abuse, the kind that doesn't show itself in a blue welt on an arm or a laceration on the back but remains outwardly invisible? Children's minds can be battered just as brutally as their bodies, but this form of cruelty is much more difficult to detect.

In the chapters that follow I shall show some of the discoveries that have been made and discuss some of the remedies that are being sought for the phenomenon of mind-battering.

8/ The Battered Mind

We have already seen that repeated bouts of physical cruelty can seriously disturb a child's psychological health and impair his mental and emotional development by creating fear and a sense of worthlessness.

But emotional cruelty separated from any physical injury is also a pernicious form of abuse, since the scarring of a child's psyche by a parent, unaccompanied by outbursts of rage or tell-tale bruises, can so often go undetected for years.

The most perplexing characteristic of real mental cruelty, inflicted by a parent on a child, is that it is so often unintentional. As Ronald Laing, the eminent analyst, writes in *Knots*, his dramatic essay on interpersonal relationships: 'Both the tier [of knots] and the tied, are unaware of how it's being done.'

Although emotional cruelty, or mind-battering, may often be unconscious, it is a powerful weapon all the same. Parents can and do quite literally drive their children insane, causing them such anguish and confusion that they can no longer function adequately in their schools or in a social context.

The rate of neuroticism in children, particularly adolescent children, has risen to a marked degree in this century, and the largest group of attempted suicides is in the teenage bracket. Isn't it a sobering thought that young adolescents, at the peak of their powers physically, should wish to court death with such frequency?

Once again, I think it is the existence of the nuclear family that we must hold partly to blame. Never before have children lived in such intense and close proximity with their parents. Unrelieved by contact with a large family or with kin living nearby, the nuclear family can become a dangerous hothouse of emotions. It has been said that when husband and wife find that their personalities clash to flashpoint level, they can always divorce. But children cannot divorce their parents. If they feel that their minds are being assaulted, their personalities undercut and their reactions minimized, they are in a 'no exit' position in the claustrophobic situation of the nuclear family. The results are known: adolescent children 'drop out' or run away, never to return; either this, or they hang on, perhaps too timid to take flight, feeling asphyxiated in the tiny, constricting world of the small family but unable to move.

When parents mind-batter, it is frequently in an unmalicious but concentrated attempt to forge the ties that bind. Mothers in the nuclear family, especially if they are without careers, are unhealthily reliant upon their children for their sensations of worth in the community, of being fulfilled, of being depended upon. The most intense mind-battering, parent to child, often occurs when the young adolescent is beginning to show his or her own identity, making healthy snips at the umbilical cord, airing individual opinions and forming new attachments, either among peers or with admired adult models.

Parenthetically, I should add here that I know that adolescent children on their part can be fractious and rebellious, callous and hurtful to their parents, and that the parent-child psychological warfare that exists during this period is not all unilateral. But in discussing the kind of mind-battering which can destroy, or partially destroy, a child's personality, I am referring more to the adolescent who is usually defined as a 'good' child by his parents; the more timid, the more isolated and dependent child, whose efforts to pull away and create some sort of separate identity are tentative and shaky.

I have taken the liberty in this chapter of extrapolating from the joint work of Ronald Laing and Aaron Esterson, *Sanity, Madness and the Family*, certain parental techniques which I think are ably shaped to batter the mind of a dependent child. In writing these case histories, Esterson and Laing were interested in the nature of schizophrenia; the girls and women they studied in a family context were all diagnosed as schizophrenic. However, as the authors explain, they believe that the condition that these women were presumed to be in by the psychiatric doctors and mental hospital staff who cared for them during their off and on admittances and discharges, were states of family-induced madness.

I believe that Laing will go down in the annals of psychiatric history as one of the great innovative thinkers of this century – in spite of some of his failures, or whether one agrees with his theories or not. In a way, he has turned our conceptions about madness upside down. His belief that madness is created, not inborn, is a revolutionary concept and one that has been rejected by many in his field. According to him, people do not inherit madness but are often driven mad or forced to embrace postures of insanity as the only effective method of escaping an intolerable situation.* His is the thesis of the existential, as opposed to the biochemical, school of thought in the approach to schizophrenia. The schizophrenic, however unconsciously, has chosen his mode of behaviour or method of existing in a certain situation; it has not simply overwhelmed him like a hat over a candle, a force genetically preordained. It is in the matter of *choice* that the schizophrenic has behaved existentially: his ship may be wildly off-course, but he is still the captain of it. Such, in any case, is the Laingian interpretation of this mental illness.

When I interviewed Laing at length some years ago in his modest, brown-walled office in Harley Street, I found it hard to believe at first that the donnish, youthful Scot, now in his late forties, could be the universal guru for a whole new school of thought concerning madness. Dressed in casual tweeds, he was conventionally handsome, soft-spoken and with his Glasgow accent still intact in spite of years spent in London, North America, India and Asia. His large, deep-set black eyes were melancholic and intense, making mock of the cosy university professor façade he had chosen to adopt in his office hours (and dropped in his free time, to judge

* Laing is careful to emphasize that the thesis that madness is made, not inherited, is not his alone. In particular, he stresses his indebtedness to the writing and thinking of US anthropologist Gregory Bateson, with whom he had fruitful contact in the early 'sixties while on a study tour of America.

from the pictures taken of him relaxing on the floor in the Lotus position and wearing Indian shirts and beads). I thought then, from his eyes, that he knew madness well. He had been there, or very near – a voyager into the Inferno who had probably come close enough to some of the inner rings to get singed, at least.

An anecdote he told me at the time confirmed my view of his fellow-traveller-with-madness status. In 1952, he had worked as a psychiatrist in the British Army. Detesting the bluff heartiness of the officer's mess, the old blue jokes about sex and drinking, he escaped and sat with the people in the padded cells; they provided him with the only reasonable conversation he could have with anyone. His respect for 'schizophrenics' – a designation he dislikes, abhorring clinical categories – has never diminished since. These so-called mad men and women are in touch with a kind of truth, he feels, however distorted.

His methods for alleviating or helping to remove (he would dislike the word 'cure') the condition of schizophrenia have caused the greatest controversy. In brief, he does not feel that these sufferers should have their delusions masked with heavy drugs, or be bombarded with electric shock therapy; rather, he thinks that they should 'work through' their madness. He shares this conviction with the US expert, Gregory Bateson, who has had a powerful influence on his work. Bateson himself writes of the 'working through' process most eloquently in his introduction to the narration of a nineteenth-century schizophrenic, John Perceval (see also page 143):

> Perceval's narrative and some of the other autobiographical accounts of schizophrenics propose a rather different view of the psychotic process. It would appear that once precipitated into psychosis the patient has a course to run. He is, as it were, embarked upon a voyage of discovery which is only completed by his return to the normal world, to which he comes back with insights different from those of the inhabitants who never embarked on such a voyage. Once begun, a schizophrenic episode would appear to have as definite a course as an initiation ceremony – a death and a rebirth – into which the novice may have been precipitated by his family life or by adventitious circumstance, but which in its course is largely steered by endogenous process.

Not content to spin theories alone, Ronald Laing decided to create hostels for 'schizophrenics' where the 'acting out' process could occur without interference, without the drugs and other impedimenta of the mental institution or hospital (edifices which he feels are in every way an insult to the human spirit).

His most famous case and certainly the most publicized, that of fifty-two-year-old Mary Barnes, has also been one of his most successful. Mary Barnes, a violent schizophrenic with paranoid delusions, spent the five years from 1964-1969 at the Community, Kingsley Hall, in the East End of London, founded by Laing and Esterson. Reliving her past and regressing, she even returned to a kind of womb by curling up in a box like an embryo and being bottle-fed by the other members of the Community. Though the Community was unstructured, with therapists and mentally disturbed inmates intermingling freely, leaving visitors to puzzle out who was the doctor and who the patient, Mary received intensive professional help from New York analyst and Laing associate, Dr Joseph Berke. She emerged from her journey back into time to paint some strikingly joyous religious oil paintings (years of practice smearing her own faeces on the walls of Kingsley Hall had proved helpful to her but had earned her the widespread opprobrium of her co-residents, quite understandably). She also went on to write a vivid and sensitive account of her 'mad' years and what she describes as a 'journey through madness'.

Not all these 'journeys' have been as successful as Mary's, as the recent book, *Anna,* by David Reed (not his real name) attests. In this, a beloved wife and mother appears to be working her way towards a kind of sanity when a brief but disastrous setback causes her to set fire to herself, a self-immolatory action that kills her and is an unspeakable tragedy for her husband and children who witness this grisly end.

Recently, Laing has shown himself to be somewhat less adamant in his stand against the possibility that madness may be genetically determined. In an October 1977 interview in *Newsweek* magazine, he told a reporter: 'I've always looked forward to the possibility that advances in molecular chemistry would lead somebody to turn up precise, subtle exchanges that were found to be disjointed in some people and that a really focused chemical could make a difference, perhaps amounting to what we could legitimately call "cure" in some percentages of those people.'

When I spoke to Laing ten years ago, the idea that madness was something 'in-the-blood' was contrary to everything he believed. As some of his most advanced writing on the subject of family-induced madness came at that time, I feel justified in quoting what he said to me then:

'I think that people who believe that madness is something caused by the composition of the blood are fantastically unsophisticated. They may be unaware of the close relationship between stress and biochemistry. There have been interviews with people – rather brutal things. You know, they present someone with a photograph of a snake or treat him in a particularly jarring way and discover that the blood pressure has altered radically. Then there are some other stress experiments where they invalidate a person's perceptions by showing him pictures of a doctor bending over a patient, or of a patient in an operating room, or some such, and then ask for his interpretations. When he gives them his interpretations of these medical pictures, they tell him that his interpretations reveal a tremendous violence. After invalidating his perceptions – sometimes they switch pictures on him, too – they find he is in a complete state of biochemical chaos.'

Whatever Laing's final stand on the origins of schizophrenia are likely to be (and I am not prepared to enter the controversy about the stress versus the biochemical theory of madness), it seems to me that nothing can invalidate the work he has already done on the psychic damage that parents can unwittingly inflict on their children. Laing and Esterson have thrown light on some fairly common battering techniques that no Spock or Freud or previous guru of the nursery – or of the analyst's couch – has touched upon. And any parent who uses them, even in a small way, should be aware of employing them. Not all of us are going to produce a mad child as a result (Laing and Esterson are concerned with extreme cases, obviously), but we could produce at the worst neurosis, and, less disastrously, unease and conflict.

While the Laing and Esterson case histories are painstakingly researched and absorbingly compiled, they are a little abstruse. The interviews are lengthy, the conversations rambling, the patients' speeches confused and meandering. I also found the hypotheses concerning the damaging techniques employed by the parents so deeply buried inside the overall material that they are at times difficult to isolate – though, to judge from what others have said about the hodge-podge of taped material they were originally forced to beat into shape, the two analysts performed miracles. (Joseph Berke writes in his book, co-authored with Mary Barnes, that he could only listen to an hour of the tapes at a time without feeling madly restless. Other therapists felt the same and would join him in a relaxing bout of dancing around the tape-recording room to unkink their muscles. Joseph Berke writes this in such a deadpan manner that the reader does a double-take. The picture of Laing, Esterson and team dancing around these tapes is a bizarre and somewhat pagan one. However, that was in the mid-'sixties, one recalls, when progressive therapists were becoming more consciously 'physical', eager to tune in on their own bodies and also to employ much body contact with their patients. Joseph Berke and Mary Barnes were constantly engaged in bear-hugs and wrestling matches, exercises which relieved tension and communicated affection.)

In any event, the tortured ramblings of schizophrenic families make for a rough read. As Berke emphasizes, they talk *at* each other, not *to* each other. So I have tried to extract and clarify some of the mind-bending methods Laing and Esterson discovered as having been used by the parents.

In *Sanity, Madness and the Family,* Laing and Esterson interviewed eleven schizophrenic women and their families; six of the women were in or just out of their teens, struggling to break free from the chrysalis of their childhood dependence upon their family. Their fictitious names and real ages were: Sarah Danzig, 17; Ruby Eden, 17; June Field, 15; Hazel King, 16; Agnes Lawson, 19; and Mary Irwin, 20. The remaining five were mature women over the age of twenty-one, who had had sad careers of repeated blind-alley incarcerations in mental hospitals and equally fruitless discharges back into the family 'nests'. They were: Maya Abbott, 28; Lucie Blair, 38; Claire Church, 36; Ruth Gold, 26; and Jean Head, 24. In many instances, the tape-recordings of the patients and their families (who could just as well be described as 'patients') would take some thirty to fifty hours – sessions which stretched over weeks and months. The structure of the interviews depended on the degree to which a family was prepared to co-operate; often they were composed of the therapist alone with the mother, the daughter, the father, a brother or sister, followed by marathon sessions with therapist, mother and daughter together (twenty-nine hours of the latter in one particularly extensive case). It is significant that, although fathers were often instrumental in creating much of the mental stress suffered by their daughters, they were just as often loath, if not downright opposed, to being interviewed, as if their 'machismo' were being challenged by such intrusiveness. Mothers, wrong-headed as they had been in parental practice throughout their daughters' lives, were pathetically keen to be of help to the therapists, although many of their answers were of the self-justificatory 'I-was-a-wonderful-mother' variety.

The families selected were ordinary, middle or lower middle-class Londoners, some from the professional classes (biochemists, teachers), others from the skilled labour (plumbers) and semi-skilled professions (store managers). They tended to be 'essentialists', believing in set ways of behaving and conforming within their social strata. However, their simplistic approach to achieving respectability in their various communities was freqently tainted by an extreme fear of scandal, particularly of a sexual nature. Often there was some rather unsensational skeleton rattling around in their suburban or urban bungalow cupboard – an illegitimacy, a common-law marriage, an adopted child – which haunted them with its threat of exposure. While keen to blend in with their neighbours, respectable and unnoticed, they were socially isolated, keeping themselves to themselves and restricting contact with the outside world (or 'the crowds', as one particularly paranoid mother called them).

These families tend to have what Laing and Esterson call 'sealed-off systems'. Each one is like a small autocratic kingdom with a structured power system, with mother or father (or sometimes both, but in different ways) playing quasi-benevolent despot; the object of which in most cases is to keep the unconsciously victimized child *in her place*: dependent, harmless, powerless, nearly invisible. When the child (in this case the grown daughter) 'goes mad', the power structure is severely shaken: the parents are suddenly in the limelight, becoming subject to medical investigation or social worker scrutiny. They seem beaten and sad and bewildered. What have they done to deserve this?

Laing and Esterson interpret these young women's flights into madness as actual journeys on the road to sanity and reality. As the two analysts unravel the cases, we see the girls' retreat into postures of madness as necessary escapes from a home hothouse. Their 'schizophrenia' can suddenly be seen in a socially intelligible light. What these parents have labelled mad and bad in their children is often merely a bizarre form of rebellion against the impossibly claustrophobic home power structure they have built to keep their children compliant and dependent. The girls in these sealed-off family systems (the same is, of course, true of boys, but this study concentrates on daughters, with only occasional reference to similarly stricken brothers) explode into behaviour that is unintelligible and frightening to their parents, thus forcing the cap off the family bottle. Compelled to go for outside help, this is the final shame and degradation for these fathers and mothers – letting 'them' of the outside world see their weaknesses.

But before the girls 'go mad', a rich and complex pattern of stratagems for control has grown up in the home. Laing and Esterson differentiate between the *praxis,* the 'agent' or manipulatory practice (e.g. telling the child she possesses certain attributes which she in fact does not have), and the *process* or 'illness', which is the effect of this technique.* (In this case the child, believing her parents, tries to apply these attributes to herself, but subconsciously knowing that they don't fit, feels deeply distressed at the contradictions she senses.)

The parent-child battle here is a deadly one, waged by frightened people who have made a fortress out of their home, and who manipulate their children in order to keep this fortress intact.

The first manipulatory technique is that of *mystification.* To mystify a child is to deliberately deny or invalidate his own perceptions, to distort what he or she perceives as true or false.

An example of this kind of parental mind-twisting occurred in the case of twenty-eight-year-old Maya Abbott, the fictional name given to the daughter of a general store manager and his wife. One

---

* This is best put by Laing and Esterson in their introduction as 'what is going on (process) to who is doing what (praxis)': in such complicated family interrelationships, it is difficult to know *who* is doing *what* to *whom,* however, and *praxis* and *process* can become hopelessly interwoven or 'unintelligible', in Laingian terminology.

of the girl's so-called paranoid delusions was that her parents constantly made signs and grimaces at each other when they thought
she was not looking (years of this made Maya understandably
violent and at eighteen she attacked and wounded her mother with
a knife). Laing and Esterson discovered that the parents thought
Maya had special powers and could read their thoughts, and when
they thought she was showing this gift, they would exchange
secret hand signals. When Maya taxed them with this, they
laughed her off. In this way, her perceptions – perfectly valid –
were invalidated by the two people she depended upon most. (The
therapist interviewing the Abbotts was himself made extremely
nervous by the Abbotts' persistent winkings and sign-language to
each other during their sessions. It was not difficult for him to im-
agine how disturbing this must have been for a daughter who
trusted them.)

In another case, that of seventeen-year-old Sarah Danzig, the
parents accused their daughter of delusional behaviour because
she insisted that they were listening in on her telephone calls. As the
interviews unfold, we discover that the Danzigs, afraid of Sarah's
attempts to become a social being and have boyfriends like other
girls of her age, construed her few sorties into society as potentially
dangerous sexual exploits. They *did* listen in to her conversations
with boys to check her movements and uncover the identity of her
admirers, then invalidated her perceptions by saying that she was
imagining things.

Ruby Eden, another teenager of seventeen attempting to try
her wings, was told she was mad because she imagined that her
adoptive parents (whom she had to call 'uncle' and 'aunt') thought
her a slut and a prostitute. Her uncle, who had encouraged her
tactile affection as a child (the 'petting' of his knees) had reacted
the most violently (incestuous feelings turned inward?) and made
her feel particularly whoreish, especially after she had become
pregnant. Again, with the help of the tape-recorded speeches of
the family, the reader can quickly discern that Ruby's intuition
about her parents' feelings concerning her morals was accurate.
Ruby herself was illegitimate, and her adoptive parents continually
expected her to repeat her mother's pattern. When she did, though
this is not explicit in the tapes, it was as if Ruby had dutifully acted
out what her parents had anticipated for her ('Your mother was

a whore, you shall be a whore', and so on).

Not all mystification is as blatant and extreme as that experienced by the three women just described. When I first read these
cases, I was reminded of the mystification that I had experienced
as a young teenager, something of which I had not consciously
been aware until I read the Laing-Esterson book.

My father, a diplomat, was a charming if quirky New Eng-
lander with an international background (his forefathers, the
Langdons, had been merchant shippers who had plied the exceedingly lucrative spice trade between Boston and Smyrna – now
Ismir – and so the family had split between the two cities and his
childhood had been spent in Turkey). It was his peculiar eccen-
tricity to find poverty romantic, presumably because he had never
truly experienced it except in the New England self-imposed,
character-building manner; his rich father had made him work
through his first year at Trinity College selling sausages from a
stand and sweeping dormitory floors.

I had always been told by him that, financially, we were in a
parlous state. It worried me intensely and I recall the acute shame
I felt as a fourteen-year-old when my embarrased violin teacher,
a first violinist with the Boston Symphony Orchestra, told me after
a lesson that my father hadn't paid him for over three months for
the dubious pleasure of teaching me. I mumbled that I knew my
father couldn't help it (hadn't I seen his beautiful antique desk
overflowing with bills?).

The violin teacher must have been as mystified as I was. The
mansion he visited in order to give me my lessons in the exclusive
Cliff Estates section of Wellesley Hills, Massachusetts, had eighteen rooms, one of them – on the third floor – a ballroom. The
beamed, spacious living-room was filled with museum pieces,
exquisite Chinese dynastic ceramics and Peking rugs deep enough
to make women catch their heels in them. There was also my
parents' gleaming black Buick, parked in the curved drive that
snaked up to the stucco mansion perched on a dramatic hill – some
millionaire American's dream of a Sussex manor house.

Yet Daddy was broke. Or so I was led to believe. I was totally
puzzled by the contradiction between the way we lived and what
my adored father told me. If we were poor, why did I live like a
princess? The answer was clear, of course. My father was a reason-

ably wealthy man with a private income, as well as the income he earned, who somehow felt guilty about his affluence. Hence his protestations about our financial state. (Not paying his bills on time sprang from vagueness and bookkeeping inefficiency, not from economic necessity.)

The mystification that our father perpetrated in adopting a luxurious life-style (with my mother's tasteful help) while declaring himself poor, has made my two hard-working sisters and myself somewhat neurotic about money. We are cautious, anxious to live within our means, panicky about the occasional importunate creditor, slightly obsessional about the state of our bank balances. Where spending is concerned, you could definitely say that we lack panache.

However, my father's unconscious mystification of his daughters was far less pernicious than that practised by the families of schizo-phrenics because it was not done in order to wield power; rather, it was an attempt to bring his girls into his own fantasy of 'life as a financial struggle'. While the results have been disturbing, leaving us with traces of neurotic behaviour, they were not damaging to the point of breakdown on our part. Both mild and severe forms of mystification can take place in most families. Few parents have been completely free of this particular mind-bending manoeuvre, but it is often of my father's mild, unintentionally confusing char-acter.

The second type of ammunition in the armoury of the severely mind-battering parent is the *double bind*. To double bind a child is to give him two entirely different orders or two conflicting roles to play at the same time. Sometimes in a double bind, the 'double' quality might be missing in the order or the directive given, but the ambivalence is always inherent in the statement. When a mother holds her child and says: 'You know Mummy loves you . . .', and she is, in fact, feeling a great deal of rage and hostility towards him for some reason unconnected with the child personally (marital upset, feelings of her own inadequacy, a sense of frustration about her circumstances generally), we get an example of the ambival-ence of the double bind. The child will hear the words of endear-ment, but he will know that they are not truly meant and that the parental rage is bubbling away beneath the falsely cool surface.

Double-binding mothers, Laing told me, have 'soft arms and

harsh voices' or 'hurtful arms and soft voices': they are a complete civil war in themselves. Being at the other end of their continuous, conflicting assertions is like being at the receiving end of noxious car exhaust fumes on a hot day in the city. Like some self-protective amoeba, the child splits under the assault of the maternal confusion directed his way and may become fragmented or withdrawn, catatonic or paranoid.

Laing lists a little glossary of double-binding phrases, no less sinister for being heard every day: 'It's all in your mind'; 'You haven't a headache, dear'; 'You just dreamed it'; 'That never happened at all'; 'Why don't you just forget it'; 'Why do you keep making that up'; 'You know that's not true'; 'No, you haven't, dear, mother says you haven't'.

Double-binding mothers or fathers often air conflicting views concerning their children's life plans, general intellectual potential and physical attributes, leading the children to question the very structure of their personalities ('Who am I?'; 'Where am I going?', they begin to ask themselves).

A perfect example of this kind of confusion arising from the near impossibility of resolving parental contradictions is shown in the case of nineteen-year-old Agnes Lawson, who was diagnosed as a paranoid schizophrenic. She had been repeatedly admitted and discharged from mental hospitals (where, on one occasion, she was given fifty insulin coma treatments, a drastic form of chemical assault on the system), a pattern that went on for five years. One of Agnes's 'delusions' was that her parents wanted her to stay in hospital and not return home. In conversations with her father, the therapists discovered that indeed her father had been disappointed in the hospital treatment, feeling that his daughter was still exaggeratedly 'irritable' and had not been at all happy about her return to the family bosom.

Mrs Lawson continually chides Agnes about her 'inferiority complex' in the interviews, saying that she had no reason to have one, being a lovely girl really. Then in one unguarded moment, after Agnes has voiced a wish to become a wife and mother, she hisses: 'You wouldn't be able to look after a baby.'

With some schizophrenic sufferers, even the 'voices' they hear will echo the double-binding instructions which have been coming their way all their lives. Such is the case of John Perceval, the 'insane' son of British Prime Minister Spencer Perceval, who was assassinated in the House of Commons in 1802 when John was nine years old. John was incarcerated in expensive asylums in Bristol and Sussex during his late twenties and wrote his 'Narrative' while behind walls. He writes of his 'voices':

> I was tormented by the commands of what I imagined was the Holy Spirit, to say other things, which as often as I attempted, I was fearfully rebuked for beginning in my own voice, and not in a voice given to me. These contradictory commands were the cause, now, as before, of the incoherency of my behaviour . . . whenever I attempted to speak, I was harshly and contumeliously rebuked for not using the utterance of a spirit sent to me; and when again I attempted, I still went wrong, and when I pleaded internally that I knew not what I was to do, I was accused of falsehood and deceit; and of being really unwilling to do what I was commanded.

To put it in everyday language, the person subject to double-binding is in a 'no win' situation. It is impossible to comply with two conflicting orders at the same time. Dr Joseph Berke, writing about Mary Barnes and the Kingsley Hall experiment, defines the double bind as 'a means for putting another in a straitjacket of guilt and anxiety in order to prevent him from doing something which you have already told it is O.K. to do'. He cites the example of taking out a gun and shouting at someone: 'Sit down or I shall shoot you dead;' then, when the person sits down, screaming: 'Stand up or I shall shoot you dead.' It is, he asserts, a great way to drive someone mad.

A third method of driving a child into states of mental retreat is *image-fixing*. Here we are concerned with what Laing and Esterson refer to as a 'Procrustean Identity' (alluding to the legendary inn-keeper, Procrustes, who sculpted his clientele to fit his famous bed, cutting off their feet if they were too long, or stretching them out if they were too short).

A parent, anxious to have things in the home as he or she wants them, assigns a certain personality structure to a child which he feels helps to keep the household-fortress running smoothly. Laing says this is a little like a football game in which each player is assigned his position. In such families labels are handed out as, for example: 'Jane is the strong one'; 'Ralph is the clever, quiet one';

'Janice is the social butterfly'; 'Jack is the delicate one'; and so on. Equably, a child will try to pour himself into this pre-ordained and immovable position in the team even though he may perceive of himself in a different light. 'Am I what my parents say I am or what I think I know I am?' is his agonized question.

When a child grows up and begins to gain some insight into his own real nature, the falsely assigned attributes may become intolerable – they simply will not wear. Laing and Esterson cite the case of Jean Head, aged twenty-four and married to a husband who has swallowed up all the parents' preconceptions about his wife (she is 'capable, cheerful, vivacious' but at the same time 'sensible, avoiding frivolous socializing'). When Jean is admitted to a mental hospital after some bizarre regressive childhood behaviour, she is suffering from the delusion that her husband and parents have all died, a clear case of wishful thinking.

Following therapy, Jean is well and brave enough to contradict her parents' and husband's assumptions about herself. To the declaration by her father and mother in the tape-recording sessions that she was 'always happy', Jean retorts: 'I was often depressed and frightened.' To the assertion that she was really vivacious and cheerful, she replied that she had 'kept up a front'. To their claim that they never 'kept her on a string', she counters that they have governed her life in all important respects and that her father, in particular, still terrifies her and controls her. Her husband comes in for a salutary dose of the truth, too, when he tells the therapist that he and Jean had always 'seen everything the same way'. She corrects him by saying she saw many things differently.

When a child adapts herself to her parents' labels as effectively as Jean had done, it is easy to see why a sudden *volte-face,* a total change of behaviour, appears 'mad' to parents. In Jean's case, her revolt took the form of regressing to a little girl's voice and giggle, acting like a 'puppet on a string'. To her mind, a puppet on a string was exactly what she had been all her life.

Jean's case is especially interesting because she is married and we see that the husband is merely extending the control exerted by her parents – continuing to assume that she is possessed of the attributes they have wrongly assigned to her. In the family ballgame (or *nexus,* as Laing and Esterson call it), we often see the out-fielders – husbands, grandparents, aunts, uncles – acting as helpful supports to the prinicipal players, the mother and father.

Again, a family does not need to go to the extremes of producing a schizophrenic child in order to join in the game of image-fixing. I recall a friend of mine telling me that when she was on the verge of a breakdown, following a particularly nasty divorce and custody case, her father chided her for taking tranquillizers to ward off her panic: 'But Sally,' he said in genuine bewilderment, 'you can't have a nervous breakdown – you're the strong member of the family.' The amazing aspect of Sally's story is that she did not allow herself to have a breakdown. Sometimes the attributes a family give a son or a daughter are so tenacious that the child, even when grown, feels they cannot be relinquished.

There are few children who haven't strained to accommodate themselves to their parents' image of who and what they are. However, in adolescence, as the child develops a growing sense of his own personality, the effort is often abandoned, leading many parents to believe that their children have undergone a drastic character change. What is really happening, in many cases, is that the child is feeling and being himself for the first time. Instead of becoming more authoritarian, this is the time for parents to loosen reins, to allow the child to perfect his own concept of what he or she is. The 'good' adolescent who conforms and obeys his parents to the letter is more often the potentially disturbed child. A certain hostility registered from child to parent in these years is far healthier (though, admittedly, not too amusing for the parents). As Dr Moses Laufer, Canadian analyst and expert on adolescence, says: 'This is the start of their psychological removal from their parents and very healthy. I'd be worried about a child who had no antagonism towards his parents.'

We know why a well-adjusted child experiences healthy antagonism towards his parents at certain stages in his development. The reason why some parents seem determined to attach labels to their children seems both less clear and less healthy. What I suspect is that these are the definitions, labels or attributes that the parents either feel they possess themselves or wish they could acquire. By bequeathing the false attributes to their offspring, many parents are living out their own fantasies. This distressing practice, which forms part of the device of image-fixing, is called *projective identification*.

An acute case of parent projection occurs in the breakdown history of fifteen-year-old June Field. The mother consistently tells the child that she has always been 'such a happy little girl'. As the biography of June Field unfolds, we see that a congenitally malformed hip as a child forced June to be in calipers until she was ten years old. Of course, this made her feel 'the odd one out' at school. As a toddler, she had had an even more curious career, tethered to a bedpost indoors and to a tree when out of doors, exactly like a dog. That any child could be consistently jolly in these circumstances would be indeed remarkable. However, in Mrs Field's case, we see that it is necessary for the mother to think of June as having been supremely happy, and of their relationship as being a harmonious and continually compatible one – that is, until June goes 'mad' and all these idyllic conditions are reversed.

A continuing characteristic in the parents of these disturbed children is their total lack of insight into their own patterns of behaviour, and into the underlying causes for reacting in the way they do to the actions of their children and to others in the family. They fly blind. Why did Mrs Field resent so violently her daughter's innocuous attempts at 'doing her own thing', such as wearing make-up and going to youth club meetings? Was it because she might have revelled in the crippled child's dependence upon her? Why, having had a malformed child, did she have to project upon her desirable qualities which the girl did not possess ('mannerliness, extreme academic conscientiousness, boisterousness')? Was it because of the slight shame she may have felt vis-à-vis the neighbours for having given birth to a handicapped child? Some of Mrs Field's self-protective blindness is understandable; the consequences of her all too human vanity are extremely sad, however.

Another case of projective identification can be seen in the breakdown history of Agnes Lawson, aged nineteen, the girl who accurately guessed that her parents did not want her back from the mental hospital. In the tape-recorded sessions with the therapists, Agnes's father speaks perpetually of the girl's 'irritability', saying that he cannot understand this quality in her, that he can't deny it gets on his nerves and that at times he feels like shaking her. In fact, the irascible one is Mr Lawson himself. In listing what he believes are some of his daughter's bad qualities – her secretiveness, her impertinence, her propensity to laugh to herself – Mr Lawson works himself up to a fever pitch of anger. The only feature that Agnes's attributes have in common, the therapists concluded, is that they all served to irritate Mr Lawson. He could barely keep his temper in check during the interviews. Unable to suppress his own wrath, the confused and probably incestuous father (he held Agnes on his knees and read fairy-tales to her until she was fourteen) loaded his own bitterness and frustration onto Agnes, calling her the irritable one.

Two other mind-bending processes, rather similar in that they both put down the recipient, are *minimization* and *denigration*.

Minimization occurs when parents play down an event because it may elicit a depth of emotional response from their child which they do not understand, nor wish to believe exists.

A perfect example of minimization is cited in the case of Claire Church, aged thirty-six, a mother-dominated woman who has been labelled a 'paranoid schizophrenic'. At the beginning of the treatment, she was found to display profound thought-disorder and impoverished affect (a sensation of being 'empty', as she described it). Claire's statements that her parents had neglected her and had shown little affection for her during her life, are passionately denied by the parents. The mother insists that she and Claire are practically alter-egos: 'so much alike'. Mrs Church's extraordinary assumption about the near identical nature of her daughter's character to her own, is based on the fact that her mother, too, was a career woman (Mrs Church being a successful shop manager, who carries her managerial qualities into the home, according to her daughter).

According to Claire, who dreamed of a university education, her greatest disappointment in her teens was to be prevented from completing her secondary schooling and thus from acquiring the necessary qualifications for higher education. For a child struggling to get out from underneath her mother's shadow, educational success must have seemed a most valued potential lifeline. This escape route was abruptly closed by Mrs Church who switched her daughter into business, making future university entry an impossibility. Mrs Church conceded that Claire had been made 'unhappy' by the switch. To which Claire replied vehemently: 'It was the biggest disappointment in my whole life.'

Part of the minimization practised by Mrs Church, apart from dismissing as merely 'unhappy' one of Claire's major life disappointments, is in her manner. She not only interrupts her daughter but persistently misunderstands what Claire tries to say – or she answers her tangentially. Claire is forced to use metastatements with her; that is, a statement to clarify another statement. Mrs Church blocks any conversational pass that seems to be getting close to emotional bedrock. When Claire says that her mother has made her feel aggressive, for example, Mrs Church switches her off in a positively inspired manner by asking solicitously: 'Claire, the sun isn't too much in your eyes?'

Finally, there is the process of *denigration,* one of the least subtle of the mind-rape techniques but none the less effective for being straightforward. It must be clear to subconsciously power-hungry parents that the most direct way of creating a dependant is to whittle away at his confidence in his own abilities. That will keep him at home.

The parents in the Laing-Esterson case histories are studies in hypocrisy. They will assert that they wish their daughters would be more sociable, more confident in their jobs, more accessible to outside contact generally. Yet everything they say to them effectively diminishes these girls' chances of functioning in society as self-assured, independent human beings.

Denigratory phrases and actions punctuate their daily exchanges. They undercut with poisoned remarks, poke fun with inappropriate mimicry and humour. Mrs Irwin is a case in point. Her daughter Mary, aged twenty, is in hospital with schizophrenia, the symptoms of which are revealed in delusionary behaviour and violent mood swings from emotional apathy to states of extreme excitement, which lead her to smash objects. Mrs Irwin is hurt and bewildered by the actions of her 'mad' daughter, previously so 'happy and social'.

Then we hear about Mrs Irwin's fun-loving ways when Mary was 'well'. She used to have such a jolly time when Mary's boyfriends came to call. One boy had a facial tic; he blinked and sniffed at periodic intervals. Mrs Irwin had a hilarious time imitating these tics when he came to visit. Mary did not think this had been 'fun'. (We are not told of the boy's reaction, nor if he ever returned for more; presumably not.)

During one of the sessions, Mary talks of her hesitancy at getting a clerical job, saying she feared that she would have made a mess of it. To this her mother responds, laughing: 'Yes, you probably would have made a mess of it.'

Again, the tool of denigration is not something unique to the families of schizophrenics. It is a game many families can and do play. A journalist friend of mine, aged forty, a polished writer on English customs and mores for distinguished American and British journals, was still, in her successful middle years, avid for her mother's approval. Her mother wanted her to write about *exquisite* England: stately homes, rare bookshops, exclusive men's clubs, Georgian architecture, sculpted rose gardens. My friend, anglophile to the point of mild mania, was willing and able to write about these features of British life, many of which perched on the very edge of social obsolescence. One year, however, she became impatient and took a new turning in journalism, having grown a little weary of the precious side of the nation's life. She wrote a hard-hitting piece on the increase of alcoholism among women. To the publication of this carefully researched and informative feature, her mother was uncharacteristically silent. When drawn to comment, she said petulantly: 'Why must you always concentrate on the sordid side of life?' My insecure friend immediately wrote a piece about a lovable old poet and his passion for Art Deco, getting right back on the track her mother had chosen for her. (Parental projection can also mean moulding a child to a career they themselves have missed, but the vicarious fulfilment only satisfies if the career is handled *their* way.)

It will be clear from the examples given that all the processes discussed above occasionally overlap and interweave; it is often difficult to tell where one ends and the other begins. However, it can be said that all are devices for bending the truth.

The defences that the children put up against these parental stratagems are largely inward in nature. They struggle to develop a rich inner life, a private terrain which is out of bounds to their parents. They tell themselves that their mothers and fathers cannot object to their being quiet and contemplative (in this they are often mistaken; their reclusion and silence, their retreat into bedrooms, are construed as acts of petulance and rejection).

Many take refuge in obsessive religiosity, memorizing the Bible, becoming assiduous church-goers. Others sit in their rooms and indulge in escape fantasies. Some adopt small bodily reflex actions which they think will deflect the power of the parent. Mary Irwin of the Laing-Esterson study defended herself against the torrential maternal monologues directed at her by 'holding her breath or going stiff inside'. (It is easy to see how such actions, repeatedly performed, could result in eventual catatonia, a state which is characterized by muscular rigidity and immobility – an almost literal 'turning into stone'.)

One of the most haunting fictional examples of a boy building up a defence which eventually overwhelms him, is that of Paul in Conrad Aiken's *Secret Snow, Silent Snow*. Paul, a schoolboy of about eleven, sees lovely snowflakes before his eyes and revels in their thick prettiness, the screen they form between him and the outside world. In a geography lesson, he can hardly concentrate on what the teacher is saying because he is so intrigued with his own snowfall. At the end of the story, Paul is in bed and the reader knows that his secret, silent snow is blocking out reality for him as the postman's footsteps he hears each morning become more and more muffled (so, too, we infer, do his parents' entreaties to him to return to them).

Paul's case is a severe one and, as the story ends, one has a sad intimation of a lifetime spent in mental institutions. However, many so-called normal children will also retreat into fantasy for solace against what seems to be a bullying world. In her powerful book, *Them,* Joyce Carol Oates's adolescent heroine, Maureen, uses this stratagem to preserve her reason in a chaotic home. She is almost a fictional echo of some of the Laing and Esterson real-life female sufferers. Her mother and grandmother have done their share of image-fixing ('Maureen is the solemn one, the one with the long face', they keep saying: 'Is my face so long?' she asks herself, questioning their perceptions).

Maureen follows her family's conception of her, pouring herself into the Procrustean mould. She is conscientious, studious, hard-working, quiet, tolerant of her sluttish mother, slavish in her performance of the household duties. But in her own imagination, she is obliterating the lot (all but her adored brother, Jules). Her favourite fantasy is that she will one day push them all under the porch of a house she has seen in her neighbourhood (where previously she had poked at a toad and seen it hop away under the wooden skirting). When she is not forcing her father, sister, mother and grandmother to disappear in a heap, she is being a leader:

> In her mind she shouted commands, like a soldier; all the kids obeyed her and lined up. There were no adults anywhere to punish or even to praise. It was peaceful and good without them now that she was taking their place and doing what they should have done. . . . Her heart would begin to pound, thinking of the captive children and herself watching over them, guarding and bullying them, a different Maureen from the girl everyone knew.

Violent fantasies can be comforting when a child is oppressed. I remember a recurrent one I had about a French teacher in high school in Wellesley. She was grey-haired, pert and poisonous and she picked on me (no delusion this; my classmates had noticed). While I waited in dread for her to call on me in order to laugh at my stupidity or mimic my faulty accent, I would stare fixedly at the nape of her neck; it was rather scrawny and denuded by a crisp, mannish bob. Over and over again, I saw a guillotine's blade fall upon that vulnerable nape. I would hurry over to tidy up the head after the blade had fallen, placing it in a basket, then ambling off to a nearby tumbril to join my appreciative *citoyens* for a triumphant tour around the Bastille. My French teacher had certainly awakened my interest in 'a little bit of France', her repeated wish for her students.

But there are also many children who do not fight back, who do not take flight into assumed postures of madness or in violent, comforting revenge fantasies. These are the compliant ones, the children who tend to grow up into a grey middle age, living at home with their mothers and fathers into their thirties or forties, or until the time of their parents' death. We all know those colourless, well-behaved spinsters and bachelors who have turned filial piety into a self-sacrificial life-style. These compliant ones do not go mad, but they share with the so-called 'schizophrenic' the apparent need to be a victim, a willing pawn in the family chess game. The oppressed child who grows up into dependent middle age, ministering to a tyrannical parent or propping up the ego of an insecure one, has, like the schizophrenic, turned himself into a scapegoat. In enclosed family systems, an element of complicity is needed to preserve the status quo. Gregory Bateson calls it 'sacrifice'. As he writes:

> In almost every such family, it is possible to recognise that the psychotic individual has the functions of a necessary sacrifice. He must by his schizophrenic behaviour conceal or justify those actions of the other members which evoked – and still evoke – his schizophrenia.

If there is an element of compliance or volition in deliberately assuming the position of scapegoat in the family in order to maintain its equilibrium, how did this come about? How is it that one child unconsciously takes it upon himself to sacrifice his own identity for the preservation of the sanity or ego structure of a parent?

It may be that the scapegoat child senses that he fulfils some deep need in his parent, that he is the object of obsessional concern. Reading through the Laing-Esterson study, we hear mothers claiming repeatedly that the relationship they had with their little girls before they withdrew into 'madness' was idyllic, a real 'love affair'. Disappointment with husbandly love plays a large part in the need of these frustrated women to seek love in other respectable forms; who can criticize the great totem, mother-love? Often the child has had some slight defect or handicap that has particularly awakened her mother's protectiveness (for example, June Field and her congenitally deformed hip), a protectiveness that turns into unhealthy possessiveness as the child develops from babyhood to early school age. The scapegoat child knows he should feel grateful for all this concern, however onerous and unnecessary it becomes, and so, guilt-laden, plays along with the demands of the needy parent. Some crack under the load in early or late adolescence and refuse to play the game – this is when they become 'mad' or 'bad' in their parents' estimation. But these are the rebels. And for every rebel, there are probably ten conformists, though we shall never know the exact ratio.

In compulsively fixing his attention on one child to satisfy frustrated emotional needs, the mind-battering parent is often imitating behaviour learned in his own childhood, leading one to believe that mind-battering, like physical battering, is a self-perpetuating life-style.

In the case of Mary Irwin, the 'schizophrenic' whose only sin seemed to have been 'sniffing' and occasionally defying her parents over small matters, we discover that Mrs Irwin herself had had a domineering mother who drove her into an early 'escape' marriage. Mrs Irwin describes her own mother as a 'dreadful old woman' whom she hated and who treated her as if she were ill in order to remain in an ascendant position. And yet, Mrs Irwin herself treats Mary in a nurse-patient manner, clucking over her as if she were a helpless babe, or somewhat ill. This leads the therapist to conclude that 'unbeknown to herself', Mrs Irwin behaves towards Mary as her own detested mother behaved towards her, thus unconsciously encouraging Mary to see her as she has seen her own mother. Here is a clear case of subconsciously willing patterns to repeat themselves.

Madness is catching, sad to relate. Being exposed to neurotic or psychotic tendencies in our formative years, we may learn to imitate them, unconsciously absorbing some of the anxieties, fears and tensions of our parents and learning to deal with them in similar behavioural ways.

In the repeating of patterns, physically abusive parents and emotionally abusive parents resemble each other. And they are alike in other ways. Both groups have unreal ideas about children's natural development and what is to be expected of them at a given age. Mrs Irwin's expectations of Mary's abilities were wide of the mark before she was three (she expected her to be completely toilet trained by the age of one) and yet she treated her like an infant well into her adolescence. Physically abusing parents want their small infants to act like grown-ups. Mind-battering parents reverse this process. They want their children to remain in states of near infantile dependence.

It can be seen that while these views may seem diametrically opposed, one group wishing to hurry age, the other wishing to delay it, both are neurotic and damaging attempts to derive ego satisfaction from the defenceless child.

After recovery, psychotic patients, savouring their new insights, are keenly aware that, in imitating their parents' ways, they are perpetuating the sins of the fathers. Mary Barnes, in describing her voyage through madness, writes that she often felt herself being pulled towards her mother's ways, even to the extent of wishing to buy her kind of soap and shop at her favourite fusty London department store. Mary Barnes has a sensitive awareness that parents can no more stop bequeathing their own ways to children than children can prevent themselves from adopting them. She describes this conundrum poetically:

> My Mother was caught and so was I. We wanted to help each other. Neither of us knew how. Although I was sure the trouble lay in the childhood my Mother had, and in turn how she had been with her children. I could only tell my Mother this truth. It was difficult to leave it at that. My whole being was rearing to get free.

It is difficult not to admire Mary and to conclude, perhaps unfairly, that the best children do get out, leaving their unhappy parents with empty hands, with no one to manipulate.

But manipulating parents are not to be found only among the families of schizophrenics. In so-called 'normal' families, manipulatory techniques mirroring those we have seen used in the Laing-Esterson study, are also freely used. Children in these families are not driven 'mad' but are often found to take refuge in neurotic symptoms and anti-social behaviour. Happily for these children, therapeutic techniques have been developing over the past twenty-five years which contribute towards their rescue – techniques which are covered by the umbrella term, family therapy.

9/ Family Therapy: How It Began

The studies of schizophrenics and their families undertaken by Bateson in the 'fifties and by Laing and Esterson in the 'sixties, have contributed a great deal towards our understanding of family interaction.

Analysts struggling with the families of schizophrenics, listening to them talk *at* one another or in parallel lines, dealing with their closed systems, were nearly driven mad themselves by the jangling, self-delusionary babble of these parents and their relatives. It took the therapists a little time to realize that they were learning a great deal about *all* families. The result is that we see many of today's family therapists descending directly from those analysts who taped the conversations of the schizophrenics in the 'sixties.*

A great many families share, in a more moderate form, the characteristics of schizophrenic families. The difference lies in the fact that while families producing a schizophrenic child are the 'hard core', the near incurables, neurotic families, engaged in unhealthy psychological transactions, can be helped.

The cliché expression 'family circle', with its connotations of roundness, is truer than we might at first realize. Families do make a closed circle of themselves, a circle from which the outer world

* Dr Joseph Berke for instance, the young analyst who helped Mary Barnes through her schizophrenic crisis, is the co-founder and organizer of the Arbours Association in London, a group of family therapists.

is excluded and in which neuroses can mushroom and thrive.

As Nathan Ackerman, Director of New York's Family Institute, has written, such 'pseudo-togetherness' can backfire, causing an emotional matrix (that which gives form to a thing or serves to enclose it – a term much used by family therapists) to form in the family, which breeds pathology rather than health. At the point when the family circle becomes an ugly fortress, creating mental ill-health, it is the unenviable job of the family therapist to walk in and break it up, deploying all his special skills.

And 'break it up' is exactly what the therapist does. In professional terminology, this is called 'intervention' – a key word in the understanding of family therapy. When I speak of the therapist as an invader, an intruder into the family circle, this is just what I mean. He is quite literally interrupting the family drama, coming between one member and another, reassigning roles and restructuring scenes that have become fixed, static and disordered.* But balk as they might at the shaking the therapist gives them, it is important to remember that the families have sought his help in the first place, (though it is possible that pressure has been placed on them from the outside, especially from the schools in the case of children).

Family therapy is such a remarkable new implement in the 're-modelling' of the family that I think it is worthwhile to trace its development.

Before the practice of family therapy became as widespread as it is today, a psychiatric patient, whether he was treated by Freudian, Jungian or Adlerian methods, was treated in isolation. In the 'twenties and 'thirties, when Freud's disciples began to practise widely in Europe and the US, and psychoanalysis came into extended use as an instrument to restore a patient's mental equilib-

* This kind of 'intervention' differs from the 'crisis' intervention mentioned in Chapter 7. It is more intense and requires more psychiatric training than the community services type of intervention where child abuse is concerned. The therapist is more than a protective buffer between a potentially abusing parent and his or her child: he is in a position of direct confrontation. 'Crisis' intervention is more indirect, less psychiatrically orientated, a community-based extension of a helping hand.

rium, the person suffering from breakdown was virtually segregated from his family. While, in the history of psychoanalysis, there has always been the belief that a patient's breakdown is caused in large part by a disordered relationship with a parent – frequently of a repressed sexual nature – the parents themselves were kept out of bounds.

Early psychoanalytical practice stands in sharp contrast with the methods used in family therapy today. In psychoanalysis, the patient is seen individually, even in a near segregated manner (especially if his breakdown has been severe); in family therapy, he is seen with his entire family, even some of his relatives, and is viewed as an organic part of the family environment. The result is that the patient's neuroses are often seen to be reflections of those projected onto him by his parents. (As we have already learned, neurosis is contagious and can be transmitted, generation to generation, or from husband to wife, or parent to child.)*

This does not mean that psychiatric patients are no longer separated from their families or put in a kind of quarantine. We saw it happen with the schizophrenic women in the Laing and Esterson study, who were constantly being shuttled from mental hospital to home and back to mental hospital again, the parents often being the ones responsible for sending them away, not the doctors. But it is happening less and less frequently in cases of breakdown which are clearly family centred.

What a difference from the 'thirties, vivid in my memory. In those days, a psychiatric patient was hospitalized, and parents, children and spouses were frequently denied the privilege of visiting him. My knowledge of this is first-hand. My mother, after diagnosing her own condition, was a voluntary patient at Shepherd Pratt Mental Hospital near Washington, D.C. She had been admitted suffering from panic feelings, palpitations of the heart, suicidal fantasies and chronic insomnia. Her depression was such,

---

* The fact that mental illness can be a family contagion is becoming popularly known. As I write, a case of two young parents having murdered their daughter in Lincolnshire, England, is in the papers. The couple murdered their eight-year-old child, fearing she was a devil. The father was judged insane at the time, the wife was said to have been 'merely submissive', the husband's sickness having been transmitted to her. (*Daily Express*, 20 October, 1976.)

she told me later when she had recovered, that even the birds who flew by her window looked like 'little grey blobs'.

Neither her mother (whose severe Victorian sexual repressiveness and covert hostility towards her had in part caused the breakdown), nor my father, an innocent bystander in this frightening home drama, was allowed to visit her. My father complained, with some justification, that it was hard to have to pay such crushing hospital and analyst's fees while being denied access to the beloved patient herself.

I was allowed to visit my mother once in the two years she was away, only because I had developed signs of severe separation anxiety and mild agoraphobia. I would not go out to the back yard to play, it was reported, cleaving to the cosier kitchen where my mother had spent much time before her hurried departure. My mother's analyst, a student of Freud, thought a visit would do much to dispel my anxieties, but it was clear she was making an exception in my case. I remember the visit well, though I was only five. I was fêted by my mother's new and fascinating friends on the ward. One, with a cropped, mannish haircut and a pin-striped suit, was a chain-smoker. A woman smoking! I loved it. The visit was also made memorable, if a little uncomfortable, by my mother's gift to me of a mahogany doll's trunk she had made in occupational therapy classes. The gift trunk overwhelmed me with conflicting emotions of gratitude and anxiety. I didn't want to tell her, but I had given up dolls during her absence, perhaps sensing a perilous dimension to the business of motherhood.

It is interesting to note that it is just this sort of mother-child bond that caused the profession to rethink the question of isolating the psychiatric patient from his family as long ago as 1932. In the existence of the strong mother-child tie, and the need to treat them together, lay the first beginnings of family therapy.

In 1932, an American analyst working in Vienna, Dorothy Burlingham, encountered many of the basic difficulties confronting a therapist when he tries to treat a patient, particularly a child, away from his family environment.

In a seminal monograph, which is still quoted extensively nearly four decades later, she aired her worries eloquently, speaking of the almost supernatural bond that exists between some mothers and their children and how complicated such a union can make the working life of a child analyst. As she pointed out, it was often the mother who initially sought help for her son or daughter because of the child's disturbed behaviour. However, when the child entered into a 'transference relationship'* with the analyst and began to act out some of the unconscious conflicts which had made him exhibit neurotic symptoms in the first place, the mother often objected to the curious genie that had been let out of the bottle. Their child's freer behaviour in analysis, coupled with the close relationship the child had with the therapist, made many mothers feel displaced and jealous.

According to Miss Burlingham, analysts can act in three ways when confronted by a disturbingly close parent-child relationship that has become a divisive factor in treatment: they can shut the parents out altogether; arrange for the child to be placed in foster care during treatment; or try to work closely with the mother, bringing her into the progress of the child's case.

While Miss Burlingham favoured the latter course, she was acutely aware of its pitfalls. She tells the case of five-year-old Gerti, the daughter of a passionate but rather unintelligent Austrian housewife, the devoted mother of three. Gerti's strange behaviour in kindergarten was what first brought her into Miss Burlingham's office: she refused to play with her schoolmates, sucked her thumb and daydreamed through her school mornings. Analysis uncovered a veritable mare's nest at home, to which the sensitive little girl is reacting. Her mother's marriage is in a state of chaos. She has reacted against a violent husband by refusing to sleep with him and taking a lover, while at the same time trying to expiate her guilt by frenziedly doing her housework, particularly the mountainous washing. In the course of analysis the lover leaves, and the consequent misery of the mother reverberates through the child.

In spite of such thunderous happenings at home, the analysis proceeds swimmingly. Gerti is a born actress and plays out the events that have happened at home (as children of this age cannot verbalize their conflicts, their innermost feelings are vividly depicted in 'play therapy'; the acting out of fantasies through playing with dolls and toys is often the child's only way of expressing

---

* A Freudian concept crucial to psychoanalysis. It refers to the dynamic relationship which grows up between analyst and patient, by means of which the patient re-enacts the significant relationships in his own life.

himself). In her curious, near telepathic way, she had sensed her mother's sexually frustrated feelings after her lover's departure. She acts out scenes of having babies, and draws vivid phallic pictures ('people with long noses, animals like elephants, horses and dogs with long tails', in Miss Burlingham's words). The child's freer feelings about sex may be what her analyst is seeking – guilt about masturbating having caused some of the child's most crippling symptoms – but the mother's reaction to this liberation is something less than joyous. She terminates the sessions immediately, writing to Miss Burlingham that she does not want her child to be enlightened about sex and masturbation. As the analyst probably rightly guesses, Gerti's mother is unable to tolerate her daughter having fixations so similar to her own. With considerable insight, Miss Burlingham writes of child analysis: 'One knows from the very beginning that one is carrying not only the child's difficulties but the parents' as well.'

Miss Burlingham's account of the case of the little Viennese girl and her bond with her neurotic mother, is admirable in many ways, I think. First, because she has had the courage to tell her professional associates of a resounding failure, and secondly because she brings to light the extraordinary difficulty of treating children whose neuroses are reflections of their parents' troubles, as is true in the majority of cases. Miss Burlingham was groping for the most civilized way of bringing Gerti's mother into her child's treatment without actually allowing the mother to sabotage her work with Gerti. But in such an extreme case of mother-child empathy, she was bound to be defeated, both by the defences of the child (who at times undoubtedly felt disloyal to her mother because of her attachment to the therapist), and by those of the mother, who believed that her robust sexual appetites were 'dirty' and 'wrong', and who felt that her daughter was giving her away to the therapist.

Miss Burlingham had tried the *co-operative* approach with the parent when treating the child, and it had failed abruptly in Gerti's year-long analysis – sadly, too, as the child was just beginning to benefit from it. But in considering the mother at all, she was being a pioneer; the majority of her Viennese colleagues at the time, while acknowledging that a neurotic child was reflecting or reacting to the symptoms of the parent, preferred to block off the parent altogether and concentrate on the child patient. An over-whelming sympathy for the child as an unwilling victim of a sick adult made shutting the doors in this way all too easy. Siding with the child against the parent was a prevalent reaction among thera-pists and an understandable one; the child, smaller and dependent, pincered in the family drama, is in every sense the underdog.

As Dorothy Burlingham puts it: 'It is hard for the analyst to keep his own emotions free. He is tempted to side either with the mother or, as is more frequently the case, with the child.'

The cautionary advice of Miss Burlingham, and others like her, brought a mild revolution to child therapy in the 'forties. It was reluctantly agreed that, for treatment to be at all successful, mothers had to be included. From Miss Burlingham's co-operative approach vis-à-vis the parent in the 'thirties, child therapy practice moved into the era of the *collaborative approach* ten years later. The latter approach was pursued cautiously and tentatively; it usually meant that, while the disturbed child was in analysis, the mother had sessions with a social worker. Analyst and social worker would have weekly collaborative sessions, swapping find-ings and correlating therapeutic efforts.

While conceding that the collaborative approach was necessary because of the mother-child bond, many analysts revealed a thinly-veiled irritation with the procedure and experienced markedly hostile feelings towards the parent. In treatment, they often tried to feel their way, making conjectures about the mother-child rela-tionship rather than delving more deeply into the social worker's report or trying to establish direct contact with the mother.

An interesting case, which is illustrative of such clumsy early collaborative beginnings, is that of a disturbed adolescent, Jack, aged sixteen, a chronic thief who was referred to the Chicago Institute for Juvenile Research in 1940. His case was taken on by child analyst Eugene I. Falstein, who reported on it at length in a paper presented at a 1941 symposium on 'Direct Psychotherapy in Adolescence'. Jack, a highly intelligent boy in his last year at secondary school in Chicago, had been stealing periodically since he was five – both in Russia and in the United States (Jack had lived in Russia from the age of eight until the age of fourteen). Though he had been stealing for eleven years, usually from stores or from his mother's purse, it took a veritable orgy of theft to bring his parents to the Institute for help.

Shortly before beginning treatment, Jack had stolen a radio, a gramophone, records and three guns. The last bag, blessedly, frightened the parents into action.

Dr Falstein was impressed with Jack, with his IQ of 128, his good command of English, his store of general knowledge and his dark, attractive looks. His shortcomings – apart from compulsive stealing – of deafness, thinness, excessive perspiration and hypertension, elicited sympathy from the analyst. Jack's mother, who was thought to be largely responsible for the teenager's problems ('Jack's stealing began when he felt frustrated and deprived by his mother,' Dr Falstein writes), aroused the analyst's distaste. He draws this unappealing portrait of her: 'The mother is short, unattractive, highly intelligent and aggressive; the younger of two children, the elder being a boy. She was always strict, domineering and punitive toward her son. It has been apparent that she showed him very little real affection and it is doubtful whether she could so do.'

Dr Falstein sees Jack forty-two times during the full fifteen months of treatment, and the therapy seems admirably successful. From a troubled thief, Jack becomes an honest paragon under Dr Falstein's guidance, ending up as his school's class orator, associate editor of the paper and president of the school debating club, among other honours. Most remarkably, he becomes a municipal college fund-raiser after graduating, collecting 1,000 dollars in the campaign without touching the sum entrusted to him, handing it in to the committee intact.

Many reasons are given for the success of Jack's treatment. First of all, he was desperately eager to rid himself of his neurotic habit of stealing. Secondly, he opened up to the therapist with unaccustomed alacrity after the first few slow sessions and allowed an easy transference to take place, with the therapeutic ego-building which followed to consolidate his progress. Dr Falstein suggests that the neurotic adolescent who himself welcomes treatment, is often the ideal psychiatric patient.

The psychiatrist gives little credit to the mother for the boy's quick recovery, although a careful study of the case reveals that she behaved with laudable co-operation. For some reason, never explained, the mother is not seen by the social worker until Jack's

ninth session with Dr Falstein. Then she has six interviews with the
social worker.

Before this, Dr Falstein does his 'blind flying' with his young
patient. He writes – putting himself in the third person – of his first
gropings, the early fits and starts:

> The vicious circle of emotional difficulties responsible for his steal-
> ing and other anti-social behaviour had not as yet been penetrated,
> and it took four or five weeks to obtain a fairly adequate under-
> standing of the boy's immediate problem. As you may recall, the
> mother was not seen between the first and ninth interviews, and the
> boy's attitude and story were available for purposes of evaluating
> his emotional stress. The therapist had to bide his time, made few
> direct interpretations, and utilised in the main a tolerant under-
> standing and friendly attitude toward the boy, permitting him to
> give free vent to his pent-up feelings.

One wonders whether Dr Falstein couldn't have saved more
time by contacting the mother from the offset. However, these
were early collaborative days, and the analyst had not shown himself over-fond of the mother. As far as Jack's father was concerned,
he received no attention whatsoever ('we do not know much about
the father other than what might be concluded from the boy's
attitude in the therapeutic situation,' Falstein writes: 'That he did
not fully meet the boy's needs seems fairly obvious . . .').

The mother, domineering, masculine and unloving as she is
purported to be towards Jack, tries to make amends after talking
to the social worker. She ignores her son's bolder attempts to rile
her by stealing, gives him as much affection as she can muster, and
confides a little pathetically to the social worker: 'I am looking
after him more like a baby and I am making some effort to antici-
pate his wants. Somehow I think he may have been deprived
during our wanderings.'

Typically, most parents being loath to blame themselves, the
mother attributes Jack's troubles to their peripatetic life-style
rather than to her early attitude towards him. However wrong-
headed this may be, she does alter her ways towards him, and
doubtlessly this facilitates Jack's recovery – something that goes
unrecorded in this absorbing paper.

Three years later, in 1943, at another Chicago conference on child psychotherapy, Dr Adrian Vander Veer of the University of Chicago's Psychiatry Division, moved one step further than his distinguished associate, Dr Falstein, by bringing a father into collaborative therapy. From the case history of twelve-year-old William, a boy with severe dizzy fits, falling spells, and fear of winds and open spaces, it was obvious to him that the anxiety of *both* parents was being transmitted to the son and that seeing the mother alone would not be enough to help the boy.

It is often said that one of the most positive factors in family therapy is that the father has finally been brought out of the cold and considered as an integral part of any family, whether it be of its weaknesses or of its strengths. This being the case, one should feel gratitude towards this Chicago pioneer in family-orientated treatment.

William's case history is as tangled as a Chinese puzzle. Both parents were hypochondriacs, the mother obsessed with unfounded fears of having diabetes, the father with memories of the death of his twin brother from pneumonia. Neither parent particularly liked or wanted children and William was only conceived in order to reassure the mother of her own womanliness, she having previously harboured fears of being barren. The mother had been forced by circumstances at the early age of twelve to rear a younger brother, and having thus been robbed of her own childhood by the responsibility of a favoured younger male in the household, was intensely anti-male.

The parents hovered over William, spoon-feeding him until he was three and a half, busily trying to convince themselves that they were good parents and not really as hostile to William as was, in fact, the case. Children are not easily fooled, and while William was able to adjust to outside life, making a pleasant enough career for himself at school, he soon cracked under the strain of the family *gestalt.** Full of guilt at his oedipal longings for his mother, who unconsciously stoked them by undressing in front of him and sleeping with him when the father was away on business, William became paralysed with panic, and the extreme symptoms of agoraphobia developed. Before seeking psychiatric help, William was

* The pattern of configuration a family creates which comes about in a way that eludes scientific explanation – like Topsy, it seems to have 'just grown'. Another frequent term in family therapy.

taken to a battery of general practitioners and his falling fits were put down to a variety of physical causes: brain tumour, epilepsy, heart trouble. None of these diagnoses proved to be correct though, at the age of ten and a half, the boy had indeed suffered from a physical ailment – ear trouble – which forced him to undergo a mastoid operation. The exceedingly painful mastoidectomy seemed to the boy to be a form of punishment for his 'bad' thoughts and deeds (curiosity about his parents' sex life, inchoate desire for his mother, and his own masturbating). Thus his breakdown came not long after this operation.

Treatment was lengthy. He had over seventy-five sessions with Dr Vander Veer, in which he aired his fantasies and aggressive feelings with great candour, calling his father a 'fat jerk' and draw-ing pictures of a dancer, who resembled his mother, doing the can-can with a great show of black lace panties (his obsession with underwear, guilt feelings about masturbation, and his use of underwear to aid him in this activity, pointed to a dangerous veer-ing towards fetishism).

William was a gifted young cartoonist, and with the real-life backdrop of World War II to fire him, he sketched fiendish Jap-anese pilots being summarily done in by brave American GIs, the violence pictured obviously relieving his own aggressive feelings. He also drew a huge, gorilla-like figure called 'Butcher-Knife', who could split men in two with a scimitar (putting paid to Daddy?). In the comfortable presence of his analyst and with the help of his cartoon strips, the young patient's anxieties diminished.

The parents saw a social worker concurrently, though Dr Vander Veer is dismissive about the help this gave them, particu-larly in the case of the mother. However, the analyst does occasion-ally compare the material he gleans from his sessions with the boy with the social worker's consultations with the parents. He does this reluctantly, feeling as if he might be betraying William's con-fidence. In Dr Vander Veer's case, as in Dr Falstein's, we see a heavy prejudice in favour of the child against the parents. He is at pains to dissociate himself from them in his sessions with William, assuring the boy at all times that his attitudes and feelings are diametrically opposed to those of the parents.

To his colleagues at the Chicago Conference, Dr Vander Veer voices his reservations about collaborative, or *concurrent*, therapy:

I think this case demonstrates the utility of a collaborative approach. Wholesale treatment was helpful in decreasing communicated anxiety which enslaved this family. . . . Collaborative therapy, however, has its disadvantages. It is hard for all members of a family to meet after their respective interviews, full of freshly mobilized guilt toward one another. It is also, at times, disquieting for one therapist to know all the contemporary material. This extra knowledge highlights the distortions of one's own patient and may provoke a negative counter-transference or rivalry with another therapist whose patient seems to be progressing faster. Finally, there is the danger of subordinating important trends in one's own patient to some current need in another member of the family. Co-ordination of the material is helpful, provided the therapeutic emphasis always remains individual.

It is obvious from these rather contorted objections to concurrent therapy, that Dr Vander Veer still felt that the individual patient might be sold short if the therapeutic emphasis was placed too heavily on all members of the family. Apparently, it does not occur to the analyst that cutting the Gordian knot of anxieties and hostilities which enslave the entire family could benefit all equally.

By the early 'fifties, there was widespread recognition that a child's behavioural disorders could be manifestations of family pathology, especially where neurotically close mother-child relationships were concerned. Dr Donald Winnicott, the British child analyst, who worked at Anna Freud's famous Child Therapy Clinic in Hampstead, London, all that time, wrote of such a symbiosis. He referred to these mother-child unions as 'couples'. One little boy involved in such a pairing came to Winnicott's office with his face screwed up in pain. When the doctor asked him what was troubling him, he said: 'Please, Doctor, my Mum complains of pains in my tummy.'

It was Anna Freud who took the bold step of having mothers analysed simultaneously with their children at her Hampstead Clinic, a much more intensive treatment than had existed previously in the Chicago cases I have outlined, when only a social worker saw the mother. The flaw in the practice of analysing mother and child, of course, is that it leaves the father out of the picture; also, it does not take into account any other highly-charged relationships in the family matrix, such as those with grandparents, siblings, and so on. Nevertheless, it was a big step forward in the development of family therapy.

It is interesting to try to visualize the growth of family therapy in mental pictures. First you have the child being analysed separately in an office, in a clinic, or at a child guidance centre, with his mother or parents being interviewed by a social worker down the hall or perhaps on another floor. Then you have the mother and child being seen together, but in the most tentative way, sometimes with the mother sitting in an adjoining room while her child plays in the therapist's office (the 'couple' is together but still a little apart, as if they were too explosive a combination to be in truly close proximity in a therapeutic setting).

Dr Melitta Sperling, a New York child analyst, evokes a vivid image of such tenuous early seating arrangements in a case history presented to her colleagues at a psychoanalytic meeting in 1950. A fascination for the transmission of neurosis, mother to child, had led her to treat twenty pairs of children and their mothers, both simultaneously and consecutively, and it was part of the material gleaned in these sessions that she relayed. She was particularly intrigued with the way the conflicts and unconscious wishes of a mother could be conveyed to the child responding subconsciously, resembling, she said, 'a person carrying out commands under hypnotic influence'.

She tells the case history of five-year-old Hilda, a child referred to her by the small school she attended because of her extreme school phobia. Hilda refused to go to school unless her mother stayed with her throughout the school period. She exhibited clinging behaviour at all times, even standing outside the door when her mother went to the bathroom. The other children made fun of her, but this did nothing to dent her compulsion to be with her mother.

Hilda had a one-year-old sister who had to be taken care of by a nurse while the mother, apparently helplessly, allowed herself to be bullied by her older child. The mother seemed most tolerant of the child's authoritarianism, even refusing to go out to dinner with her husband in the evenings, in response to the little girl's tyranny. She put the daughter's bullying tactics down to a fall from a ladder, saying that this had been the incident which had altered Hilda's behaviour so dramatically. As the simultaneous therapy unfolds, Dr Sperling begins to see that it is in fact the timid, fearful mother who wishes to cling to the child, and who does not want her out of her sight. The ladder incident had thrown the mother into a panic, and she later confessed that, after it, she never wanted Hilda to be separated from her.

It is generally believed that, in many cases of 'school phobia', it is the mother who is reacting against the separation caused by school attendance, not the child. The child, in protesting against going, is actually responding to a mother's unconscious wish. The child is reversing the roles in demanding to stay home, wanting to allay the mother's anxieties, parenting the parent.

Dr Sperling had to move cautiously in her dealings with the symbiotic pair. She describes how she coped with them in the analytic setting. For many of the sessions, Hilda's mother sat in the same room, knitting, while the child played. But then the doctor attempted a mild separation:

> When Hilda seemed more relaxed and interested in her play with me, I hinted to the mother that she should leave the room. Unlike most mothers in such a situation, she seemed to have difficulty in taking my hints. . . . Hilda accepted my suggestion that she come in without her mother under the following provision: She told her mother to sit in a certain chair and not to move from it and asked that all the doors be wide open, through which she could watch the foyer which led to the waiting room. She kept running to the waiting room constantly to make sure that her mother was still sitting in the same place. . . . After I had worked out with Hilda her fear that her mother would disappear if she didn't keep close watch on her, there was a marked improvement in Hilda's behaviour to the extent that she could stay during the entire play session without having to look for her mother.

This began a severing of the over-close ties that bound mother and daughter, and soon the mother began to give Hilda the normal amount of freedom a schoolchild needs, allowing her to develop her own identity independently. In affecting a mild spatial separation in her office setting, Dr Sperling was doing much more, as we have seen. The analyst was presaging a prime factor in family therapy; placement in therapeutic sessions as a dynamic factor in treatment. *Where* members of a family place themselves is strongly symbolic of where they are situated in the family circle. Part of a therapist's intervention, as we shall see, is rearranging this pattern, repositioning the family.

In Dr Sperling's treatment of Hilda and her mother, we see how crucial it was for the analyst to see the 'couple' together. Paradoxically, the analyst had to see them together in order to separate them. She could not have cut the mystical and unhealthy bond if she had seen them in separate sessions.

Clinging behaviour between mother and child is a feature of family life with which anyone who has had occasion to observe parents and children in a pre-school or primary school setting will be familiar. The voltage issuing from such a scene – the wailing, pummelling child, the frantic, tearful mother – can be extremely upsetting to see. In a small way, particularly during the first days of a new term, most mothers will have experienced milder manifestations of this wrench with a young child. However, when the tumultuous parting occurs each morning for months on end (if, indeed, the child doesn't emerge victorious and return home, exhausted, with the mother), then it is time to examine the union more closely. Why is the bond so close that it interferes with the normal functioning and school life of the child?

Dr Jules Henry, the St Louis family therapist who has made a study of mother-child relationships in primitive Indian cultures, has his own explanation of the phenomenon. He thinks that such apparently 'loving' behaviour in Western cultures is nothing of the kind. Mother and child are in fact locked in a neurotic love-hate relationship born of hostility on the one side (the mother's) and insecurity and feelings of submission on the other (the child's). The mother feels guilty about her hostile feelings, which may have nothing to do with the child but be a replay of earlier resentment against a younger sibling. To counteract these feelings, she becomes over-protective. The child, an emotional scapegoat, senses her ambivalence towards him and alternates between clinging to her and provoking her. (If the mother were a physically battering kind, the child would be black and blue. As she isn't, he is merely sucked into her pathology and treated like a lover in a turbulent adolescent love affair.)

It is the therapist's unenviable task to untie this ugly love knot by coming between the two. While such intervention is usually sought on a conscious level by the parent, who realizes that the relationship is socially unacceptable ('Johnny won't leave my side and everyone thinks it odd', etc.), it is often the mother who resists the separation when it is effected. Dr Henry cites the case of a five-and-a-half-year-old boy referred to his clinic because of his extreme fear of injury, lack of friends, absence of self-confidence and refusal to accept food except from a bottle. The mother is very critical of him, calling him 'dumb' and 'worse than a baby'. The father plays no great part in this duo, viewing it passively and a little wearily. After innumerable sessions with both mother and son, Dr Henry scores a victory. The boy throws his bottle away. It is then that the mother sobs, 'I've lost my baby!'

By throwing his bottle away, this little boy was fighting back. And it is fair to say that the children in these 'couple' situations are not always passive victims. A little four-year-old treated at the Hampstead Child Clinic in the late 'fifties was reported to have 'gained the upper hand' when he hit his mother so hard that she stopped retaliating. They were, nonetheless, like so many of these duos, inseparable.

Such a mother-child configuration, a sick interacting of needs, rarely occurs in simpler cultures, Dr Henry believes. In his study of the Pilaga Indians of Argentina, he noticed that mothers felt no guilt at all about their babies, largely because the process of carrying them is treated more casually. They believe that the infant is shot into their wombs, small but totally formed, by the male ejaculation of semen and that their bodies are no more than nine-month-long feeding stations. This makes for a more casual post-natal approach and a lack of guilt when, and if, they express irritation and hostility towards their offspring. Although Dr Henry does not say so, he does put the thought in one's mind – reminiscent of Henry Kempe's reference to the Madonna fixation of Western mothers – that the too high expectation of motherhood as a near celestial vocation, can backfire badly. By investing the role with too much mystique, we also open the way for much disordered behaviour.

Even though Dr Henry described his bottle-sucking child patient and tormented mother as long ago as 1951, it is clear that he is on the right track. He has no doubts about tackling the two together in order to divide their unwholesome union. He does not try to side with the child against the mother. But the logistics of treating them come close to defeating him. He saw the pair, which he calls the 'L' family, for a period of three years, during which time the material concerning them accumulated alarmingly. He writes:

> In a child guidance clinic the materials for the understanding of a patient may be spread among three or more persons; for a psychiatrist and psychologist may work with the child, and a psychiatric social worker with the mother . . . the volume of material in the record becomes great and the personnel handling the case in therapy may change a number of times. Hence comprehension of the case becomes even more difficult. . . . There are two ways in which the interactional analysis can be validated. The first is through having an observer live in the home of the patient. Psychiatric research will one day have the courage to undertake this. The second is by having two or more analysts code the same material in order to see whether they come out with the same results. Neither of these techniques have been used here. However, the purpose of the present paper is not to present a valid interpretation of the pathology of the L. family but rather *to suggest a method of approach to a better understanding of behaviour disorder as a manifestation of family pathology.*

The method of approach for which Dr Henry pleaded over twenty-five years ago has been quite a long time in coming – and, though it does not operate in quite the way he prescribed then, it has come in the form of family therapy.

In the next chapter I shall look at some recent developments in this new and highly promising therapeutic development.

10/ Family Therapy:
How It Works

Family therapy has raced along in its development since its beginnings nearly twenty years ago. As we have already seen, it grew in part out of child analysis and the realization that a child was not producing a symptom in isolation but often reflecting parental disturbance.

One can also trace its roots in marriage therapy and counselling, with its focus on the interlocking neuroses and needs between couples. Therapists and marriage guidance counsellors began to notice that some partners were locked in an unhealthy symbiosis, one spouse appearing to need the erratic or sick behaviour of the other (it has been demonstrated that the 'well' member of a duo, for instance, will go into a neurotic decline when the so-called 'sick' one has been cured by analysis or psychotherapy).

Family therapy should not be confused with group therapy. In essence, group therapy depends upon the dynamic engendered among a number of *strangers* led by a trained therapist; these strangers will indeed interact and produce a momentum of their own, allowing some of the sufferers to voice feelings and inhibitions which they may never have faced before. However, group therapy is an *ad hoc* process; the members form unions and divisions in a day by day, ongoing way. Family therapy is vastly different in that the therapist is dealing with a configuration, a *gestalt,* that has been fixed and formed and made unhealthily static long before the

172

family seeks help.

Couples can become locked in this kind of static posture as well. A revealing study of unwholesome symbiotic need in marriage was carried out in 1968 by two American psychiatrists, Robert L. Dupont and Henry Grunebaum, with sixteen couples at the Massachusetts Health Center. The women had all been admitted for treatment in various stages of paranoid illness. It was found that their husbands shared many of these characteristics; they were compliant, conventional, hard-working and passive. The marriages had all been 'happy', according to the couples, but were characterized by isolation. The women's breakdowns occurred shortly after cessation of sexual relations with their husbands. This close-down on the part of their men had driven the women to jealous fantasies and erratic behaviour. The husbands stood by stolidly in a 'Look-at-her-isn't-she-behaving-weirdly?' sort of way, but it was obvious to the therapists in charge that the husbands were men with suppressed and angry feelings of sexual frustration – the wives having 'submitted' to sexual relations with them up to that time, but without any evidence of shared pleasure. The husbands' reaction to this unresponsiveness, finally, was: 'If she doesn't like it, she won't have it at all. . . .'

It seems that the husbands needed to see their wives behave angrily and erratically because they themselves were incapable of doing so, and that their sexual withdrawal was an unconscious means of pushing their wives into such behaviour. It was a system that satisfied needs in both spouses (the need of the husband to be retributive, and of the wife to be shrewish). In marriage, it often happens that one party becomes a mouthpiece for the feelings of the other. These men wanted to lash out and behave unreasonably. Instead, they precipitated their wives into doing so. Without realizing what they were doing, they became puppet-masters.

Studies such as this one led therapists to scrutinize entire family systems – parent to child, husband to wife – in an effort to discover whose neurosis, or psychosis, was satisfying whose need.

In the early 'sixties, in family therapy clinics springing up in the leading Eastern seaboard cities of the US (Philadelphia, New York, Boston), the father was suddenly brought out of the shadowy corner in which he had been standing, figuratively-speaking, in preceding decades. Fathers were no longer allowed to be mere voyeurs of their own family disturbance; they were drawn into the centre of the family stage, where they belonged.

Other relations were beginning to be included as well – siblings, members of the extended family such as paternal and maternal grandparents, aunts and uncles, cousins, in-laws, spinster sisters – whoever had been influencing the family *gestalt*.

In a curious way, since those early beginnings, family therapy has grown to become an antidote to the tight nuclear family configuration. Therapists, recognizing that a parent may be a force in a grown spouse's marital set-up, are now asking him to join the therapeutic group. The irony here is that manifest family dysfuntion had to occur before efforts were made to extend the family circle.

Working with hundreds of disturbed families over the years, therapists have observed a number of common characteristics that link them. As long ago as 1951, the prescient St Louis psychiatrist Jules Henry was feeling for this concept when he wrote of a family where *'dominance, provocation, clinging tendencies* . . . interrupt *communication* between themselves and other members of the family or between others and the outer world.'

In referring to the type of family who make communication with the outside world almost impossible, Dr Henry might have been talking about those Laing-Esterson families of schizophrenics. One realizes that such families chatter cryptically at each other in an unconscious attempt to use language as a barrier against outside intrusion into their bizarre worlds.

Attempting to classify disturbed families in the early 'fifties, Dr Henry already recognized one of the types of family later observed in his own large practice by Dr Horst Richter, a West German analyst and expert in psychosomatic illness. In his book *The Family as Patient,* Dr Richter writes of what he calls 'the paranoid family', whose members withdraw into an 'illusory, narcissistic, private world' in order to hide their own explosive, aggressive tendencies from themselves.

Other types he has come across are 'the hysterical family', who make a kind of colourful, perpetual theatre of their lives, and the 'anxiety neurotic' family, a panicky, phobic group who make a kind of sanatorium of their homes, shutting out the disturbing world outside.

Dr Richter describes these noisy, theatrical, and exclusive families in a dramatic, readable way. Two American therapists, Salvador Minuchin and Nathan Ackerman, study them more clinically but make them no less interesting for this. They also discern a number of basic behavioural patterns that frequently emerge in dysfunctioning families.

One of these is what they call *complementarity*. Here, a flaw or behavioural quirk in one member of the family will often satisfy a need in another (like the extreme example of the paranoid wives and the secretly aggressive husbands previously described). I think the term as used here is confusing because it turns the verb 'complement' upside down. We have always understood complementarity in two people to be a good thing (simple example: 'she is an extravert, her husband is an introvert, so they complement each other perfectly'). However, used in family therapy the term means an unhealthy fitting together of two character qualities in the group family setting. Nathan Ackerman describes it as 'a form of circular support'.

Families who are functioning unhealthily are also often seen to have formed *coalitions*. Although unconscious, these can be as strictly aligned as any governmental coalition (perhaps more so). The most common coalition one finds is that of the mother and her children against the father. A certain degree of dissembling is usually employed, the mother appearing to submit to all her husband's wishes, to look up to him as the law-maker. She will encourage her children to feel that her husband is a sort of benevolent despot, too. In fact, what she has often done is to render him powerless and to push him to the outer perimeter of the family circle, where he is merely a peripheral member, superfluous except in his role as breadwinner.

It is not difficult to see the propensity of mothers in the home to castrate their husbands in this way as a form of backlash in an age-old war of the sexes. At the same time, it is interesting to speculate on how increased equality, since the advent of the Women's Movement, may actually come to the rescue of the father in the home. If being a mother is no longer viewed as a form of banishment from the male world where the power really belongs, it is possible that women will rely less on such compensatory factors as matriarchal domination to soften the humility they have felt for their second-class citizenship status.

The coalition between mother and children is not the only type one finds in a family structure. There can be siblings against parents (this is especially true of adolescent children), father and children against mother, mother and parental child against younger children (the eldest child is usually the parental child, the one who has taken on the functions of either the father or the mother; the parental child is particularly evident in single family situations).

Another characteristic of the dysfunctioning family is its propensity to erect rigid boundaries, a rigid disposition being necessary to form an effective coalition. When a therapist moves into the vortex of a disturbed family, it is his task to differentiate roles so that *each* member can begin to have his own individual autonomy and thus weaken the rigid coalition.

Salvador Minuchin, a Philadelphia-based psychiatrist with an Argentine background and one of the most innovative of family therapists, writes that one of the best ways to discover whether a child is part of a rigid coalition system is to ask him a direct question in therapeutic sessions (example: 'When do you go to bed at night?'). If a child answers for himself, then Minuchin is assured that he has a slight measure of autonomy. If the child has to look to a parent for a cue before answering, then his individuality is being curtailed. Also, it is a way of discovering who heads the coalition. If the child looks to the mother for a cue, then the therapist can begin to see where the coalition exists and who it is who heads the party. Should the child look to the father, or to the parental sibling, he will be able to discover how the family hierarchy is constructed and who leads it.

Another feature of the unhappy family is its propensity to project. This quality has already been amply demonstrated by the families of schizophrenics, where a parent has been shown to bestow feelings of guilt or shame upon a child because it has become intolerable to carry them on his own shoulders. In such a situation the parent is staving off his own breakdown by projecting his conflicts onto someone else. This 'someone' may be a marriage

partner or, more often than not, a child. As Nathan Ackerman
writes:

> In family process one conflict may be substituted for another, or
> the pathogenic focus of conflict may be displaced ... at the level of
> group defense, there may be an increased rigidification of role
> patterns ... a recourse to diversion and escape, or an indulgence
> in *prejudicial scapegoating* ...

I have italicized 'prejudicial scapegoating' in this passage
because it is crucial to the understanding of what often happens
in a dysfunctioning family. To keep up its unhealthy defences, the
family will select a scapegoat. As Dr Ackerman says, if the victim
happens to be a child, the 'projective accusations' become even
more intense – undoubtedly because a measure of subconscious
guilt is at work in the psyche of the parent who has taken this mani-
festly unfair course.

The role of the scapegoated child in a sick family is to act as a
lightning rod, attracting all the electric tensions generated in the
home. He may begin to behave anti-socially, be silent and withdrawn at home or at school, or unruly and vandalistic (both
extremes are signs of distress). Or he may develop psychosomatic
symptoms: asthma, appetite disorders (over-eating or self-starvation), bronchitis, skin rashes. All these symptoms – anti-social
behaviour or psychosomatic illness – may be 'conflict-detouring'
mechanisms, in Minuchin's phrase, deflecting attention from the
real centre of disorder in a family (often a conflict between husband and wife).

What happens in this context when a child is scapegoated and how
does the therapist literally come to the rescue? I have concentrated
here on some famous clinical examples of child scapegoating and
therapeutic rescue, realizing that other members of the family – a
mother, a maiden aunt, a grandfather – can also be treated pre-
judicially. Sadly, however, it appears that in the majority of cases
the victim is a child, and as I am primarily interested in parent-
child relationships, I have focused on malfunctioning in this area.

The complexity of family therapy lies in the fact that many

parents need their child's sickness and may therefore feel ambivalent about the therapist's intention of curing him. When a husband and wife are at emotional loggerheads – competitive, aggressive, sexually incompatible – their child's 'illness' may serve to unite them.

But often the child's problem begins to get too big even to serve as a welding process for the parents (it could be that the child, weary of his hidden role as a conflict-detourer, starts to exaggerate his symptoms as an unconscious protest and a cry for help). Alarmed at these exaggerated symptoms, one parent will ring up a therapist ('Jane plays with matches', 'Ralph won't eat', 'Johnny has a phobia about going outside', etc.), and offer their child as 'the presenting problem' – the elected banner-leader of the real and suppressed family malady.

Another term for the child in this role is the 'Identified Patient'. It has become so customary in the history of family therapy for families to come to a clinic in desperation with all floodlights on the one symptom-filled child, that such children have been given a clinical nickname, the abbreviated form of 'I.P.'.

Ten-year-old Sally Brown, a case treated by Salvador Minuchin, is a well-known 'I.P.' in the literature of family therapy. Although Dr Minuchin does not exclude other neurotic symptoms from his treatment, he has become particularly well known for his treatment of child sufferers from anorexia nervosa, or self-imposed starvation. Sally Brown was in a serious physical condition, having lost fifteen pounds in ten weeks and weighing only forty-two pounds when she was admitted to hospital. When Dr Minuchin visited her, she had lost two more pounds and looked, he said, like 'an emaciated old woman with a sad, fixed smile'.

The Brown family confessed themselves utterly bewildered by Sally's refusal to eat because they – successful architect father, mother, and three other siblings (Michael, fourteen, Robert, twelve, and John, eight) – were such a happy 'normal American family', as they protested frequently to the therapist.

This strange and continuous assertion of absolute normality quickly alerted the therapist to the possibility of family neurosis. When a family denies the existence of any conflict, as if believing that having 'trouble' would automatically put them in the pariah class, the doctor's suspicions are immediately aroused. Their claim to normality often disguises a mass of unresolved conflicts. In this case, the starving Sally is the perfect focus in the family drama. Rather than voice their own conflicts, the parents and siblings can rush to the afflicted child, exclaiming over her strange behaviour, raising so much dust that the real issues are effectively screened from view. As Minuchin puts it: 'The psychosomatically ill child plays a vital part in his family's avoidance of conflict by preventing a focus for concern.'

Dr Minuchin penetrates the family circle in a direct approach that is fascinating to observe. With anorectic patients, he employs the technique of eating with the 'I.P.' and his or her family, able thus to watch the full panoply of tensions, submerged angers and family alignments while the tense activity – in this case, that of eating at table – is performed.

If one were not so worried about the seriously ill Sally, the transcript of his luncheon sessions with Sally and her family would be faintly comical. Sally herself sounds like the figure in an early W. C. Fields film as she wails: 'I don't want the hamburger. I just want the ice cream. Let go of me!' (A Fields figure would have given her the ice cream, but as to how and where would be a matter for the slapstick scriptwriter.)

But Minuchin is infinitely patient and skilful. While she is in hospital, he manages to urge Sally to order her own meals from the hospital kitchen, thus giving her a sense of independence and an interest in food. By prodding, ignoring her petulance (incessant 'I don't knows' when asked about her preferences), he manages to extract from her the statement that she will eat the hospital menu of chicken, potatoes and peas. This strategy offered immediate results, he writes; she started eating during the session at his practice, and thereafter in the hospital and after her return home. She regained her previous weight in a month.

With the danger to Sally's health passed, Minuchin is able to scrutinize the family's troubles more closely. It is significant that often, when the Identified Patient is cured of her dangerous symptoms, the problems of the parents come into sharp relief. In the Brown family, Mrs Brown had formed a coalition with some of her children, pushing Mr Brown to the outer edges of the family circle and acting as the controller of communication between the children and the father. Thus isolated, the husband-father has been made to appear an absolute despot. As Minuchin writes, Mrs Brown's relationship with the children is 'overcontrolling, intrusive and over-nurturing'. She has made a weak puppet-dictator out of her husband.

Sally, too, is excluded and isolated from the coalition of brothers and mother, and, perhaps because of this, she subconsciously sympathizes with her father. The selecting of food as a flashpoint is not random. One of the disagreements the two spouses have had over the past twenty years is in the realm of table manners (the mother criticizes the husband's). By not eating, Sally is both asserting herself and putting herself in a position of covert ally to the father.

The sick quality of Sally's unconscious manoeuvre is that, left unchecked, it manages to satisfy all members, making the family's rigid role-playing even more intractable. The mother can fuss over Sally and thus satisfy her need for being over-protective, the mother-brothers coalition is reinforced because they can go into a huddle over their concern for the odd one out, and even Sally – the former outsider – has a measure of satisfaction in being able to assert herself in a dramatic way.

Minuchin sets about freeing the child from this enmeshed system. First, as we have seen, he relieves her of her dangerous symptom of self-starvation. Then he tackles the communication system of the entire family. At the crux of the family dysfunction is the inability of the Brown parents to negotiate or communicate with each other. The therapist brings these real, submerged conflicts to light – the father's impotence both as a disciplinarian and as a bed-mate, the wife's feeling that she does not have her husband's interest or support. Most importantly, he allows them to drop their hypocritical façade of being apple-pie normal and one hundred per cent 'happy'. (In fact, after long therapy, they did begin to approach their previously imagined goal of 'happiness'.)

Horst Richter has defined the 'sick' family as one which 'drives some member of the family into a state of symptom formation'. Often the person who retreats (or protests) against unhealthy family interaction by developing psychosomatic symptoms, is a pre-school child. The ability to pick up what the flower children of the 'sixties might have called the 'bad vibes' in a family setting seems to have no age limit.

Three California child psychiatry casework specialists, Augen-
baum, Reid and Friedman, cite the case of a two-year-old, Lynn
Morris, who suffered from recurrent bouts of diaorrhea associated
with temper tantrums. The child was bright, pretty and intellectually alive, the parents a pleasant, appealing pair in their late
twenties. Another happy family, one might suppose. However,
upon close analysis, and after several interviews with the family,
the intervening therapist discovered that the couple were in severe
discord about how to discipline Lynn. The father was indulgent,
the mother less so, but both felt tyrannized by the child's uncon-
trollable reactions to having her way curtailed.

In one session, the therapist deliberately took one of Lynn's toys
away to test her reaction to such frustration (this ploy is referred to
as 'tickling the defences' in the language of family therapists). He
found her reactions mild. Concluding that the child was anxious
for unambivalent control, the therapist guided the parents towards
a more unified response towards setting limits for her.

When the parents began to act in harmony towards Lynn, the
child's diaorrhea and temper tantrums ceased. The therapist
believed that the child had sensed the rift in her parents' approach
to discipline and was manipulating their disharmony for her own
ends. While one is tempted to view Lynn as a little devil for playing on her parents' dissension in this way, it is obvious that she did
not like herself for doing so; the tantrums and the unconscious
psychosomatic symptom of diaorrhea undoubtedly caused misery
both to herself and to her parents.

The child who detects discord in the family and reacts against
it by developing symptoms, is a little like a rebel in chains. There
are not many verbal protests a young child can make. But he can
react with his body. He can stop eating or eat compulsively. He
can control his bowel movements, or not control them. As Horst
Richter emphasizes, a child's psychosomatic symptoms often
represent what remains of his psychological health. When a
therapist intervenes, he does so not with the object of encouraging
the child's outspoken rebellion, but in order to deflect the energy
being put to use in such a direction, and to channel it towards more
creative ends.

Reacting psychosomatically to family dysfunction is not the
only form of protest a child can make. Performing poorly in school

is another symptom a child may register against over-controlling or emotionally disruptive parents. Or, as I have mentioned previously, he may indulge in petty thieving or vandalism. The latter course is the most self-destructive and the one most often registered by young adolescents whose parents are repressive, unable to loosen the reins and allow the child to make the transition from childhood to adulthood (it is not only the parents of schizophrenics who indulge in this form of over-control). Here, too, the child may be helped most effectively when a therapist can see the family *in toto,* a situation which will allow the parents to gain insight into the reasons for their over-zealous control, and the effect it is having on their child's behaviour.

Nathan Ackerman gives a vivid example of a family in turmoil over what turns out to be adolescent rebellion of an easily understandable nature.

The adolescent 'I.P.' in this case is fourteen-year-old Henry N., the third child in a family of four children, two college-age boys of seventeen and nineteen, and a younger sister, Jane, aged twelve. His father has telephoned Dr Ackerman in distress over Henry's behaviour. The boy had planned the hold-up of a store but had himself warned the school authorities of the plan. This incident had followed a series of petty crimes, such as pilfering from Boy Scout funds and stealing petty cash from his parents and brothers. The parents are recent Jewish emigrants from Austria to America, having escaped the Nazi terror, and are intellectually ambitious for their children. The father is a hypochondriac, fussing over his haemmorrhoids, dominated by his overpowering wife and haunted by the memory of his profligate, gambling Austrian father. In Henry's behaviour, the father perceives horrifying reflections of his own black-sheep father.

The N. family have 'sent Henry to Coventry': he has been ostracized. All five – his parents and three siblings – seem appalled by him. The mother is repelled by his 'otherness', his refusal to become a scholar, his preference for the outdoor life, his pursuit of agricultural rather than purely cultural interests. His father finds everything about him almost a personal insult to himself – his criminality, his preference for an older neighbour (who takes Henry shooting and fishing), his withdrawal from his proffered affection. The other children, eager students, decry his anti-intellectualism. Henry's own attitude in therapy is that of an outsider: 'Henry acted like a criminal and an outcast,' Ackerman writes. 'He was isolated and stiff; he slumped in his chair and showed a blank stare, a face without feeling or expression.'

Probing the family picture more deeply, the therapist comes across underlying conflicts far deeper than Henry's understandable wish to steer an unusual course for himself in the otherwise united family direction. Deep down, the mother and father are at daggers drawn; the father calls her the 'General' (or, almost worse, in one slip of the tongue, 'mother') and feels castrated by her; the mother is uneasy in this situation of reversed roles, subconsciously loathing her position as the 'General' and wishing for more emotional support from her weak, self-absorbed husband. Henry, sensitive, flees the uneasy home configuration of contorted parental relationships, seeking the fresh air of an outdoor sporting life. In the boy's own words: 'I like hunting and fishing. Father doesn't like it, can't go with me.' As Ackerman explains, the boy really wishes to 'lose' his father, to express his 'uniqueness' in a conformist family.

Though Henry has proven that he prefers the healthy outdoor life to one of criminality, his family still harps upon his past thieving. They are offhand about his gesture of courage in warning the school principal of the projected hold-up (for which he received the opprobrium of his 'buddies' who were going to join in the robbery). Rather, they elect to point an admonitory finger at him for choosing to be unlike them. In cultural terms, we can see that these frightened refugees, with their collective memories of the ghetto, are trying to pull Henry into the classical Jewish emigrant net, urging professionalism upon him as a mode of leaving persecution and oppression behind him forever. Henry, in his turn, has opted for the open spaces, in a manner reminiscent of the founders of the State of Israel, many of whom disdained the old virtues of intellectual excellence as a badge of the formerly ostracized and oppressed.

On a psychological level, the parents punish the boy in order to hide their own unresolved marital conflicts. By picking on him indiscriminately, the father can also release the unexpressed feelings of aggression he felt towards his own ne'er-do-well father.

As Ackerman says, the father 'had unwittingly cultivated in Henry the characteristics that had so disturbed him in his own father': the boy was being pilloried for feelings his father had about a grandfather he had never even seen.

It should be emphasized here that it is not only infants who can trigger off emotional irrationality and abreactive behaviour in a parent. An adolescent who begins to resemble or to behave like a hated grandparent, as Henry did, can bring seemingly inexplicable wrath upon himself as well. In receiving parental abuse for no rational cause, Henry is another case of the 'Sins of the Fathers', resembling in some part the battered infants who trigger off violence in a mother or father because they have inadvertently awakened memories of a past unhappy parent-child relationship.

Therapy was successful with Henry, and soon after the N. parents sought help from Dr Ackerman, the closely-aligned family ceased to ostracize him. Most important of all, the father, realizing that his hostility to Henry was not something the boy himself was responsible for, stopped scapegoating him. The therapist had mounted a very real rescue job for the victimized teenager.

Trying to describe the delicate task of intervention, and the often near-miraculous results they achieve, it is not unusual for therapists to find themselves in real difficulties with words.

In Ackerman's complicated definition, the therapist is – 'activator, challenger, supporter, interpreter and integrator' – a set of active roles that would exhaust lesser professionals (and, presumably, elude those who haven't the 'feel' for such delicate intercession).

In simpler language, how exactly does the family therapist work his magic? Salvador Minuchin describes his own technique of opening up contact with the family by acting as a 'host-guest' in the initial session; he puts the family at ease, gets to know their names, indulges in relaxing small talk, shows the young children where a few toys are kept. While this warming-up process goes on, the therapist is watching the individual members carefully, seeing how they position themselves.

Positioning is deeply significant in family therapy, as the way members choose to place themselves will reflect their life postures and feelings about one another. Families tend to give significant non-verbal cues; how a husband and wife sit, position their knees or their shoulders, space their chairs, mirrors the proximity or distance of their feelings for one another.

Noting these undercurrents as revealed in their seating plan, the therapist then plunges in with a general question, usually asking what it is that has brought the family to him. While eliciting their answers and reasons, he tries to make contact with each member, hoping to relate equally to each one. He then attempts to spark them into a general conversation with each other. When they do, he acts as a sort of Olympian cameraman, zooming in on the relationships (the dyads: mother-and-father, mother-and-son, father-and-daughter; or the triads: mother-father-child, mother-son-daughter), examining them with his wide lens, allowing them to interact as naturally as this setting allows.

At this point, as Minuchin points out, the therapist functions very much like the director of a play. He will direct certain members to talk with one another, bring up certain disagreements, see how they cope with these disagreements, explore the liaisons. After he has observed this dynamic scenario, he begins his therapeutic strategies.

These strategies are deceptively simple. They often consist of moving the chairs about and thus rearranging the original seating plan, the unconscious and highly revealing one the family has adopted. As the seating was deeply symbolic to begin with, the re-arrangement is correspondingly charged.

In the case of Sally Brown, the anorectic child, for instance, Minuchin devises certain significant moves. It will be remembered that Sally was isolated from her siblings and protesting, in her own manner, about this unfair ostracism. Aware of this, Minuchin asks that

> the three younger children occupy the centre of the room, with the mother and father helping them from outside the circle. John and Robert are directed to play with Sally. But when the three play a board game together, the game becomes enmeshed and chaotic. Therefore, the children are assigned the task of playing board games at home. The parents are to buy the games and then see that the rules of the game are followed.
>
> Robert, the brightest and most psychologically minded of the family, begins to ally with the therapist, sitting near him and com-

menting on the family's functioning. He begins to have more school friends and spends more time with them in an age-appropriate process of contacting the extrafamilial. Sally and John grow closer.

What starts as a mere spatial rearrangement (bringing the three children into the centre of the room with the parents at the *outer* ring), breaks up a coalition – that of mother and three children, with Sally as the outsider. The husband and wife are asked to view the children as a *couple* (their chairs are outside the inner ring of siblings). This brings them together. Robert begins to have more friends outside the family circle, helping to break up the coalition of older siblings. Most crucial of all, Sally is brought closer to John, the youngest of the brothers, and is no longer an outsider. In the case of the Brown family, Minuchin states, therapy was successful after nine months, with Sally no longer a worry to the family.

Reading the literature of family therapists, one is struck by the fascination they have for their own techniques. They often make themselves sound like guerilla warfarers hacking their way through the densest jungle in order to make a surprise attack – fleshed out Action Men, padding adventurously into the family psychodrama. Ackerman writes of the therapist entering the nuclear family set-up like a catalytic parent figure, moving right into the centre of the distress. Using the tactic of catching the family members by surprise, he thus undermines their fixed patterns of coping and defence by provoking painful but honest confessions of submerged, interpersonal conflicts.

Perhaps such self-consciousness regarding technique can be forgiven when one realizes that the relatively new form of therapy is still virtually in its infancy, under twenty years of age, compared to the ripe fifty or so years of experience held by the practitioners of individual therapy.

It may be unfair to point out dangers when a new technique for cure is as hopeful in outlook and as young. However, family therapy does have one serious potential pitfall – that of becoming a little mechanical. The therapist writing of his technique in mechanistic-sounding language, or sitting in a room manipulating placement and emotions like some compère in a game of musical chairs, must be wary of treating humans lke robots.

New York family therapist Celia B. Mitchell has warned her colleagues most eloquently against a 'systems' view of the family. While conceding that our lives are unavoidably influenced by cybernetics, computers being so much a part of existence today, she asks them to guard against perceiving of the family as 'a sort of clogged computer that needs to be reprogrammed and jogged out of its bogged-down state by reprocessing procedure'.

Having mentioned its dangers, we must also ask the most bedevilling question of all. Can family therapy live side by side with the more classical forms of therapy for the individual? Morton Schatzman, a New York psychiatrist now in charge of a family therapy association in London, is quite sure that it can. He feels that both disciplines must remain in action, complementing rather than excluding each other. As he says, family therapy is only useful for those who have to live in the family circle – younger children and spouses. For the single person, the independent man or woman who does not live in a family, or whose parents may no longer be living, individual psychotherapy is still the answer to any psychiatric conflict he or she may be experiencing.

'For young adults, family therapy is sometimes not a proper substitute,' Dr Schatzman told me. 'Young adults may want to leave the family. But for a child or adolescent who must still remain in the family, it is frequently the most efficient approach in terms of the therapist's time and in coming to understand what is really happening.'

These reflections conjure up a rather hideous jingle – 'the family who is treated together stays together'. But there is some truth in this fantasy advertisement. Family therapy, by viewing the family as an organic whole – though at times a dysfunctioning one – is helping to consolidate both the concept and the reality of this social unit. One must welcome a new technique that may well cure the malaise of alienation within the family.

11 / The Effects of Divorce

Divorce, like love, marriage and procreation, seems to be here to stay. In fact, resembling some human cell gone wild, it appears to be multiplying.

In the US, one out of every three marriages is doomed; in some states, like California, one out of every two. In Britain, the rate has soared to dizzying heights since the new, simpler procedures were initiated (what the Americans, in a succinct phrase, call the 'no fault' divorce). In 1975, there were 120,000 divorces listed in the United Kingdom. A year later, a twenty-three per cent rise was reported, leading a High Court judge to recount sadly that, in England and Wales at any rate, the country was catching up with California.*

Whatever interpretation these rising statistics suggest, divorce is no longer an exceptional event. It has become a familiar circumstance in human relations, an accepted option when a marriage is over. But does this mean that its effects on the family concerned, and particularly on the children, have become any less serious than

* Sir George Baker, President of the Family Division, High Court, expressed his concern at a Law Society annual conference at Harrogate on 7 October, 1977, saying: 'We used to view California's one divorce in every three marriages with horror. . . .' He then pointed out that, in England and Wales, there had been one divorce for every two marriages in 1976. However, it must be remembered that such statistics should be used with caution; the couples divorced were not the same as those who had got married.

in the past?

The answer is an emphatic 'no'. We can say for certain that, wherever children are involved, the child is in every sense the 'fall guy' when parents split up. He is totally helpless in a situation brought about by the flawed judgement of his parents.

One of the reasons why we can laugh in a pained way at film comedian Woody Allen's comment on divorce in *Play It Again, Sam* ('My parents never divorced: I begged them to, but they wouldn't . . .'), is because we are fairly sure that such a plea is unlikely ever to be made. For every child who might *want* his parents to divorce, there must be thousands for whom it is an unmitigated disaster.

However, there is little to be gained from emphasizing the tragedy inherent in divorce for a child – divorcing or divorced couples feel guilty enough already. And guilt is an unproductive emotion, particularly where a life-mistake has been made (people who feel no guilt whatsoever tend to psychopathy, so I do not wish to dismiss the emotion altogether – only in relation to divorce).

What is useful is to gain an understanding of the effects of divorce on children by looking at some recent research, and to try to modify the usually adverse affects wherever we come into direct contact with them, either personally or professionally.

In understanding the effects of divorce, we owe a great debt to the American psychiatrist, Louise Despert, whose special field was poor performance at school as a result of emotional crisis in the home. Her seminal book, *Children of Divorce,* first published some twenty-five years ago, overturned our ideas about the effect of divorce on children. Until that time, it had always been thought that the child of divorce was as unfortunate as the victim of a car crash; at best, he would be left with a kind of spiritual concussion and feelings of being battered by the accident between his parents; at worst, he might be crippled for life by the experience.

According to Dr Despert, this was not the case. Divorce need not necessarily be a destructive experience for the child. Much depended upon how the break was handled. In fact, divorce could be a positive and mentally healthy step for a child rendered uneasy and puzzled by the ugly atmosphere in the home. As far as her personal experience with disturbed children of divorce (at the Payne Whitney School in New York) led her to believe, it was often the events *leading up* to a break that were damaging to a child and not the actual legal action itself.

Dr Despert tells us that this discovery had come to her as something of a shock. When she had begun her study, she had, like most people, believed that the children of divorce would have a high rate of emotional disturbance. Gradually, she discovered the opposite to be true. She writes:

> Astonishingly, I found far fewer children of divorce among these [those children requiring therapy] than are found proportionately among the general population, which includes both well-adjusted children and children in difficulties. There was trouble between the parents of every one of the children in my files, but surprisingly few of them had been divorced.

The evidence in her files led her to another startling conclusion: that 'emotional divorce' is far more disturbing to children than physical divorce. By 'emotional divorce', she meant the condition of tension between parents that is characterized by 'chilly silences and empty courtesies', as she puts it. These bad adult feelings, unidentified but palpable, can seem far more threatening to children than something they can readily identify – like the actual split when it comes.

Despert records a conversation she overheard in school between nine-year-old Pete and several of his classmates. One child had said that divorce was worse than death for his parents and Pete retorted passionately:

> No, it isn't. Look at my mother and father. Before Mother got her divorce they were always fighting or just about going to fight, and it was horrible. John and me were scared all the time and sometimes I felt like dying. Now we're not scared any more. Mother and Father are good friends again. They're happy now that they're not married and we all get along together fine.

As Dr Despert observes, Pete had not come to this healthy conclusion unaided. He and his brother John had suffered greatly before the final parental break. In fact, they had been brought to her school originally because the home situation had seriously affected their capacities to study, bright and willing as they were.

The parents discussed the boys' dilemma with the headmaster in weekly meetings, and the co-operation between school and parents as well as the cooling-off of temperatures brought about by the divorce itself, helped the boys to gain an optimistic acceptance of their parents' break and helped their working standards.

One could perhaps dismiss Dr Despert's findings as being too narrow a sampling seriously to influence our attitudes about the overall effects of divorce. Indeed, the young children she observed at Payne Whitney could hardly reflect a general social situation. However, earlier studies on the connection between an unsatisfactory home life and delinquency had pointed in the same direction. (I should mention that Despert was something of a lone figure in the 'fifties when she conducted her studies: sociologists have been very slow to scrutinize the special problems of the child of divorce.)

However, a few years before Despert published her illuminating comments on children and divorce, sociologists studying another problem area, juvenile delinquency, were unearthing facts that would support her views about the damaging effects of a disturbed home life on children, and the actual amelioration of these effects *after* separation and divorce.

In a study on the relationship between juvenile crime and a bad home situation and other factors, published in 1957, F. Ivan Nye, an American sociologist, also contested the view that the presence of two parents necessarily created a better child-rearing situation.

He discovered that adolescents from divorced homes adjusted far more successfully than those from dissident unbroken homes. According to him, the crucial factor in the adjustment of children is the social-psychological success or failure of the family, not whether nor not it is legally or physically broken.

Nye's findings were corroborated by another research sampling conducted in the 'fifties, an American study undertaken by N. C. Elmer on 18,000 delinquent children. This revealed that only a small percentage (one-tenth of delinquent boys and one-fifth of girls) came from homes broken by actual separation and divorce.

Reading Elmer's findings at the time that she was observing her young pupils at Payne Whitney, Louise Despert became all the more convinced that the pangs of 'emotional divorce' were worse for children than the actual rift itself. Most of these children, she asserts, would have been better off if their parents had brought their disharmony into the open and divorced. In her pleas for the 'clean break', she writes:

> Divorce also often brings the child's buried anxieties to the surface. The divorce has not created these anxieties. They have been there throughout the period of dissension. . . . We would much prefer that parents loved each other and their children simply and wholesomely and that homes remained intact emotionally as well as legally. But since unsuccessful marriages cannot be wished out of existence . . . it is reassuring to know that under certain circumstances the divorce can bear good fruit.

What are the circumstances in which divorce can bear 'good fruit' for the children involved? How can the effects, once the break has been made, be mitigated?

Dr Despert goes on to say that a certain degree of amicability between the divorcing or separating parents will obviously ease the divorce passage for children. If at all possible, parents should plan their children's future coolly, with a modicum of self-abnegation, an ability to place their wounded feelings or sensations of failure in the background and concentrate on the child. Despert calls this 'planned protection'; a necessary cocoon spun around the child or children by both parents in co-operative union.

She suggests that this is of paramount importance in a marriage break-up and should take pre-eminence over other considerations, such as property divisions, finance, place of residence of the departing partner, and so on.

Parents have too long put themselves first in the divorce situation, regarding children as afterthoughts – there to trouble their consciences, already weighty with guilt. If they were to put their children first, planning their futures like a quiet military manoeuvre jointly conceived, it is likely that they would not only be protecting their children from harm, but might also be indulging in therapeutic behaviour for themselves. Squabbling, hostile parents often lose what they value most – the respect of the very child they're struggling to possess.

I recall one case of a friend of my daughter's at boarding school. The thirteen-year-old girl, Alice, had been dumped at boarding school (Despert calls these casualties 'boarding school orphans') while her parents conducted their battle royal over custody. The placing of Alice at the school was the only wise course they took, though the decision had not been thought out. Alice, withdrawn and timid at first, soon became a popular member of a 'swinging' group of teenagers, and during the holidays, elected to visit her friends' families instead of her own. As she grew older, her refusal to join either of the parents when not at school, conveyed a real message to her mother and father: she wanted no part of them. When the mother did finally win full custody of Alice, it was a Pyrrhic victory for her. Alice had effectively left home already.

A recent study, conducted by Dr John McDermott, consulting psychiatrist at the Children's Play School, Ann Arbor, Michigan, has shown that the least damaged child in a divorce is the one whose parents have practised 'planned protection', the most damaged the one who, like some neglected wraith, is left to suffer in limbo between two self-absorbed parents.

The study concentrated on sixteen children, aged three to five, whose parents were in the process of divorcing. McDermott felt that such a study was significant in many ways, not the least of which hinged on the fact that, as the highest proportion of divorces occurred after the first five years of marriage, it is frequently the very young child who is directly affected. While McDermott concedes that the 'emotional divorce' immediately preceding the legal break may have involved far greater discord in the home, he also sees the actual break as a time of acute stress for the child.

He makes the rather obvious point that this is so because the child is subjected to a disruption of his regular life with two parents. It is only the rare child who rides through this without feeling bruised, he says. What we are dealing with in the children of divorce, then, is not the absence of hurt, but the degree and quality of hurt sustained. For some it is slight, for others overwhelming.

The objectives of the McDermott study were to see how long the period of significant stress lasted for the children, how the school was able to assist them during their periods of stress, and – of special relevance here – which conflicts and anxieties rose to the surface and how the children adapted to them.

(It should be emphasized here that teachers have a crucial role to play in softening the effects of a parental split. A conscientious headmaster, headmistress or form teacher can keep a watchful eye on the child, subtly looking for signs of strain and removing pressure when he thinks fit. As a teacher can play such an important part in guiding a child through the worst immediate after-effects of a split, it is absolutely essential that a concerned parent put the teacher or school head in the picture about the impending divorce, either by letter or by a visit. No one can expect a teacher to divine what is happening; he should be apprised of all the facts – change of address, date of departing spouse, formal custody, and so on. Obviously, in the new situation, he will also need the new address of both parents.)

In McDermott's study the teachers recorded the behavioural changes in the sixteen children from week to week. (The children had all attended the nursery school between 1956 and 1966, although not all had been there at the same time.) The careful records kept showed that out of the sixteen, ten boys and six girls, ten of them manifested acute behavioural changes in the period immediately following the parental break.

It is interesting to note that, while young children do not have the same means to remedy their hurt feelings as adults, their reactions to grief are depressingly similar. The ten worst affected children met their trauma with 'shock, anger, depression, and defences of denial and aggression, blaming others for their problems', as McDermott reports. The emotions are familiar to any adult who has sustained grief, although the children expressed them in typically childish ways:

> . . . they become possessive, noisy, restless, and pushing, kicking, hitting and occasionally biting peers in contrast to previous behaviour. One child would hit others, become startled by his own actions and begin to cry, saying that he didn't know why he did it. Another child began finding angle worms to kill in the backyard.

> One child, a four-year-old boy, who was previously regarded as well socialised . . . began knocking down blocks and throwing other children's toys, dishes, and puzzles. . . .

> Two children in this group demonstrated a depression which disrupted their play. . . . Extreme boredom and inhibition were typically seen during 'free play' periods when the activity was left up

to the child. During free periods their comments were typically, "What can I do, I can't think of anything to draw".

The signs of aggression which erupted from the otherwise quite peaceable four-year-old boy, remind me of the six-year-old son of a friend of mine who divorced two years ago. Bruce, usually a mild boy, adopted a Capone-like swagger and bullying manner towards his peers almost the week after his father left. The father's departure had been made even worse for Bruce and his mother because they were forced to look for smaller quarters while the richer, more powerful father and his new girlfriend kept the family town house.

Some time later, Bruce and his mother passed by the old house, which they had been forced to leave in such an undignified hurry (it had not been a civilized divorce!), and Bruce looked up at the house and muttered through his clenched teeth, gangster fashion: 'I'd like to break in there and get my teddy bear back. . . .'

Bruce's mother told me this story to make me laugh, but it made me wince with pity instead. Children's defences against personal catastrophe seem extraordinarily pathetic. Psychiatrists tell us that the child of divorce often resents the custodial parent (usually the mother), sensing, rightly or wrongly, that she has driven the father away. Bruce's instant swagger was a way of clinging to what he remembered of his much missed, absent father (the split had been too bitter for the cool setting out of access or visitation rights; consequently Bruce hasn't seen him since the final rupture).

Children's reactions to divorce are varied. In severe cases, the child may regress dramatically, begin to bed-wet, thumb-suck and sleep poorly. Often associated with this type of depressive behaviour are feelings of an acute loss of identity. In this state a child may have the need to become more acutely conscious of his body. He may insist on wearing tight shoes, lacing them up painfully, hitching belts a few notches more tightly than is comfortable, wearing jeans or underpants that are too small. In cases where the desire for a heightened body awareness tumbles into severe disturbance, the child may masturbate incessantly. By creating an erotic sensation, children at least know they are there.

Another symptom of upset is an apparent need for self-punishment. The child in this state of despair uses his body as an automotive object; hurtling into chairs and against doors, crashing into circles of other children, careering into swings and tricycles. This accident-proneness and hyperactivity are blind and sad signals of distress, which sensitive pre-school and nursery school teachers should pick up and handle as warmly as possible. Young teachers are often instructed to be extremely tactile and holding when dealing with such overt cases of distress. Touching, rocking and embracing upset children who are not receiving enough body contact at home, is a valuable way for teachers and para-professionals in nursery schools to counteract the pain children are experiencing as a result of this lack of warmth.

Another defence that many young children employ in these times of crisis is to become a 'little parent' to their own parent. Girls are particularly adept at this. Bossiness comes easily to confident small girls, and when they are temporarily rocked by an event, they may exaggerate this quality of imperiousness and order their mother and teachers about. 'Put on your slippers this minute, Mummy!' they will scold, in a parody of the commands their mother makes to them.

One little girl like this is described graphically in the McDermott study:

> . . . bossiness and pseudo-mature mannerisms were a way of dealing with conflict. For example, one of these girls seemed quite popular with her peers, but on close study her relationships were quite superficial. . . . She looked and acted like a caricature of Shirley Temple . . .she was a fussy dresser who wore clothes too elegant for nursery school and often demanded compliments from the teachers. . . . She used grown-up expressions, at lunchtime exclaiming, "This is absolutely delicious!"

McDermott explains these characteristics as a kind of identification with a real or imagined part of the mother, which has great meaning for the child at the time of divorce. He believes that the child has copied the less agreeable personality traits of her mother – bossiness and nagging – qualities which the child may subconsciously suspect were the ones that drove the father away. Grafting on the mother's most negative aspects is counterphobic: the child fears them, they were in part responsible for the rift, therefore – in a magical way – she can defuse them by appropriating them herself.

While all this may seem very complex behaviour for a nursery school child, one must accept that the young, bruised boy or girl of divorcing parents *is* a complicated, sentient being, who picks up and reflects, without proper understanding, a multitude of adult currents and unresolved conflicts.

While it is useful to explore the ways in which children reflect their disturbances at the time of divorce, one must also focus on those who appear relatively unscathed from the experience. What can we learn from their behaviour and their success?

McDermott mentions three children – two boys and one girl – who were apparently unaffected by their parents' split. He suggests that in these cases the parents had anticipated the emotional difficulties that their divorce might create – feeelings of guilt, blame and anger – and had worked through them with their children. He is convinced, for example, that the parents must have explained their reasons for living apart carefully at the time of the split. These undamaged children appeared to have a good, solid relationship with each parent – so solid that their feelings for them remained unchanged after the divorce. It was evident in all three cases that the parents were not using the children for the purpose of mutual emotional blackmail, that they still retained a great deal of respect for each other, and that everything had been done to keep the visitation rights of the non-custodial parent as flexible, open and easy as possible.

Evidence for this amicable relationship during separation or divorce was revealed to the teachers in a variety of ways; the parents came together at parent-teacher meetings, took turns driving the children to school or picking them up, accommodating to their children's needs in these practical but essential ways. (That one little boy had no trouble in adapting to his new situation was shown at Christmastime when, with no apparent mental conflict, he made two separate presents for each parent while the other children were making joint gifts. He did this naturally and unselfconsciously.)

It is certain that the child who knows his parents have divorced and who has digested the knowledge, is emotionally healthier than the child who is left in the dark about the real situation. When a child is not told the truth, he senses that the parental rift may come under the heading of 'unmentionable'. He therefore represses it himself, pretending that it has not happened and refusing to discuss it with his peers. In later years, during early adolescence, he may indulge in fantasies to friends to explain the prolonged absences of a parent: 'Daddy lives in Argentina and runs a gold mine there – that's why I don't see him very much – but he is going to buy me a motor bike soon', and so on. These adaptive techniques are sad and may run a child into deep psychological trouble (especially when he himself comes to half-believe his own fantasies, which can happen).

But though it is a truism to say that the child who knows his situation is better armed to combat the hurt it may bring, it is astonishing how few parents do tell their children. American anthropologist Paul Bohannan, in his study on divorce, found himself appalled by the lack of honesty among parents vis-à-vis their children. He writes:

> One of the most consistent and discouraging things found in interviewing American divorced persons came in the response to my question, "What have you told your child about the nature of divorce in general and your own in particular?" This question was almost always followed by a silence, then a sigh, and then some version of, "I haven't told them much, I haven't had to. They know. You can't kid kids".

I know from personal experience that one can make a grave sin of omission with one's child, and thus build up a cluster of half-truths and misunderstandings in his mind by being inexplicit about one's plans. Waiting for the required two years' separation from my husband to achieve Britain's 'clean' divorce – the uncontested one, on the grounds of 'irretrievable breakdown' – I was, of course, a 'separated' but not a divorced person for the required period. By chance I happened to mention to my son, then aged ten, on a summer trip to the States, when we were in a close mood of confidentiality brought on by our amusement at the gadgetry of our Boston motel, that I would be getting my official divorce in several months' time. His face fell.

'Oh dear,' he said in a crestfallen way, 'I thought as long as you were just separated and not divorced, there was maybe a slight chance of you two getting together again.'

It is clear that I should have mentioned the divorce regulations in Britain, and the reason why his father and I were separated people for a period of time and not automatic divorcees. After I had explained the situation, he accepted the inevitable, recalling that five of his schoolmates also came from divorced homes. Children derive great comfort from knowing they are not alone: where a divorce is concerned, a parent should feel no compunction about comforting his child with statistics. It is not even spurious, I believe, to point out that many famous men and women come from broken homes (Anthony Eden, Adlai Stevenson and, most recently, Peter Jay, the glamorous new British Ambassador to the USA, are, or were, grown-up children of divorce). Children can absorb the truth, but they cannot seem to tolerate half-truths and concealed hints about their real situations.

A little girl in the McDermott Ann Arbor nursery, one of the well-adjusted children of divorce, neatly told an assembled gathering of playmates and teachers: 'Do you know that not all married people love each other?' She found this fact unremarkable – and acceptable.

It is reassuring to think that many parents can go through divorce in a civilized manner, considering the emotional welfare of their children above all – but what of the others? How about the bitter divorcees, the ones whose desire to possess the child or children obliterates all other considerations? How do their children fare?

One only has to reflect upon one year in the life of three-year-old Caroline Desramault, the child of an English mother and a French father who fought their custody battle over three countries. In May, 1971, a Versailles Court ruled that Caroline should be provisionally entrusted to her parents alternately for three-monthly periods. M. Desramault balked at this decision and fled with his child to Switzerland, rather than allow the mother to have temporary custody (the alternative, the judges decreed, to the split custody decision). The child then shuttle-cocked between her grandmother, her father (hidden in small hotels) and temporary care. The newspapers showed a picture of a very stunned-looking child when her relieved and long-suffering mother finally achieved custody. One wonders whether Caroline will ever recover.

I suppose everyone must be acquainted with such embittered parents. I know of a Canadian engineer who left his Catholic wife and four children in Montreal to work with a British company in Manchester. Their marriage had been mired in 'emotional divorce' before he left, and she construed his departure as a rejection, and has refused to communicate with him for the past four years. In all this time, the father has received only three smudgy crayonned picture 'letters' from his twin girls in return for his stream of presents to them. He pins them over his bedstead as if they were votive offerings.

As if this situation were not difficult enough for this father to bear, he also has to accept the allegation of being a 'deserter' because he has not been able to afford the expensive air trip home. Society is not very forgiving to either of the divorcing partners, but the one who departs the country, never returning to see his children, is the one who earns most of the opprobrium.

This Canadian father is miserable about his situation and goes into deep mourning each time he buys a present for his children on their birthdays. His argument that, even if he could save the money for the flight, the visit would be disturbing for his children because of the bad atmosphere between his wife and himself, does not convince his associates.

Curiously, however, this unhappy father has some weighty support from an unexpected source – the revered Anna Freud. In her arresting and controversial book, *Beyond the Best Interests of the Child*, written in collaboration with Joseph Goldstein and Albert J. Solnit, she makes a plea for the tranquil, uninterrupted residing of the child with one 'psychological' parent (one of the blood parents, or the parent figure to whom the child feels most attached). Also, when the divorced parents are warring, she sees nothing to be gained by visits from the non-custodial parent. They contribute to what she calls 'discontinuity', a rather heavy term but clear enough in its support of the continuous, good, stable care by one parent. She explains this position:

> In addition, certain conditions such as visitations may themselves be a source of discontinuity. Children have difficulty in relating positively to, profiting from, and maintaining the contact with two psychological parents who are not in positive contact with each other.
> Loyalty conflicts are common and normal under such conditions

and may have devastating consequences by destroying the child's positive relationships to both parents. A 'visiting' or 'visited' parent has little chance to serve as a true object of love, trust, and identification since this role is based on his being available on an uninterrupted day-to-day basis.

Anna Freud's belief that there is more continuity in living with the sole 'psychological' parent, and that the mental health of a child is safeguarded by a minimum of 'discontinuity' and visitations (usually referred to as 'access' in Britain), is not shared by everyone.

I recently attended a conference in London of a relatively new self-help group, Aid in Divorce, directed by a former policeman, Barry Powell. With an almost evangelical fervour, this divorced father of two said he felt the happy future of divorce lay in smooth joint custody. Many in the audience felt that this was a Utopian ideal and one that would be difficult for divorced couples to achieve. A spokesman for the National Council for the Divorced and Separated pointed out that such idyllic situations could only come about when financial arrangements had been dealt with to the satisfaction of both parties. It was a fascinating conference because of this clash of viewpoints; the idealistic one as proposed by AID, and the sceptical, down-to-earth convictions of the National Council.

In the US, perhaps because divorce has become so prevalent, there has been a movement towards 'accentuating the positive' in a split; this feeling was best summarized by the author Mel Krantzler in his book, *Creative Divorce,* in which he expresses the belief that divorce can be a way for the partners involved to find 'a new opportunity for personal growth'.

Apostles of the 'creative divorce' concept find that the most positive expression of this 'modus vivendi' between parents is achieved when they become harmonious joint custodians of their child or children. One such couple, writing in a 1976 issue of the *New York Times* magazine, described how they elected to live within minutes of each other after their divorce so that their children could visit them at will, on alternating nights if they so desired.

Personally, this sounds to me as if it might make for maximum confusion and Anna Freud's 'discontinuity'. The logistics of the arrangement alone sound rather defeating: what if the children disagreed about which parent they wished to visit on a particular night? I don't wish to be sour about any innovation in the post-divorce lives of children, because whatever makes them feel better about a split must be acceptable. But I do worry a little about parents deliberately seeking the limelight with new exhibitionistic life-styles. Are they pleasing themselves or their children?

Divorce is a time when the maturity of parents is tested to the fullest. Mrs Margaret Bramall, Director of Britain's National Council for One Parent Families, summed up this need concisely when the Council extended its role in 1973 to include not only un-married mothers but single parents of both sexes. She said:

> The amount which the child suffers as a result of break-up depends greatly on the maturity of the parents. If they put their child's interests first, before their own bitterness or hurt, and achieve a reasonable relationship, the children will benefit. If the parents are immature, or so bitter and insecure as a result of the break-up that they mistrust the relationship of child and absent parent . . . or use the child as a pawn, the whole situation can be grossly destructive.

The National Council for One Parent Families was anxious to let people know that, when they spoke of supporting the single parent at that time, they also meant fathers. (The Society say there are 100,000 lone fathers caring for their children in Britain today.)

There has been a growing movement towards fathers' custody, and organizations created to help fathers fight for their parental rights have proliferated on both sides of the Atlantic. Fathers have banded together to try to combat what they believe to be the in-built prejudice of the courts, who automatically believe fathers lack the necessary nurturing abilities to make them proper parents. The British Society, 'Families Need Fathers', begun in 1974, blames much of the bitterness in these custodial battles on the adversarial system of the courts themselves (pitting one parent against the other). Also, they believe that the judges do not have the requisite training, either psychiatric or social, to qualify them to make custodial decisions.

Fathers are finding that group action and legal self-help are methods of assisting them to reform the present divorce laws, so that these operate more in their favour. Any father who seeks his child's custody will receive the best legal advice the Society 'Families Need Fathers' can muster.

In two US states, New Jersey and Texas, groups of fathers are suing the states' courts themselves, alleging judicial prejudice in custody cases. These men belong to a growing number of men's rights organizations who say that they – like women – want equality in all things, and this includes equality in the fight for custody.

What shows up glaringly in all the discussions regarding custody, is that the parent to whom it is granted is regarded as the winner, while the non-custodial parent, with visitation or access rights only, emerges as the loser. The winner-loser configuration of divorce is one of its most unpleasant characteristics.

While I admire parents who can phase this flavour of sparring ill-will out of their divorce lives and construct a successful joint custodial arrangement, I suspect that they are in the minority. Harmonious joint custody may be the future goal towards which divorcing or divorced couples should aspire, but the reality is that most children of divorce live for the majority of their growing lives in the home of one parent.

12 | Is One Parent Enough?

We have already seen that Anna Freud believes that one parent is enough – provided it is the one the child wishes to go to (she thinks that young adolescents have the right to choose). In *Beyond the Best Interests of the Child* she writes:

> Only a child who has at least one person whom he can love, and who also feels loved, valued and wanted by that person, will develop a healthy self-esteem. He can then become confident in his own chances of achievement in life and convinced of his own human value.

It is just as well that we have these comforting words on the validity of the one-parent family from one of the world's leading child analysts. Comforting because the lone parent is a growing phenomenon; as divorce increases, so does single parenthood. In Britain, more than 620,000 parents manage alone, of whom 500,000 are lone mothers (some divorced, some unmarried, others widowed). In the US – at the last count, in 1972 – there were nearly six million lone mothers and over a million lone fathers.

Single parents have a constellation of emotional problems. As Mike Wilson of the National Council for One Parent Families told me when I interviewed him last year: 'A single parent is in a particularly vulnerable position, likely to sink in the nearest ripple. She or he has lower expectations, lower self-esteem. The odds against a single parent are very high. Yet given adequate financial assistance and community provisions, the one-parent family is a viable unit and the children need not suffer any great emotional deprivation.'

The National Council for One Parent Families has marshalled a long list of facts concerning the plight of lone parents, which stresses that their largest problem may be financial. In this hard-hitting list, the Council asks whether we know that:

> One-parent families are the fastest growing group at poverty level in Britain?
>
> Nearly 250,000 one-parent families are living on supplementary benefits?
>
> In 1971 there were day care facilities for only 14·5 per cent of children between two and five years of age?
>
> A third of one-parent families had to find new accommodation when they divorced?

The lowered self-esteem of which Mike Wilson spoke arises from a punishing combination of being alone and poor at the same time. Margaret Bramall, the Council's Director, spoke eloquently of these struggling parents and their reduced financial status in a a paper presented at the Royal Society of Health at Eastbourne in 1973:

> Many one-parent families suffer acute or relative poverty of a crippling intensity. The restrictions of a life lived for long periods on statutory means-tested benefit, the problems of living on or below the poverty line, even if the parent is at work, the difficulty of parents of either sex who try to re-enter employment after a period of absence and the inferior position of women in the labour market all result in a financial stringency which can cause lone parents to feel a double failure as parents. They cannot prevent their children from living in poverty in an affluent and material-istic society, and they have failed to provide or keep a second parent for the child. Lone parents have to fulfil the roles of pro-vider, home-maker, loving parent and authority figures, with no one with whom to share the joys and anxieties of parenthood.

Most crippling to the single parent is an overall fear of failure, compounded of the feeling of being stigmatized by society and a belief that their children's behaviour is caused by being without a father or mother (for which they feel responsible and thus guilty) rather than by a natural striving for independence.

That a parent should be weighed down with emotional stresses as well as being poorer than before seems almost too much to bear. But most of them do bear it, and with impressive strength.

There is a complicated, unidentified factor in the make-up of most lone parents, which I have never seen properly analysed. The rawness of their situation, the social ostracism, the indignity in many cases of having to live on social security – all these disadvantages pale before a grittiness that takes over. Single parents live with symbolic fists balled. Because they feel they have failed their children in one aspect – by having divorced – they appear determined to be better parents than ever. And it is this gritty ingredient that often makes them become much better parents than the average.

Last year I interviewed twelve single parents for my newspaper, the *Daily Express* – six mothers and six fathers. I spent a great deal of time with each of them, met their children, had tea at their homes. In the end, the paper only ran a quarter of the interviews, having decided, in the restless way of newspapers, that they no longer wanted to run long serials. I was sorry that my interviewees talked long and hard for so few rewards (not even a captioned photograph in many cases), but I shall never regret the assignment.

They were communicative and warm; there were no problems of reticence. Lone parents feel they have nothing much to lose; false dignity and paranoia towards the media do not colour their attitudes. They talk freely. In many cases I found I had to censor *them*. For instance, I saw nothing to be gained by reporting that one father, a bluff and hearty North Londoner, had been deserted by his wife because she had fallen in love with another woman. He did not feel emasculated by the fact, nor like the butt of a music hall joke (though he was humorous enough to see that this could have been the case).

I think I discovered a great deal about the situation of the lone parent and the fact that I was one, too, gave my interviewees a friendly fellow-feeling towards me they would not otherwise have had.

As I have said, many lone parents seem to keep a firm grasp on

their survival kits. They speak like survivors of an earthquake or
of a military skirmish. One beautiful actress, Yolande, a South
African in her early forties, with two young teenagers – a boy of
twelve and a girl of fourteen – peppered her phrases with almost
warrior-like images to describe her state:

> When you're a single parent, it's rather like being a soldier who's
> been shot in combat; the soldier runs until he gets back to camp
> and it's only then that he can collapse. I'm still at the running back
> stage.
>   Maybe when my children are grown up then I can collapse,
> relax my tension, consider myself back at camp.
>   But I like the challenge of being a survivor. No one is going to
> get me alive. I don't know what the suicide rate is with single
> parents, but I would think it's quite small.

This propensity to view life as a savage challenge can have its
attritive effect on a lone parent. With women particularly, the
effort of being a warrior vis-à-vis bureaucracy, of having to cope
with housing officials, social welfare workers, the divorce courts –
when increased support payments are needed as the children grow
and their needs become more sophisticated – can result in a temporary loss of the sensation of being a woman.

This was the case with Judy, aged thirty-one and struggling to
bring up her appealing, doe-eyed son, Paul, aged seven. She had
gypsied around with Paul since her marital split, living in squats
and caravans, but had tired of this existence, feeling that it was unhealthy for Paul to have so many different homes or abodes. When
I met Judy, she had finally found comfortable accommodation
with her steady boyfriend. Her only problem was being 'hassled',
as she put it, by the Social Security officers who suspected her of
'co-habiting' with her friend (she was). The theory behind the
refusal to give a single parent social security benefits if she (or he)
is living with an employed person, is that she can live 'off' her
partner and thus does not need assistance. I gather that this kind
of intolerable interference into the lives of single parents is soon to
cease, but Judy was still being subjected to it when we met.

Judy continued to live with her boyfriend in spite of the
'hassling', but she had other problems – emotional ones. As she
explained to me:

When you're fighting, the feminine side of you is in danger of disappearing altogether. I think it's because a single parent has to be both man and woman.

Before I met Tom, I used to take real pride in the fact that I could lay carpets, paint and decorate. I found I was buying all my clothes – always pants, of course – at men's shops. I still wear pants, but now I try to wear pretty tops with them and earrings.

But femininity is hard to recover. When Tom gave me a nightgown for Christmas, I said, 'What are you, crazy or something – I haven't worn a nightgown since I was four.'

Judy has focused on one of the most difficult aspects of being a lone parent; the need to be both mother and father combined. Most single parents are conscious of the need to be tender, as a mother should be, and of also having the authority of a father. However, the ambivalent role is an almost impossible one to maintain. (The Women's Liberationists feel that these roles are sexist and false, in any case, the results of childhood conditioning; whether they are right or not, the fact is that these are still the expected male-female attitudes in child-rearing.) Many feel it is best to abandon the schizophrenic position altogether, and to opt for being either mother or father, seeking sex-role substitutes for one's children outside the home. Single women rely heavily on the school to provide male sex-role models for their growing boys – teachers, camp directors, football instructors, swimming coaches. This is especially true if the father has deserted them.

Men seek surrogate mothers in their women friends – found at work, at community centres or among unmarried relatives, at singles clubs or church socials.

One widow I interviewed had analysed the ambivalent role required of a single parent and thrashed out her own difficult solution. This was Ruth, aged forty-five, the mother of four children – two of them (a boy and a girl) in their teens, and two younger ones. The younger children presented her with no emotional difficulties, but coping with her older teenagers had forced her to come to grips with the male-female role dilemma. She told me how she resolved it:

For a time, especially when my eldest son was experimenting with marijuana, and had dropped out of school, I decided I'd try to be a strict disciplinarian. But after a while, I just knew I couldn't make it. I felt split down the middle. I decided to let a great deal of discipline go by the board in order to remain happy with the children. I couldn't stand myself as the nagging matriarch.

This meant that both the eldest had some considerable troubles over schooling, and one with playing around with soft drugs. I'm sure their father could have prevented much of this. But if I had prevented them, I would have lost their confidence and friendship. So I abandoned the male role. To go on would have meant forfeiting a lot of the fun and gaiety we've had together.

The sensation of denying one's children the requisite portion of masculinity or femininity is one that disturbs most single parents. This feeling was expressed passionately by one lone father, Mike, fifty-five, a man with a distinguished war record, living entirely on social security with his two children, aged three and four. Their mother had run away with another man, and only rarely visited the children. He had knuckled down with military efficiency to the practical business of keeping two active young children in clean clothes and with full stomachs. But he had the feeling that he was depriving them of something – female comfort, he thought. As he said:

I hand-wash their clothes on Mondays and then have one day of wild cleaning, usually Wednesdays. On Saturday mornings, I stock up on tinned food. They eat out of tins a lot, I'm afraid, but I'm rather imaginative with them. For instance, I have devised the perfect stew made out of tinned spaghetti and meatballs added to a tin of potatoes and a tin of carrots. They love it.

Actually, they're pretty happy kids, I think. But they miss cuddling at night, I'm sure. They would love something warm and soft and cuddly to lay their heads on. And as handsome and distinguished as I may be, I am forced to admit that I lack a pair of breasts.

Mike was remarkably unembittered about his wife's desertion. I was astounded at how philosophical these male interviewees were about having runaway wives (another sad, growing social phenomenon). I do not know whether I can draw any conclusions about lone fathers in general from such a small sampling, but I came away with the distinct feeling that abandoned fathers do not spend their time in bitter recriminations.

Lewis, a warehouse manager, aged thirty-six and in charge of three small boys, two of them teenagers, said he had no time for harbouring bad feelings about his wife who had left him abruptly the year before – more for a high-paying job, it seems, than for another man. He felt that bitterness about her might communicate itself to his sons. Philosophically, he associated her departure with the Women's Movement and its logical consequences for those women who had felt oppressed by marriage and child-rearing. As he put it:

> I think women in the past put up with unhappy marriages because they couldn't do anything else. Now they can take the initiative and it makes them more independent. My wife began working in the first place so that she could supplement my income, so I can't blame her for that. But I'm sure that if she hadn't been working, she couldn't have walked out because she wouldn't have had the money to do it.

But while Lewis was immensely forgiving of his wife for having left him, he was not happy about the social adjustment he was making and had, rather joylessly, set about taking ballroom dancing lessons to try to recover a former talent and perhaps to meet a new partner one day. Why not on the dance floor, he asked? Certainly, he was never going to meet another woman watching television with his ten-year-old in the evenings.

In many cases, the social adjustment for a single parent is just as difficult as the financial one. Patty, aged thirty-nine, an American novelist living in the elegant London suburb of Barnes with her three-year-old daughter, was scathing about the bourgeois attitudes she encountered concerning her single-parent status. She described these to me:

> People are very couples-minded, especially in suburbia, where I live. If I am asked to dinner, I am usually asked to bring someone with me. I find this rather insulting. In middle-class circumstances, you're not regarded as people, but as couples. When I do go out alone, I'm made to feel a bit odd, especially by wives who have no career.

In these circles, men have a happier time of it socially than

women. A single man, fairly or unfairly, is usually considered a
social asset. The fact that he is bringing up children alone often
enhances his attractiveness, particularly for motherly women.

Bob, a forty-five-year-old public relations man for a publishing
firm, said that his girlfriends always included his pretty blonde
nine-year-old daughter in their plans for him, asking her for weekends in the country and for dinner at their homes. He himself was
very concerned about the way his beloved daughter was coping
with living with one parent – much more so than about his own
flourishing social life. He thought he had done the correct thing in
always being honest with her about his divorce and about his feelings towards her mother. As a result, he says, she is almost blasé
about divorce:

> Three of her close friends have divorced parents, and when she
> speaks of people splitting up she says it as naturally as if she were
> saying, 'It's going to rain tomorrow.' I have always tried to make
> the point that people are fallible and frail, that they either grow
> out of each other or grow into someone else. I think she accepts
> that marriage is a dying art.
>
> But I notice that she always talks about having a family . . . get-
> ting married. I never hear her talking about falling in love and
> going to live with someone.

Bob was touching upon another truism concerning the children
of divorce. They often idealize marriage because of their parents'
failure to make a success of theirs. However, the children of divorce
frequently divorce in later life themselves, and it is sometimes said
that there is a pattern of intergenerational repetition at work here.
Personally, while I believe that many neurotic behaviour patterns
can be transmitted from generation to generation – as I hope my
book has shown – I do not think it applies here.

The failure of many children of divorce to achieve a happy
marriage themselves, may well have much more to do with having
unrealistic expectations. It is natural for a child to believe that he
will succeed in an area in which his parents have failed. As children
of poor parents are often desperate to become financially successful
in adult life, so the children of divorce feel driven to contract
marriages that will last. Frequently it is this very 'clenched-teeth'
approach ('I *shall* have a happy marriage unlike theirs') which pre-

disposes the marriage to fail.

But I return to Bob. What Bob did not tell me, although it became obvious to me as I came to know him better and watched him with his daughter, was that this child had become a little surrogate wife to him. One of the dangers of the single-parent situation, especially when there is an only child involved, is the propensity of the child to become over-possessive. 'Our children become our parents,' one single parent put it a little wearily.

David, aged forty-eight, a grocer in North London and the father of one son, John, aged fourteen, said that his son's possessiveness actively interfered with his love life. At first, he had capitulated to his son's demands and given up his plans to spend weekends with his girlfriends, taking John away to the seaside instead. But when I met him, he had struck his first blow for freedom and was going on a communal seaside holiday organized by Gingerbread, a self-help group of single parents with branches throughout Great Britain. He explained:

> Of course, John is coming too, but he can damned well have his own bedroom this time. I love having him with me at all times, but I've decided I need a sex life, too, and who is going to want to bed with me with a snoring, hefty teenager in the room? He won't like it. He's always highly critical of my women – but this time, he'll have to lump it.
>
> I don't mean to sound harsh. John will always come first with me. But I think he has a problem. You know, he has to pile all his feelings into one parent instead of two. I think I'll find what I'm looking for by finding a nice lady friend. Well, hopefully. . . .

David's projected sortie into communality in order to get away from the emotional constrictions of the one-parent family, is highly significant, I think. It may well be that the single parent who takes this necessary plunge into a more extended form of social existence will be enriching his life tremendously.

It has been suggested that the most hopeful aspect of the future of divorce vis-à-vis the children involved, is that these children may be brought into contact with other lone parents and their children. Many sociologists are coming to believe that the nuclear family at its most claustrophobic, is a much less fortunate family structure than that of the lone parent who enters into communality and a form of extended family life.

It would be ironic, indeed, if the future were to show us that the event of divorce – until now considered worthy only of pity and general dismay, and a major catastrophe for the children – could open up a new and more refreshing form of family existence.

What is needed most urgently, I believe, if children are to benefit from the advent of divorce, is more personal choice for the child in the selection of his custodial parent. This reform seems to be on its way, borne on the new wave of the Children's Rights movement. Young teenagers in some states of America – in Florida, for example – can already opt to live with one parent or another. In Britain, the Children's Bill, which has been unfolding in slow stages over the past few years, will soon give young children a say in whether or not they wish to be adopted by the custodial parent's new spouse in the event of a remarriage.

Though it is far from easy to be a single parent, I do believe that their special dedication, coupled with increased government support, will make them more than equal to their difficult task.

I do think it is important to realize that one good parent is better for a child than two inadequate, warring ones, and that the life of a single parent need not be all struggle, sacrifice and social ostracism; on the contrary, it can be an enriching experience, enlarging social horizons.

References

INTRODUCTION

Rutter, Michael and Madge, Nicola, *Cycles of Disadvantage,* London: Heinemann, 1976.

CHAPTER ONE

Avery, Gillian, *19th Century Children,* London: Hodder & Stoughton, 1965.

Branch, E. Douglas, *The Sentimental Years,* New York: D. Appleton-Century Co., Inc., 1934.

Farson, Richard E., *Birthrights: A Bill of Rights for Children,* New York: Macmillan, 1974.

National Society for the Prevention of Cruelty to Children, 1 Riding House Street, London W1.

Pinchbeck, Ivy and Hewitt, Margaret, *Children in English Society,* Vol. II, London: Routledge & Kegan Paul, 1973.

Spargo, John, *The Bitter Cry of the Children,* New York: Macmillan, 1906.

CHAPTER TWO

Earle, Alice Morse, *Child Life in Colonial Days,* New York: Macmillan, 1909.

CHAPTER THREE

Holt, L. Emmett, *The Care and Feeding of Children,* New York and London: D. Appleton & Co., 1894.

Inglis, Ruth, Streich, Corinne and Spencer, Herbert, 'Dr Spock & Sons', *The Observer Magazine,* 9 November, 1969.

King, Sir Frederick Truby, *Feeding and Care of Baby,* London: Oxford University Press, 1913.

King, Mary, *Truby King – The Man,* London: George Allen & Unwin, 1948.

Schatzman, Morton, *Soul Murder: Persecution in the Family,* London: Allen Lane, 1974.

Schreber, Daniel Gottlieb Moritz, *Kallipädie oder Erziehung zur Schönheit durch naturgretreue und gleichmässige Förderung normaler Körperbildung,* Leipzig: Fleischer, 1858.

Spock, Benjamin, *Baby and Child Care,* New York, Giant Cardinal Edition, 1957 (58th edition of original published in 1946).

——, *Bringing Up Children in a Difficult Time,* London: Bodley Head, 1974.

——, *Decent and Indecent,* London: Bodley Head, 1969.

CHAPTER FOUR

Bettelheim, Bruno, *The Children of the Dream: Communal Child-Rearing and Its Implications for Society,* London: Thames and Hudson, 1969.

Caffey, John, 'Traumatic Lesions in Growing Bones', *British Journal of Radiology,* 1957.

Cameron, J. M., Johnson, H. R. M. and Camps, F. E., 'The Battered Child Syndrome', *Medicine, Science and the Law,* Vol. 6, No. 1., January 1966.

Griffiths, David and Moynihan, Francis, 'Multiple Epiphysial Injuries in Babies', *British Medical Journal,* No. 5372, 1963, pp. 1558-61.

Harlow, H. F. and Harlow, M. K., 'Social Deprivation in Monkeys', *Scientific American,* Vol. 207, 1962, pp. 137-46.

Josselyn, Irene, 'Cultural Forces, Motherliness and Fatherliness', *American Journal of Orthopsychiatry,* Vol. XXVI, 1957, pp. 264-71.

Kempe, C. Henry *et al.,* 'The Battered Child Syndrome', *Journal of the American Medical Association,* No. 1, 1963, pp. 17-24.

Leboyer, Frederick, *Pour Une Naissance Sans Violence,* Paris: Seuil, 1974. (UK: *Birth Without Violence,* London: Wildwood House, 1974.)

Pavenstedt, E. and Bernard, V., 'Child Abuse: A Symptom of Family Crisis', in *Crisis of Family Disorganization,* New York: Behavioural

Publications, 1971.

Rodenburg, M., 'Child Murder by Depressed Parents', *Canadian Psychiatric Association Journal*, Vol. 16, February 1971.

Scott, P. D., 'Parents Who Kill Their Children', *Medicine, Society and the Law*, Vol. 13, April 1973.

CHAPTER FIVE

Belucci, Matilda T., 'Group Treatment of Mothers in Child Protection Cases', *Child Welfare*, Vol. LI, No. 2, February 1972.

Burland, Alexis J., Andrews, Roberta G. and Headsten, Sally J., 'Child Abuse: One Tree in the Forest', *Child Welfare*, Vol. 52, November 1973.

Court, Joan, 'The Mother Who Injures Her Child', *Social Work Service*, December 1973.

De Courcy, Peter and de Courcy, Judith, *A Silent Tragedy: Child Abuse in the Community*, New York: Alfred Publishing Co., 1973.

Elmer, Elizabeth, *Children in Jeopardy*, Pittsburgh: Pittsburgh University Press, 1967.

Giovannoni, Jeanne M. and Billingsley, Andrew, 'Child Neglect Among the Poor: A Study of Parental Inadequacy in Families of Three Ethnic Groups', *Child Welfare*, Vol. LII, No. 3, March 1973.

Klein, M. and Stern, L., 'Low Birth Weight and the Battered Child Syndrome', *American Journal of Diseases of Children*, No. 122, September 1971, pp. 259-60.

Oliver, J. E. and Taylor, Audrey, 'Five Generations of Ill-Treated Children in One Family Pedigree', *British Journal of Psychiatry*, No. 119, 1971, pp. 473-80.

Resnick, Phillip J., 'Child Murder by Parents: A Psychiatric View of Filicide', *American Journal of Psychiatry*, Vol. 126, September 1969, pp. 325-34.

Schultz, Leroy, G., 'The Child Sex Victim: Social, Psychological and Legal Perspectives', *Child Welfare*, Vol. LII, No. 3, March 1973.

Smith, Selwyn and Noble, Sheila, 'Battered Children and Their Parents', *New Society*, 15 November, 1973.

Steele, Brandt F. and Pollock, Carl B., 'A Psychiatric Study of Parents Who Abuse Infants and Small Children', in Helfer, Ray E. and Kempe, C. Henry (eds.), *The Battered Child*, Chicago: University of Chicago Press, 1968.

Young, Leontine, *Wednesday's Children: A Study of Neglect and Abuse,* New York: McGraw-Hill, 1964.

CHAPTER SIX

De Courcy, Peter and De Courcy, Judith, *A Silent Tragedy: Child Abuse in the Community,* New York: Alfred Publishing Co., 1973.

Elmer, Elizabeth, *Children in Jeopardy,* Pittsburgh: Pittsburgh University Press, 1967.

Galdston, Richard, 'Observations on Children Who Have Been Physically Abused and Their Parents', *American Journal of Psychiatry,* Vol. 122, 1965.

Hyman, Clare A. and Mitchell, Ruth, 'A Psychiatric Study of Child Battering', *Health Visitor,* Vol. 48, No. 8, August 1975.

Littner, Ner, 'The Importance of the Natural Parents to the Child in Placement', *Child Welfare,* Vol. LIV, No. 3, March 1975.

Martin, Harold, 'The Child and His Development', in Kempe, C. Henry and Helfer, Ray E. (eds.), *The Battered Child and His Family,* New York: Lippincott, 1972.

Stephenson, Susan P. and Lo, Nerissa, 'When Shall We Tell Kevin? A Battered Child Revisited', *Child Welfare,* Vol. LIII, No. 9, November 1974.

Terr, Lenore C., 'A Family Study of Child Abuse', *American Journal of Psychiatry,* Vol. 127, November 1970, p. 5.

CHAPTER SEVEN

Belucci, Matilda T., 'Group Treatment of Mothers in Child Protection Cases', *Child Welfare,* Vol. LI, No. 2, February 1972.

Blos, Peter, *On Adolescence: A Psychoanalytic Interpretation,* New York and London: Free Press, 1962.

Clegg, Alec and Megson, Barbara, *Children in Distress,* Harmondsworth: Penguin Books, 1968.

Court, Joan, 'The Battered Child Syndrome – The Need for a Multi-disciplinary Approach', *Nursing Times,* 3 June, 1971.

D'Agostino, Paul A., 'Dysfunctioning Families and Child Abuse: The Need for an Interagency Effort', *Public Welfare,* Fall, 1972.

Davies, J. M., 'Detection and Prevention', *Nursing Mirror,* June 1975.

De Francis, Vincent and Lucht, Carroll L., *Child Abuse Legislation in the 1970's,* Denver: The American Humane Association, Children's Division.

Fontana, Vincent, *Somewhere a Child is Crying,* New York: Macmillan, 1973.

Gil, David G., 'What Schools Can Do About Child Abuse', *American Education,* April 1969.

Irwin, Theodore, *To Combat Child Abuse and Neglect,* Public Affairs Pamphlet No. 508, New York: Public Affairs Committee, Inc., 1974.

Kaufman, Irving, 'Psychiatric Implications of Child Abuse', from *Protecting the Battered Child* (pamphlet), Denver: The American Humane Association, 1962.

Murdock, George C., 'The Abused Child and the School System', *American Journal of Public Health,* January 1970.

Non-Accidental Injury to Children, Memorandum sent to British Area Health Authorities by the Department of Health and Social Security, April 1974.

Parents Anonymous, Inc., 2009 Farrell Avenue, Redondo Beach, California 90278. (Contact P.A. for addresses in other parts of the US and in Canada and Britain.)

Parents Anonymous Lifelines, a new group established in the London area in 1978. An emegency telephone number for abusive or potentially abusive parents, 01-643 8878, is manned from 6 p.m. to 6 a.m.

Pringle, Mia Kellmer, 'How to Cut the Cruelty', *The Sunday Times,* 9 October, 1977.

Reinhardt, J. B., 'Love of Children – A Myth', *Clinical Pediatrics,* December 1968.

'Summary of the Battered Child Syndrome', prepared by the NSPCC's National Advisory Centre on the Battered Child, 1975.

CHAPTER EIGHT

Aiken, Conrad, *Secret Snow, Silent Snow,* New York: Scribner, 1934.

Barnes, Mary and Berke, Joseph, *Two Accounts of a Journey Through Madness,* London: MacGibbon & Kee, 1971.

Bateson, Gregory (ed.), *Perceval's Narrative: A Patient's Account of His Psychosis, 1830-1832,* London: The Hogarth Press, 1962.

Laing, R. D., *Knots,* London: Tavistock Publications, 1970.

Laing, R. D. and Esterson, A., *Sanity, Madness and the Family,* London: Tavistock Publications, 1964.

Oates, Joyce Carol, *Them,* London: Victor Gollancz, 1971.

Reed, David, *Anna,* London: Secker & Warburg, 1976.

CHAPTER NINE

Ackerman, Nathan, *Treating the Troubled Family,* New York and London: Basic Books, 1966.

Burlingham, Dorothy, 'Child Analysis and the Mother', *Psychiatric Quarterly,* Vol. IV, 1935, pp. 69-92.

Falstein, Eugene I., 'Case Presentation by Eugene I. Falstein', *American Journal of Orthopsychiatry,* Vol. XII, 1942.

Hellman, Ilse, Friedmann, Oscar and Shepheard, Elizabeth, 'Simultaneous Analysis of Mother and Child', in *The Psychoanalytic Study of the Child,* Vol. XV, London: The Hogarth Press, 1960.

Henry, Jules, 'Family Structure and the Transmission of Neurotic Behavior', *American Journal of Orthopsychiatry,* Vol. XXI, 1951.

Sperling, Melitta, 'The Neurotic Child and His Mother: A Psychoanalytical Study', *American Journal of Orthopsychiatry,* Vol. XXI, 1951.

Vander Veer, Adrian, 'Psychotherapy for Children', *American Journal of Orthopsychiatry,* Vol. XV, No. 1, January 1945.

CHAPTER TEN

Ackerman, Nathan, *Treating the Troubled Family,* New York and London: Basic Books, 1966.

Augenbraun, Bernice, Reid, Helen L. and Friedman, David B., 'Brief Intervention as a Preventive Force in Disorders of Early Childhood', *American Journal of Orthopsychiatry,* Vol. XXXVII, 1967.

Dupont, Robert L. and Grunebaum, Henry, 'Willing Victims: The Husbands of Paranoid Women', *American Journal of Psychiatry,* Vol. 125, August 1968.

Henry, Jules, 'Family Structure and the Transmission of Neurotic Behavior', *American Journal of Orthopsychiatry,* Vol. XXI, 1951.

Minuchin, Salvador, *Families and Family Therapy,* London: Tavistock Publications, 1974.

Mitchell, Celia B., 'Problems and Priniciples in Family Therapy', from Ackerman, Nathan W., Beatman, F. L. and Sherman, S. N. (eds.), *Expanding Theory and Practice in Family Therapy,* New York: Family Service Association of America (44 East 23rd Street, New York, NY 10010), 1967.

Richter, Horst E., *The Family a Patient,* London: Souvenir Press, 1974.

CHAPTER ELEVEN

Bohannan, Paul, *Divorce and After,* New York: Doubleday Anchor, 1971.

Bramall, Margaret, from a press release issued in November 1973 by the National Council for One Parent Families, 255 Kentish Town Road, London NW5 2LX.

Despert, Louise J., *Children of Divorce,* New York: Dolphin Books, revised ed., 1962.

'Families Need Fathers' Organization, 97c Shakespeare Walk, London N16.

Goldstein, Joseph, Freud, Anna and Solnit, Albert J., *Beyond the Best Interests of the Child,* New York and London: The Free Press, 1973.

Krantzler, Mel, *Creative Divorce,* New York: Evans, 1974.

McDermott, John F. Jr., 'Parental Divorce in Early Childhood', *American Journal of Psychiatry,* Vol. 124, April 1968.

Nye, F. Ivan, 'Child Adjustment in Broken and Unhappy Unbroken Homes', *Marriage and Family Living,* November 1957, pp. 356-361.

CHAPTER TWELVE

Bramall, Margaret, 'The Single Parent Family', paper read to the Health Congress of the Royal Society of Health, Eastbourne, 1973. Copyright of the Royal Society of Health.

Gingerbread, Self-Help Organization for One-Parent Families, 9 Poland Street, London W1.

Goldstein, Joseph, Freud, Anna and Solnit, Albert J., *Beyond the Best Interests of the Child,* New York and London: The Free Press, 1973.